The Awkward Thoughts
of W. Kamau Bell

The
Awkward Thoughts
of W. Kamau Bell

Tales of a 6'4", African-American,
Heterosexual, Cisgender, Left-Leaning,
Asthmatic, Black and Proud Blerd,
Mama's Boy, Dad,
➡ *and* ⬅
Stand-Up Comedian

W. KAMAU BELL

DUTTON

□

DUTTON

An imprint of Penguin Random House LLC
375 Hudson Street
New York, New York 10014

Copyright © 2017 by WKB Industries, Inc.
Penguin supports copyright. Copyright fuels creativity, encourages diverse voices,
promotes free speech, and creates a vibrant culture. Thank you for buying an authorized
edition of this book and for complying with copyright laws by not reproducing, scanning,
or distributing any part of it in any form without permission. You are supporting writers
and allowing Penguin to continue to publish books for every reader.

DUTTON is a registered trademark and the D colophon is a trademark
of Penguin Random House LLC.

LIBRARY OF CONGRESS CATALOGING-IN-PUBLICATION DATA
has been applied for.

ISBN 9781101985878 (hardcover)
ISBN 9781101985892 (ebook)

Printed in the United States of America
1 3 5 7 9 10 8 6 4 2

BOOK DESIGN BY AMY HILL

While the author has made every effort to provide accurate telephone numbers, Internet
addresses, and other contact information at the time of publication, neither the publisher
nor the author assumes any responsibility for errors or for changes that occur after
publication. Further, the publisher does not have any control over and does not assume
any responsibility for author or third-party websites or their content.

Penguin is committed to publishing works of quality and integrity. In that spirit,
we are proud to offer this book to our readers; however, the story, the experiences,
and the words are the author's alone.

*This book is for Sami and Juno . . . because pretty much everything
I do is for Sami and Juno.*

CONTENTS

Contents

INTRODUCTION

Hello, reader.

Before you start reading, I have a question: Why are you reading this particular book?

Do you have a dead spot in the pit of your stomach that has been there for months and isn't going away? Are you kind of afraid that it never will? Are you feeling stuck? Trying to figure out your next move? Questioning everything that you held dear and wondering how you could have been so wrong about what everybody else in this country was holding dear? Are you unsure of how you are going to continue dealing with the level of hate in the world and, worse, the level of hate you have to deal with when you want to talk about the level of hate in the world? (Just me??)

"Let's talk about the racism that we all deal with every day!"

"You *would* want to talk about the racism, YOU RACIST!"

"Wait, what?"

"[Expletive.]" "[N-word.]" "[Thinly veiled death threat.]" . . .

Are you (like me) hoping that the recent events in American history will kick-start the 1960s all over again? Or are you secretly happy that all of this happened because your life is pretty much golden and you were hoping for things to get more interesting because TV hasn't really been interesting since the final episode of *Mad Men*? . . . Or was it *Breaking Bad*? No . . . it was definitely *The Sopranos* . . . unless it was *The Wire* . . . Yes! TV hasn't been good since the last episode of *The Wire*. Ahhhh, doesn't it feel good to be distracted again?

Wait . . . Is that why you're reading this book? Is it serving as a distraction until the new season of *Game of Thrones* (or *Luke Cage* or *Insecure* or *Empire* or *Veep*) begins? OH MY GOD, *VEEP* IS SO GOOD! Julia Louis-Dreyfus is on the Mount Rushmore of comedy!

If it's a distraction you want, you might be in the wrong place. I like getting distracted, but I can't seem to turn away from everything that is happening right now. It feels like things are slipping away. It feels like just showing up isn't enough. It feels like the day before the beginning of one of the *Mad Max* movies. Maybe that is the distraction we need. I want to see what exactly happened the day BEFORE the world turned into a post-apocalyptic desert and people began paying thirty bucks for an ounce of water. I want to see a just-pre-post-apocalyptic film. Like the eve of the post-apocalypse. Maybe that will help us make sense of things. What happened that night? I'm betting those people didn't know it was the night before the apocalypse. I bet they were just sitting around saying something like, "Wow! I never expected that candidate to win the presidency! . . . Oh well! We'll get through this! Like we always do!"

Cut to the next day and a bald-headed Charlize Theron is driving a car across a barren wasteland for ninety minutes. Because, eventually . . . You. Don't. Get. Through. It.

That's what happened in that movie, right? I never actually saw it. I prefer my post-apocalyptic movies to be more like *The*

Book of Eli, because you literally . . . Can't. Go. Wrong. With. Denzel. Washington.

Are you reading this book because you feel like this may just be the just-pre-post-apocalypse? Like maybe we are currently living through the sequel to the fall of the Roman Empire? (Makes sense. We love sequels.) Are you reading this because this is just about the end and this book seems like a good read to end the world with?

Well, I don't know that I have any answers for the end of the world. And any distraction I have to offer comes in the form of awkward tales from my past. (Like the time when I was a kid and I wore fur-lined leather boots, which I LOVED, to elementary school, only to learn later that I was made fun of all day because they were girls' boots. My first window into the idea that gender is a continuum . . . like flavors of chocolate. Milk chocolate, YES! Dark chocolate . . . Well, I guess. Just this once.) But I'm sitting here writing this book as a way to grapple with some of the questions that this crazy, upside-down time has produced, both in me and in the world.

Maybe that is why you are here? To watch someone grapple with some questions? Perhaps you have heard me do just that on my podcast *Politically Re-Active*. Or are you one of the small but mighty who still feels like my yearlong FX (and later FXX, and after that FXX-ed) show, *Totally Biased*, was 1. groundbreaking and 2. canceled too soon. (Hint: 1. Could be. Who am I to say? 2. Definitely not.) Maybe you were shocked by how my seemingly ridiculous fanboy podcast *Denzel Washington Is the Greatest Actor of All Time Period* has turned from a weekly examination about the underrated greatness of Denzel Washington into a larger discussion about representation in Hollywood? Maybe you have seen my CNN show, *United Shades of America*, and you're wondering how crazy I must be to have gone and asked questions of the Ku Klux Klan? Maybe you've seen me wrestle with racism onstage as a comedian, online in blogs, in print, or (at some of my lowest moments) with Internet trolls. Maybe you've appreciated seeing my struggle to articulate (my word, not yours, so I can call myself articulate) how I feel and what I think.

Or . . .

Are you reading this because you just don't think I'm funny at all? Not even one bit? (Have I never made you laugh? Or even smile? Not even one time? What are you doing here?) Maybe you think I'm just some sort of affirmative action hire sent to make guilty white liberals feel better about themselves so that even though they don't have any Black friends, they can tell their white friends, "But my favorite comedian is J. Jamocha Fudge . . . I mean, W. Kamal Brown . . . I mean, that guy who looks like Questlove but isn't him . . . At least I don't think it's him." That makes sense.

(By the way, I spell "Black" with a capital *B* because I subscribe to all the Black intellectuals and academics and barbershop sages who say that Blackness is as much an uppercase identity as Chinese-ness or Christianity-ness or any other proper-noun identity is. And if Wikipedia is going to insist on capitalizing "Klansman," then I am certainly going to insist on capitalizing "Black." No matter what every editor of everything I write tells me—except for the editor of this book. Thanks, Jill.)

Or are you here for the same reasons I am? Have we gotten here, to this page, together because in the past few months it feels like the United States of America has turned upside down and we have to review some of what's happened in order to think through what comes next? Are you thinking (perhaps awkwardly) that you need help sorting through the stuff that makes up America in order to attempt to figure out how we should remake America? And have you seen or heard enough of my work that you know I'm awkwardly thinking the same? And often thinking it out loud? And what's more awkward than having to permanently commit my awkward thoughts to the page for all time, or at least until the current administration takes us firmly into the apocalypse, where there is no electricity for your smart devices and all actual books are used as firewood to heat the underground caves that we all call home?

If that's why you're here . . . welcome to my awkward thoughts.

CHAPTER 1

My Awkward Youth

My mom is Janet Cheatham Bell, and she is awesome. Seriously awesome. And I'm not just saying that because she's my mom. She is empirically the greatest mom of all time period. Everybody likes her. Everybody wants to be her friend. Everybody wants her approval. Everybody wants her to think that *they* are cool. I have friends who let me know when she "likes" their posts on Facebook. And these aren't my emotionally needy friends. These are my kick-ass, activist, artist, take-no-prisoners-and-free-ALL-political-prisoners friends. And they turn all gooey when my eighty-year-old mom likes their status update that quotes James Baldwin's prescient criticism of modern-day conservatism. And if she comments on their post . . . fuggedaboutit! I've seen less enthusiasm from those people who get brand-new homes on that show *Extreme Makeover: Home Edition* or from that dude on *Maury* who moonwalked when he found out that he was "not . . . the . . . father."

My mom is a race warrior and educator in the true senses of

the words. My dad is Walter A. Bell. And, weirdly, he is also every-thing my mom is: popular, charismatic, loved and admired by all who know him. But they took it two different directions. To para-phrase Malcolm X—and who doesn't like paraphrasing Malcolm X whenever you can?—my mom is a field negro. My dad is a negro in the house . . . which is different from a "house negro." My dad is a field negro who worked his way into the house, bought the house, and turned the slave quarters into a wine cellar. And he didn't lose any (or not much of) the "field" in the process. Both my parents seem regal. They both turn heads when they walk into rooms. But where my mom feels like a *Matrix*-style oracle, my dad seems . . . well . . . famous. People stare at him even if they don't know him. Part of it is because my dad is tall, like *for reals* tall. I'm six foot four, which is like regular tall, but my dad is six foot six, which is like actual-for-reals NBA tall. My dad is also really good-looking. (There was a point in his life when he was regularly getting mistaken for Dr. J., aka NBA legend Julius Erving—if you're not nasty.) And I've known all my life that my dad is better-looking than me. Like, a lot better-looking. I know it sounds weird to think of an eight-year-old looking at his dad like, "Damn, that dude is good-looking!" But it's true. He is good-looking, and on some level, even as a child I was jealous. My dad was a semiprofessional photographer, turned oldest rookie bank teller ever at forty, turned insurance salesman, turned vice pres-ident of a Fortune 500 company. And other than both being Black, my parents have only two things in common:

1. Me
2. They are both hustlers in the best possible way.

As I said, my mom is an outside hustler. She has been self-employed since the mid-'80s. Back around 1984, she left her job as a textbook editor in Boston and moved us to Chicago. Chicago had just elected Harold Washington as mayor, and she said she wanted to be in a city that was run by a Black person. Chicago was about to go through a golden age. Because 1984 was also the year Michael Jordan was drafted to the Chicago Bulls, and it was the year that a former news anchor named Oprah Winfrey took over a half-hour talk show called *A.M. Chicago* and decided to try to give Phil Donahue a run for his money. Phil Donahue hasn't been seen since.

Once my mom got us to Chicago, she set to work self-publishing a book called *Famous Black Quotations*. It was a compendium of African-American quotes, at a time when that did not exist. And my mom was already with the tiny-tech revolution, because she made sure the book could easily fit into your pocket. Now there are many books of African-American quotations, and really, who needs a book? You can just Google "inspirational quotes by Oprah from this morning" and be all set. But back when my mom was self-publishing books, it was a major task. She had to collect the quotes on her floppy disk. She had to take those quotes to a typesetter to get the book laid out. Then she needed to take all that to a graphic designer to make the book look good. (And yes, I mean she had to "take" this stuff. There was no e-mail.) Then she had to find a printer that would do a short run of books since she wasn't ordering a million copies. And then, once the book was done, she spent lots of time in her car hand-selling them to individual bookstores (many of which were Black owned). And now in the year 2017, everything

I described can be done with Microsoft Word and Amazon.com. But back then, it took serious work.

But my dad is an inside hustler. He's got that Kevin Hart "While you're sleeping I'm doing sit-ups, Instagramming, having a meeting about *Ride Along 3, 4,* and *5,* and I'm on my way to do nineteen sold-out shows at Madison Square Garden" thing. That's my dad, but replace sit-ups with leisurely treadmilling, Instagramming with monitoring his investments online, movie pitches with actuarial charts, and Madison Square Garden with nineteen meetings in various corporate boardrooms around the country and occasionally the halls of government in Bermuda. (Yup. Bermuda.)

I am an only child, and the youngest grandchild on both sides of my family by a mile, so I was always "the baby." My mom was thirty-five when she had me. And in 1973 that was like one of those stories you read today about a sixty-five-year-old woman giving birth. My mom's brothers and sister had gone what was then the traditional route of getting married out of high school and immediately having kids. And her oldest brother went the also popular route of having a kid in high school and not telling anybody so there could be a surprise forty or so years later.

And since both my mom and dad come from big families, there were always lots of cousins around. And when the cousins would gather, I was always on the outside because I was the youngest. I ended up feeling like a mascot and not quite like one of them. But I didn't always hate it. I just knew that no matter how entertaining they found my trailing behind them, at some point they would be like, "OK. See ya!" And then I would be left to my own devices. My device of choice was television. Still is today.

I was also the youngest because my mom put me in school a

year earlier than she should have. She said I was bored at home at five, so she just decided to put me in first grade. Apparently you could do that back then. It's not like now. If I wanted to get my two-year-old daughter, Juno, into the three-year-olds' class at her preschool, me and my wife, Melissa, would have to submit a birth certificate, blood samples, fingernail clippings, and a recent stool sample. Kinda like what President Obama went through to stop the current Birther in Chief from taking his job away.

"I'm sorry, Mr. Bell. According to our tests, your daughter is only two and three-eighths, not quite old enough for you to have the privilege of having her nap here instead of at home with you."

So for the first half of my life, being the youngest was a big part of my identity. Everybody else hit those age markers way (or what seemed like waaaaaaaaay) before me: work permit, driver's license, voting age, drinking age, losing-their-virginity age. OK, that last one wasn't a fault of my youngness, but it certainly felt like it at the time.

(I was twenty-one. It was to a jazz singer. Not a woman who liked to sing jazz but an actual professional jazz singer. And it was amazingly . . . awkward. I was all knees, elbows, and technique-less, like a turtle darting in and out of its shell trying to not get hit by the rain. If I ever see her again, I'd immediately apologize. Also, I hope I never see her again.)

Conventional wisdom says that the youngest kid has the least amount of pressure on them. But in another way I wasn't the youngest, because I was also "the only." Now, in an effort to not totally lose my stepsister from the audience of this book and thus the coveted stepsister demographic, I should say I am the only biological child of my dad. Although by the time Ashley and her mom, Loresa, came into my life, "only child" was such a huuuge part of my identity that I wasn't interested in newcomers. I was six. Already stubborn. Already King of the Grudge Holders. Already stuck in my head and imagination. Plenty happy with the TV, comic books, action figures, paper and pencil. I was never lonely. Never bored. And minus action figures, those things pretty much still define my happy place, although I've replaced comic books with actual books for the most part.

Wait. Why am I lying? I've replaced comic books with multiple browser windows open to articles about how the world is getting worse as each minute goes by, mixed in with whatever my current, purposefully distracting YouTube videos of choice are. (Recently it has been Dr. Pimple Popper—aka Dr. Sandra Lee, if you like nasty videos of pimples being popped. Many of the articles never get read, but ALL the videos get watched . . . sometimes more than once. But be careful, grasshopper. Dr. Lee ain't for the faint of heart.)

My parents have always had high expectations for me for vastly different reasons. For my mom, I think it had something to do with how hard it was to actually have me, and again how late in her life that it happened.

My mom was born and raised in Indianapolis, Indiana. She was born in 1937, which meant she was around for separate drinking fountains for Blacks and whites, "Whites Only" signs, Black people being forced to sit in the balcony at the movie theater, Black people being forced to sit at the back of the bus (as opposed to when I was a kid and choosing to sit there), and everything else that came with those realities. My mom was around during the time when the word "colored" was said by white people who were *trying to be nice.*

My mom has all the classic American Black folk stories. Her dad was an elementary school dropout and yet always worked three jobs at a time in order to help support his wife and four kids. My mom's mom was a teacher and a seamstress who devoted her life to the church. As a kid my mom loved to read and was good at it. But when schools were integrated when she went to high school, they put her in remedial English because she wasn't reading at the level of the white students her age. They. Thought. She. Had. A. Learning. Disability (except I'm sure they didn't say it that politically correctly). In reality, my mom did not have a learning disability. What she had was a syndrome called "Years of being educated at Black public schools that didn't have the greater resources of white public schools because of racism-itis." Heard of that syndrome? Turns out this country still has it. But because my mom didn't play the "Believe whatever people tell you" game—especially when those people were white people in Indiana in the first half of the twentieth century—in a short period of time, my mom went from remedial English to regular white-people English and then to proving to herself that she was at least as smart as anybody in that damn school.

This was a time when people got married right out of high school and had babies right away. But my mom didn't do that. When she first got married, she was only twenty-three but already considered an "old maid." (I'm pretty sure "old maid" was the term they used before people felt comfortable saying the word "lesbian.") At that age she had gotten married to a man—who isn't my father. (Thank you, Black Jesus!) And they had a son named Paul who was born sick and died as a baby. That marriage ended shortly thereafter. Then later she got married to a white Jewish man whose name, when it rarely comes up, serves exclusively as the punch line of jokes about male insecurity and male chauvinism. My mom swears up and down that when this man was introduced to a new woman, he would pinch her breast as a way of saying, "Nice to a meet ya!" What in the name of *Mad Men* was he doing? I have no idea. Fortunately, this marriage also only lasted briefly. They didn't have any kids. And from the way my mom tells the story, they didn't even try to have any kids. (Again, thank you, Black Jesus!) It doesn't sound like she even enjoyed the rehearsal process of trying to have any kids. When I ask her why she married him at all, she sort of always seems to frame it like it was a way to get out of her parents' house and ultimately out of her hometown of Indianapolis. "What's wrong with Indianapolis?" you ask. Well, it is alternately referred to as India-no-place and Naptown. Yup, Naptown. That's the nickname Indianapolis gave itself! New York is the city that never sleeps. And Indianapolis is the city that gets sleepy around three p.m. and has to shut it down.

So by the time my mom was pregnant with me, she was thirty-five, unmarried, and twice divorced. That may not sound like a big deal (or any kind of deal) now. In fact, now we've kind of flipped the whole thing. These days it can seem weird if a woman is pregnant in her twenties. MTV has based a whole genre of programming around the weirdness of a young woman having a kid at the age that women have historically always had children: *16 and Pregnant*. Ummm, you mean like all of our great-great-great-great-grandmothers?

But in 1973, my mom was a pioneer (which she often is in her life). In 1973, women didn't just have kids, for the first time, at thirty-five years old . . . with no husband no less(!) . . . unless a lot of bad shit had happened to them leading up to that point. But there's no way my mom would have defined herself as the "victim of two divorces" *or* as an "unwed mother." Naaaaah. She was single. She had a relationship with the child's father (my dad); she would have been happy if their relationship had worked out, but she wasn't depending on him to help make this kid's life happen. These were *her choices*. And she was *making them*. Her choices weren't *making her*. She was a pioneer. My mom basically invented the idea of a woman waiting until *she was ready* before she became a mom. You're welcome, Madonna, Halle Berry, Mariah Carey, Geena Davis, and Sandra Bullock.

And now, whenever my mom gets to talking about the subject of my birth, she will often tell the story of how she had to assure the people at the ob-gyn's office that she actually did want to keep the child, and that she really wasn't interested in an abortion. And when my mom tells this story, it is not a cautionary tale or some sort of anecdote about a woman's right to choose. My mom is definitely pro-choice (as am I), and she laughs when she tells this story. I think in her mind she thinks the doctors were actually asking her, "You really want to keep this kid? . . . REEEALLY? But you're single, Black, AND female? Really, you want to keep this child? But what will you possibly do with him once he's born and there's no man around to put food on the table? And you're sooooooooooooold? You're more like a grandmother than a mom. . . . Oh my God! And I almost forgot to mention that you're Black? Is the father Black too? JESUS H. CHRIST! So there's like a 100 percent chance that your baby will be Black too! You know what, ma'am? . . . Why don't you take another brochure explaining the benefits of not giving birth to fatherless future criminals."

Now, there are two things I take from that story. One, I have known it all my life. My mom has told it to me—and in front of me—as far back as I can remember. Which means I was probably (definitely) too young to hear it the first time. But that's how my mom was. She was raising someone to be her equal, so she treated me and talked to me like I understood everything. Which pretty much guaranteed I was always trying to. Although when you think about it, what is the societally acceptable age for a child hearing the "doctors kept wanting me to abort you" story?

The second thing I take from all of this is that my mom is very funny and has a very stark sense of humor. Not a specifically dark sense of humor, but a stark sense of humor. She likes it when jokes cut through and clarify. She's a big fan of jokes that aren't a traditional setup and punch line. She likes jokes that are just statements that make you go, "DAAAAAAAAAAAMN!" My mom's favorite Chris Rock joke is: "A man is as faithful as his options." Damn.

That tells you a lot about her relationship history, and a lot about how she is using that joke to cut through some obvious pain. But if you hear my mom repeat that line, she will laugh like she's never heard it before, and like she didn't just say it. As if she was hearing Chris Rock say it again for the first time. And my mom knows how to laugh. It is a big, mouth-agape, cacophonous explosion. It is the laugh that makes people turn around and wonder if everything is OK, even though it is very definitely a laugh. People turn around, even if they are also laughing at the same thing that she is. When I'm onstage, I can hear that laugh above hundreds of other laughs in a crowded club. But my favorite version of her laugh comes when nobody else (or nearly nobody else) in the club finds what I just said particularly funny, and my mom doesn't care or doesn't notice that they didn't laugh, and she laughs anyway. It is a kind of laugh that I associate with Black women over the age of fifty. A laugh that says, "I made it this far. I've fought all the battles they brought to me—racism, sexism, ageism, everything-else-ism—and now, I'm just going to have a good time. And nobody is going to stop me."

My mom wasn't exactly a single mom. She and my dad were still together when she was pregnant. Theirs was a heavily on-again, off-again relationship. They were, however, never married. Despite the fact that they were never married, my mom changed her last name to Bell, just like my dad's. When my dad asked why she had taken his last name when they weren't married, my mom had her comeback ready to go, just like she always did. She told him, "I didn't take your last name. I took *Kamau's* last name." Damn. Check and mate. My mom knew that as much as my dad was annoyed that she had his last name, he absolutely, positively, definitely, without a doubt, 100 percent wanted me to have his last name. My mom's response immediately ended the conversation as a topic of his consternation once and for all. According to my mom, my dad actually wanted me to have his entire name: Walter Alfred Bell. He says that's not true. And that's not even close to the number of things they have told me about their relationship that have totally contradicted each other. That would have made me Walter Alfred Bell Jr. Sometimes I think about who that guy would have been. I think he would have gone by Al. Yup, good old Al Bell. I feel like wearing sunglasses indoors would have been a big part of Al Bell's life. Maybe he's a guy who had a record player the whole time. A guy who never gave up on vinyl. Never bought into the CD craze. Al Bell feels pretty good about that now. And he holds it over all his friends' heads. And he's definitely a weed smoker. Not a wake-and-baker but not *not* a wake-and-baker. And Al Bell lost his virginity at thirteen, not twenty-one like Walter Kamau Bell. Al Bell is also six foot five, not a measly six four like me. Al Bell is the best.

But my dad says he wasn't interested in making me a junior. I don't know who to believe. But I do know that when I was born, my parents were spending a lot of time in East Palo Alto (EPA), California, which at the time was the Oakland to Palo Alto's San Francisco (i.e., waaaaaaaaaay more Black folks in EPA). And in the early 1970s, EPA was thick with Black people and talk of the revolution. My parents were hanging out with a group of people who had formed a tribe. They all had taken on African names. Just around each other. They didn't go changing them legally like many Black people did back then. I often wonder why they didn't. Although at that point changing your name to an African or Arabic name was probably the equivalent of calling the FBI and saying, "Hello, could you please put me on a list, please? . . . Thank you!"

I've been told that I was the first baby born into the tribe, so I was given an actual (and legal) African name all my own. "Kamau" is a Kenyan name. It is Kikuyu, one of the main dialects in Kenya. "Kamau" is a very common name in Kenya. Often it is a last name. "Ka" means "quiet." And "mau" means "warrior." For those of you even tangentially familiar with Kenyan history, you will know that the Mau Maus were known as the warrior class of Kenya. As an only child who didn't talk much but who felt a lot of intense feelings, I thought the name made sense for me. I've known the meaning of my name my whole life, but if I ever happen to forget it, I'll be all right because every Kenyan I meet (and

I meet a lot more of them since I've been on TV) always, always, *always* tells me the history of my name and what it means. They don't ask me *if* I know the meaning. They just immediately tell me the meaning. When this first started happening, I would interrupt them and say, "I know. I know." But now I realize that this is their way of saying, "I like you right now, but you better be good enough to carry this weight. This. Is. Not. A. Game."

And as an American Black person who has no real idea of where my "African parts" came from—and who is also pretty sure that none of his "African parts" are Kenyan, since most of America's human forklifts were stolen from the west side of Africa—honestly it feels pretty awesome to be "adopted" by the motherland in this small way.

And apparently my parents weren't that bothered about the fact that they weren't married. They tried to get married once, but there was some sort of blood test problem. They were together the first couple of years of my life, but I literally have no memory of that. And I mean "literally." I have seen a few pictures of the three of us together when they were still a couple. Everybody looks happy. It is definitely a family. But it's not my family. My family is me and my mom . . . and my dad. We aren't one unit. And that's fine. That's how family is sometimes. But when I look at pictures of my family now with my wife, Melissa, and our two daughters, Sami and Juno, and me, I know that I don't want that to come even close to happening to us.

But with my parents, staying together wasn't the right choice. I don't blame them at all for splitting up. They are such different people. I can't quite imagine them—again, literally—agreeing on anything. I can't even imagine them agreeing on anything long enough to decide to have sex with each other. It was not meant to be. And whenever I see them together I'm always reminded by their terse (yet friendly, in a professional associates way, like two lawyers who often try cases against each other) conversation of how not-meant-to-be it really was.

My mom has told me lots of the juicy details about how they broke up. And again she told me when I was probably way too young to know them. But my dad has never told me anything about his relationship with my mom. He never talks about it. Like never. And let me be clear, my dad is a talker. He's got opinions on everything. And not just opinions. He *knows* he's right about everything. And he is a smart guy in the boardroom and in the back alley, so it kind of sucks for me that he does know a lot. But when it came to my mom, especially when I was growing up, it seemed like my dad thought of my mom as if she was a highly sensitive explosive material that was best to steer clear of. Part of this may have been because he knew how close I was to my mom. As much as it may have frustrated him, I know he respected it because he had been super close to his mom, Gladys . . . which let's just stop and recognize that "Gladys" is the most perfect old–Black lady name ever.

But all this is mythology, anyway, because I was too young to experience most of it, and what I do know, for the obvious reasons stated above, comes from my mom. I did grow up knowing that my parents had never been married. I always knew that they'd met in a class in Northern California, at a junior college named Diablo Valley College, where my mom had moved after getting divorced for the second time and after leaving Indianapolis. My mom was teaching a class, and *he was one of her students.* Six years younger, in fact. To be clear, though, he was in his midtwenties and she was in her early thirties. But even though it was college and not high school, where their age difference would have been really scandalous, I still go, "OOOHHHH... So 1980s TV Movie of the Week, *or* ... So 2017 Lifetime Movie Any Night of the Week."

At the time, my mom was in the PhD program at Stanford University. She was there to get her doctorate in African-American literature. She is not a PhD today, because she says that at the time (the early '70s) Stanford wouldn't give her a doctorate in that because it wasn't a valid field of study. (Let that sink in. Remember Maya Angelou, Richard Wright, Zora Neale Hurston, James Baldwin, and Ralph Ellison had all ripped the earth asunder with their writing by then.) She described my dad as the hip, cool guy who you kinda want every Black guy to be in the 1970s. If you see pictures of my dad from back then, he has a huge Afro and looks amazing. He looks like Jim Kelly from *Enter the Dragon* (Bruce Lee reference number one of many, many in this book) or Black Belt Jones. I've always been aware that I'm not as cool as my dad. Even at my age now, I'm not as cool as my seventy-three-year-old dad today. My mom is cool too, but it's a different cool. My dad is cool the way that a Black James Bond would be cool. He's tall, he's slender, he's poised. And now that he's seventy-three he's become even cooler, *because he's seventy-three.* My parents both look waaaaay younger than their ages. It's like my people always say: "Good Black don't crack." If you thought he was fifty-two—and you probably would—you'd think, "Hey, that dude's pretty cool. Wait, he's seventy-three? Holy shit!"

My dad was always the cool guy, which is funny because I've

NEVER been the cool guy. I guess it skips a generation? Because my daughters, Sami and Juno, are really cool. My wife, Melissa, was always a popular kid too. It's weird to live in a home surrounded by the cool kids. I live in fear of walking into the living room, seeing them all talking and immediately stopping when they notice that I'm there. I ask them, "What's going on?" My two-year-old, Juno, responds, "Nothing." Then they all turn to each other, laugh conspiratorially, and walk out of the room together while looking back at me like, "Dork!"

My mom always described my dad as the love of her life. And I think that's true because she never had a serious relationship afterward. Despite what happened with her first child, who when I was kid I thought of as my brother, my mom knew that she wanted to try to have a child again. And when my mom first saw my dad, she said she looked at him and thought to herself, "Oh yeah, that's the man I want to have a kid with. That's the right guy." Which again is even more awesome when you think about the fact that their first meeting was in a classroom.

My dad is from Mobile, Alabama, born as poor as Black people in Mobile, Alabama, tend to be born. Mobile has two interesting but unmarketable facts going for it. One fact most of you reading will not believe. And the second fact is gonna bum you out. Let's do it!

Mobile is the actual birthplace of Mardi Gras. Yeah, see, I told you. You don't believe me. (I even just Googled it right now to double-check because I know it to be true but . . . it still *doesn't sound right*.) But it *is* true. Mardi Gras did not start in New Orleans even though it seems integral to the very existence of New

Orleans. It's so integral that after Hurricane Katrina devastated much of the city, many people's big question was, "Are they going to do Mardi Gras next year?" Not one voice—outside of Mobile—said, "Don't worry. Everybody can just go to Mardi Gras in Mobile, Alabama! Since Mobile has been doing Mardi Gras since 1703 and New Orleans has only been doing it since . . . Well, it's complicated. A French guy celebrated Mardi Gras near New Orleans in 1699, but he only invited his friends. Whereas Mobile has been doing organized celebrations since 1703 and . . . Hey . . . Where you going? . . . Oh . . . New Orleans . . . Yeah, I get it." For the record, New Orleans did celebrate Mardi Gras the next year it came up on the calendar right after Hurricane Katrina, and apparently it was amazing . . . because of course it was. IT'S NEW ORLEANS!

The second notable fact about Mobile that is sure to bum you out, even if you know it already—at least I hope it bums you out, because if it doesn't then you're in for a long ride with this book—is that Mobile is the place where the last ship containing newly enslaved Africans landed. It was September 22, 1959. Just joking. It was really sometime in the fall, one hundred years earlier. (I just Googled that too even though I already knew it. Did you know that the word "slave" is on Mobile's Wikipedia page eighteen times? I didn't, but I had to "command F" that word to find out if I was correct. Eighteen? Wow! Seems high. Like whoever wrote Mobile's page thought, "I'm going to get the word 'slave' in here as many times as possible!") Now, it is definitely notable that Mobile was the last place that Africans ever got off the boat in the States and said, "WHAT THE FUCK? . . . FOR FREE? . . . YOU GOTTA BE KIDDING ME!" A whip cracks across his back. "OUCH! Oh, you *aren't* kidding . . . Not even one bit. Got it now!" But that's not exactly something you can build a city's identity around. Maybe a museum, but not anything marketable to tourists. Nothing easily put on a T-shirt the way San Francisco has the "I got crabs in the wharf" shirts. Nobody wants an "I got my freedom papers in Mobile, Alabama" T-shirt. Nobody but me!

My dad certainly wasn't thinking about all that when he was growing up. He was one of five kids, but it was more complicated than that, as it tends to be in the South. It was one of those families where his oldest sister (who was older than him by a country mile, apparently) had a kid who was only a few years younger than him. His sister died. (I'm not sure how or why.) And so his niece was raised like his sister. That niece—who is really my cousin—was so much older than me that she was always referred to as my aunt. In fact, her daughter, Nora, was only a few months older than me. It's Alabama, Jake!

After high school my dad bounced around from one college to another. He moved north and lived in Connecticut with his brother for a while, then California. When I was a kid and Vietnam was the war of choice, I often wondered how he didn't end up there. He would have been twenty-two in 1965. But instead of being at the Gulf of Tonkin, my dad ended up at the Watts riots but not as a rioter. Somehow my dad had gotten himself in the National Guard. As grateful as I am that my dad didn't have to fight in Vietnam, I also think it had to be weird to be a Black man and to be on *that side* of the Watts riots. Not that my dad is out in the streets right now with Black Lives Matter or anything. But his granddaughters are!

By the time he got to the Bay Area, my dad was a photographer and a poet, and he listened to John Coltrane (which is how my mom first heard Coltrane). My dad was living the classic Bay Area artist's life. (The one that is nearly gone in the current Bay Area, thanks to gentrification, tech money, and rents that make the people on the island of Manhattan scream, "Are you effin' kiddin' me?") But back then my dad actually owned and rented a few houses, because at that point, you could put down like $1,500 and get a mortgage to buy a house. And if you met my dad today, you would not think that he had ever been a bohemian. While he still owns a few different properties, now he relaxes in polo shirts and loafers while perusing CNBC to check the market.

But I didn't grow up with this current version of my dad. And I didn't really know the bohemian either . . . well, at least not for long. I do have faint memories of the end of that guy's tenure. Memories of hand-rolled cigarettes (or maybe they were "cigarettes"?) and eight-track players in giant, boat-size, '70s-era Buicks. I even have a faint memory of being in a boat with him as a kid, but I don't know who's boat, why he had it, and if it even really happened. I think I remember it because in my "memory" it was just the two of us, which was something I craved from my dad when I was a kid.

What I definitely know as true is that eventually my dad moved back to Mobile (after a brief stint in Indianapolis with my mom). And in Mobile, over the course of several years, he completely reinvented himself, from a part-time professional photographer, amateur poet, and Miller High Life drinker, living at his mom's house, into a banker, then an insurance salesman, and currently a pillar of any community that he chooses to place himself in. And even though he has traversed the globe many times over for work and has lived in New York City two different times, he still prefers his community to be Mobile, Alabama. I do have love for Mobile, but I wouldn't live there. This is one of 120 things that separate me from him. Also, he pronounces "fajita" with a hard *j*.

(For the record "Mobile" isn't pronounced the way you pronounce the type of phone you have in your pocket. "Mobile" is pronounced as if you were from the Deep South and somebody asked you if you would like some more "beel," and then you would say, "I would like mo' beel." I have to do at least one thing in this book that I know will make my dad happy.)

So by the time I was two, the pattern had been set. My parents were never together again. During the school year, I lived with my mother, although we moved around pretty frequently. Before I was thirteen, we had lived in Palo Alto, Indianapolis, Boston, and Chicago. But with all that movement, I would spend every summer with my dad in Alabama. Initially we lived in Gladys's house. My grandmother had a classic Southern-grandma house. There was a front yard with a fence around it, and a dog named Freeway who barked at cars. It was regularly well over ninety degrees in the summer, but using the air conditioner was an absolute worst-case scenario situation. And even when it was used, it was so "Grandma." We would close all the doors to every other room in the house except for the den, where the air conditioner was located, in a window above her chair. (Yes, I said *her chair*. Sit in it. I dare you. Even though she passed away more than twenty years ago, she'll come back and get you for sitting there.) And we would sit in that room, where the temperature would drop to arctic levels. It was so cold I would sometimes get up and go into one of the quarantined "hot rooms" just to get blood moving again.

Many of my happy childhood memories in Mobile are of

lying on the floor and watching TV with my grandmother. The mornings would start with game shows, because that's when God intended game shows to come on, in the morning. Not in primetime, now that Hollywood has completely run out of imagination. We'd watch *The Price Is Right, Wheel of Fortune, Password*, and the "even-more-*Password*-y" *Super Password*. There were also the game shows that have long been canceled and mostly forgotten. Shows like *Deal of the Century* and *The Joker's Wild*. But that was just getting the TV warmed up for her "stories," all the various soap operas we liked. (I say "we" because I liked them too.) Even though my grandmother was a proper Southern Baptist churchgoing (EVERY SUNDAY!) lady, she loved the ridiculous, bawdy scurrility of shows like *Another World, Days of Our Lives*, and *Texas* (later, that time slot was filled by *Santa Barbara*). For the already soap opera initiated, you can tell that my grandmother's house was a strictly NBC soap opera house. We didn't mess with none of that ABC *General Hospital* or that CBS *Young and the Restless* balderdash.

And then once the afternoon hit and Grandma was busy with one of her friends who had stopped by, or she was working her sewing machine over like it owed her money (she was an expert seamstress), or she was simply asleep in *her chair*, that's when I got the TV to myself. And that meant cartoons. Blessed, blessed cartoons! *Tom and Jerry, Looney Tunes, The Flintstones, Super Friends, ThunderCats, G.I. Joe, Voltron*, and others. But not *Transformers*. Never got it then, and still don't get it now. And then there were reruns of sitcoms that I had no idea at the time were reruns! Blessed, blessed reruns! *The Brady Bunch, The Monkees, The Partridge Family, Soap!*

So when I think about my time in Alabama, I think a lot about Grandma. And also I think about my cousin Nora. Again, Nora was (and still is) the daughter of the "aunt" who was really my cousin. Nora and I had a natural friendship, because we both felt out of place in Mobile . . . and maybe even the world at large. While Nora lived full-time in Mobile with her mom, her dad lived in Brooklyn. So like me, Nora knew there was a world out there much bigger and grander than Mobile. I often felt bad for Nora having to live in Mobile. It just didn't suit her. We were these two weirdos. She liked to write outlandish fantasy stories, and I liked to draw. I had my own fantasies of being a comic book artist. But reality caught up with me when I was in about sixth grade and kids who didn't care about drawing at all could draw better than me. Nora fared much better with the writing. She grew up, and after lots and lots of hard work she is now known as writer N. K. Jemisin. She has had, at my last count, seven books published, and last year won a Hugo Award, which is the Academy Award of science fiction and fantasy writing. Blew my little Emmy nomination out of the water. And I couldn't be happier for her. Weirdos win again!

Around the time I was six, my dad moved in with his new wife, Loresa, and her daughter, Ashley, which meant I spent less time at Grandma's house in the summers. Ashley was only about a year and half younger than me, but our cultural differences were miles apart. She was small-town and had never really traveled. I was well traveled for a kid, and I loved big-city downtowns and public transportation. Still, though, she was doing fine. She was also a popular kid. I can't seem to escape those people.

The South feels like another country. I'm really happy that I spent so much time there as a kid, because it means that "the South" doesn't freak me out the way it freaks out many people I know who have never been there. I have seen the look on people's faces—people who have clearly never been to the South—when I tell them that I'm going to visit my dad in Alabama. Often their response is to contort their faces into a confused yet stunned rictus and ask incredulously, "What's that like?" To these people, saying, "I'm headed to the South" is like saying, "I'm headed to my own lynching and I decided to bring the rope just to make it easier on the Klansmen." It is one of my enduring frustrations with this country. People live in their part of the union, and if they don't travel a lot then there is a tendency to believe that whatever is going on in their part of the union is what goes on in the "real America." And sometimes it gets even worse. People think the things going on in other parts are actually anti-American. And when you combine that with the stigma of violent racism associated with the South, and then combine *that* with the chip on the shoulder many in the South have developed in response, well, then that's how you get President Donald J. Trump. (Well, that plus the electoral college's leftover slaveholder math. But I digress.)

When I took my wife, Melissa, who has traveled all over the country and the world but just not to *the South,* to Alabama for the first time, I had a great time just looking at the look on her face as she took it all in. The slow pace of life, the open and unashamed stares when people see something they don't recognize as "from around here," the accents that sound exactly like you think they will sound . . . except harder to understand, the thick layer of hospitality that covers everything, even when people don't actually like you, and the homes that can be big and palatial like the "big houses" they once were or they can be shacks that look like a stiff breeze would knock them over. And of course the food! It's all fried, and it's all good. I'm happy that I know how to speak "Southern." It's more than just a language. It's also about understanding someone's intentions. There are things people in the South say to me that I just let go, but if someone outside the South says the same thing, I'll be like, "Well, somebody's getting a joke written about them that I'm going to test out on Twitter to see if it gets any pickup before I say it onstage."

I was in a Walgreens near Danville, California, one time when I still had long dreadlocks. A white woman who also happened to be the cashier ringing me up asked in the middle of our transaction, "Can I touch your hair?" When you have dreadlocks you start to get used to this question. It happens all the time . . . which unfortunately doesn't make it any more appropriate or any less annoying. But I was used to it. I said, "No, you can't touch my hair," but I said it with a smile so that we could both move on without the situation getting weirder than it already was. But a few months later, in Mobile, I was at a Krispy Kreme with my dad, and when a different white woman asked the same thing, I said, "Sure." I could tell from somewhere in her tone that she was taking a chance by asking me this. I could tell that she had maybe never had a real conversation with a Black person before. It felt like an after-school special. Like after she touched my hair she maybe went home and told her momma (it has to be "momma." It is the South after all), "Momma, they is peoples jes' like us." There, communities are more segregated. The Southern woman had seen Black people, but she probably wasn't talking to them. People in the South feel like they need more of that "dumb question" time that can be important to dismantling ignorance. I get it. Hell, I get it so much that I built a career on asking "dumb questions." There is still such a scar on the South because of its history of racism that it feels like it has stunted its growth as an inclusive society. I give people in the South a pass that I won't give people in other parts of America. Whereas if you live in California and you don't know a Black person, well, then you might just be an asshole. That's not true 100 percent of the time, but it is something to keep in mind when someone at a Walgreens asks if they can touch your hair. So, yes, in the South, I would like to normalize Black people for you. Outside of the South, it's "No, you need to go make some Black friends."

As I've gotten older, I've seen my parents grow in very different directions. My mom is a lefty, low-to-the-ground, living truth-teller and seeker. My dad is . . . well, I wouldn't call him a lefty. I'm not sure he's a Democrat. I know he voted for Obama twice. But I also know that he worked in the administration of the Republican governor of Alabama. I know he's definitely a fiscal conservative, but he also believes in giving back to his community and to his church. And he has worked very hard to improve his community of Mobile, Alabama. I guess he's maybe an Alabama liberal, which is kind of like a San Francisco Republican. You can trust them to mostly do the right thing, but you can't let them get out of your sight. Because they might go full-on Peter Thiel on you.

The first time I was ever on Comedy Central I was on the show *Premium Blend*. It was 2005 and my act was beginning to turn the corner into politics and racism. And that was all crystallized by a joke I did about then senator Barack Obama. The joke was that the country wasn't ready to vote for a Black president, especially not one named Barack Obama. The punch line was that the name "Barack Obama" sounded like "Black Osama." (I know it doesn't sound like a great joke *now*. But at the time it was my closer. The big dismount joke at the end of my set. And a couple years later somebody from Comedy Central contacted me to tell me that according to them I had the first Barack Obama joke ever.) After it aired, my dad called me, laughing about how some of his Republican friends had called him, surprised about his son's liberal politics. I told my dad I was sorry if I had gotten him in trouble. He laughed again, and like a cowboy from one of his favorite Westerns he said, "I can take it." I still smile thinking about that now.

My dad has spent most of my life acquiring the credentials and accolades that make sure that before he walks through the door his reputation precedes him. And if you don't know his reputation, then his sheer presence will overwhelm your lack of knowledge. Bob Costas, the sportscaster, once said that even if you didn't know who Michael Jordan was and he walked into a room, you would know that he was somebody. My dad has that.

My mom has it too, but it's quieter, which is ironic because she is anything but quiet. Today, people often assume that my mother is a college professor. People assume she's a doctor and even call her Dr. Bell because she holds the space even though, because of racism, she's not. A similar thing happens to me.

People assume that I have a degree in poli-sci and that I decided to become a comedian just because that was the best way to spread my message. It's the same for my dad too. He seems like he has a bachelor's degree in economics from the Wharton School, but he really only graduated from Spring Hill College in Mobile. For all three of us, people assume that because we have the information, we must have pieces of paper that certify us as smart. Nope. We just have information because we wanted it. If there's one thing that I learned from both of my parents, it is that you don't need the paper to get the information. As much as they are so different from each other, I learned from them that nobody can beat hard work.

Awkward Thoughts about Superheroes and *Doc McStuffins*

When I was a kid I loved superheroes. I loved them in all of their forms. I loved comic books, action figures, superhero movies, and even superhero TV shows. And I was born in 1973, so superhero TV shows were weird. Take the 1970s *Spider-Man* TV show. Spider-Man wore his web shooters on the *outside* of his costume because apparently the producers thought they were too big and clunky to fit on the *inside* of his costume. And also (apparently) the makers of the TV show didn't think that we, the watchers of the TV show, would suspend our disbelief long enough for the producers to make the *fake* web shooters small enough to put them inside the *pretend, not-real, made-up freaking costume where they belong*!

There was also *The Incredible Hulk*. A TV show that I LOVED. LOVED! LOVED! LOVED! I loved it so much that my mom cut up old clothes of mine that I could wear while watching the show so that when Dr. David Banner "Hulked out," I could "Hulk out" too. I know you are thinking that it sounds adorable. But it wasn't. I was six years old, and I was a very ferocious Hulk. Very ferocious. You'll just have to take my word for it. The Polaroids have all been destroyed.

The Incredible Hulk was a TV show that could only have been born of the 1970s. At its core it was one of comic books' greatest stories. It was Stan Lee and Marvel Comics's twist on *Dr. Jekyll and Mr. Hyde* with a whole lot of *Frankenstein* thrown in. The Hulk was invented in the throes of the Cold War and America was learning to live in constant fear of nuclear annihilation. A puny—that was the word that the comic often used to describe him—scientist named Dr. Bruce Banner got exposed to way too much gamma radiation while saving a young man from an explosion of gamma radiation. This was a simpler time in superheroes that I honestly miss. Back then, a comic book writer could just write "bathed in radiation," and the reader would say to themselves, *WELL, OF COURSE! THAT'S DEFINITELY GOING TO LEAD TO MAGICAL POWERS AND NOT SOME FORM OF LYMPHOMA!* People had more room for mystery back then. Now we know too much. The reason that every modern Superman movie sucks is because we all sit in the audience thinking, *So wait . . . Lois is a Pulitzer Prize–winning journalist and she can't figure out that the key to Superman's secret identity is glasses?*

The 1970s were the last time that Superman made sense on the big screen. And the original *Superman* movie is still better than every other one since (special effects notwithstanding). I loved that movie. In fact, if you asked me who my favorite actor was in 1978, when it came out, I would have instantly said, "Christopher Reeve!" Even though I had never seen a movie where he played someone other than Superman. But when I love something I go all in. It's tunnel vision. And it's annoying. All my friends know who my favorite bands are (Living Colour, Fishbone, and Rage Against the Machine); favorite athletes (Michael Jordan and Muhammad Ali); favorite, ummm . . . Bruce Lee (Bruce Lee); comedians (Bill Hicks, Chris Rock, Dave Chappelle, Robert Hawkins, Dwayne Kennedy); and actors (as a kid, Christopher Reeve, and as an adult, Denzel Washington, aka the Greatest Actor of All Time Period). And in 1977 my favorite TV show was *The Incredible Hulk*, and my second favorite

TV show was *The Dukes of Hazzard*, where every week the bright orange car named the General Lee, with the Confederate flag painted on top, would save the day as the two hillbillies, Bo and Luke, inevitably screamed, "YEE-HAW!!!" My mom was so proud.

But back to superheroes. The reason why the 1970s were the last time *Superman* made sense as a movie is that the 1970s were also the time when Hollywood got dark and cynical. It was the rise of the auteur as filmmaker. People like Martin Scorsese, Francis Ford Coppola, Stanley Kubrick, and many others. Even Steven Spielberg decided to scare the shit out of us all with *Jaws*. And clearly the creators of *The Incredible Hulk* TV show were all about this darkness too. They took a simple comic book tale that every comic book fan could relate to (puny guy gets pushed to anger and turns into a huge green monster), and they ladled heaps and heaps of the 1970s on it. Actor Bill Bixby played the scientist David Banner. (Reportedly, the makers of the show renamed the character because they thought the name "Bruce" sounded too "gay," because "puny" is one thing, but "gay" was too weird.) Bixby played David as totally tortured and drowning in guilt. He was on the run from the "sin" of turning himself into a destructive green monster. Later, when I watched reruns of the show as an adult, I could tell that Bixby thought he was a much better actor than the show allowed him to be. He often had the look of the actor who wanted to be acting up against DeNiro and Pacino but got stuck in TV due to his roles in *My Favorite Martian* and *The Courtship of Eddie's Father*. There was a little "I can't believe this shit" in his face. The same way Harrison Ford looks throughout the first three *Star Wars* movies, as opposed to how he looks in the 2015 *Star Wars* movie: "Thanks for calling me!"

The tone of *The Incredible Hulk* was dark. The soundtrack was not the soundtrack of a fun "superhero show." It was a soundtrack filled with mourning and melancholy. And the theme song was all anxiety and foreboding, and had a sullen voice-over that reeked of terror. Whenever David was pushed into "hulking out," he was riddled with regret for what he was about to do as the Hulk.

Bodybuilder Lou Ferrigno played David's alter ego, the Hulk, as a reluctant monster. In the comic books, the Hulk was partially a comedic character, full of malapropisms and broken sentences like "HULK SMASH!" But on TV, the Hulk didn't talk. He just wailed plaintively. And the end of every show was virtually exactly the same. It featured David skulking out of town, walking down a road (usually a freeway), thumbing for rides, while the music ended on a dissonant note of dread. There was no "YAY! The hero has saved the day again!" And just to fully set it in the 1970s, David was skulking out of town in . . . bell-bottoms. And that shows you how great an actor Bill Bixby was. Bell-bottoms are the single-most difficult item of clothing to wear while also skulking.

So even though CBS had taken my simple monster tale and turned it into *Midnight Cowboy* minus prostitution plus a six-foot-five-inch bodybuilder slathered in green body paint (not to say that a six-foot-five-inch bodybuilder slathered in green paint can't participate in prostitution too)—I LOVED IT! I loved it because no matter how much of the 1970s the producers ladled on the show, the core of it still remained. A person (Banner) who felt powerless and bullied (who knew deep inside that he was smarter and more sensitive than the bullies) could rise up against the bullies as his alter ego (the Hulk). It was literally every comic book geek's dream: *No one understands how smart and cool I am. But if they keep pushing me, I'll show them.*

My love of the Hulk and Spider-Man lasted through my teenage years. Superman got left behind in the '70s. I still watched the movies when they came out, but I didn't buy the comic books. Superman becomes boring real fast. He's too strong. Too powerful. He is invulnerable. And his weakness is boring. It's a rock. A rock from his home planet, Krypton. Who cares? I couldn't relate to being invulnerable. I was a Black kid growing up in America.

The Hulk and Spider-Man were regular people who had extraordinary abilities. I was also a regular person. I also had extraordinary abilities . . . I mean, I thought I did . . . I hoped I did. And there was something else here too. The Hulk and Spider-Man weren't white. I mean, yes, they were white people. David Banner and Peter Parker were both white men (OK, Spider-Man was a teenager when he began his superhero career), but when they were superheroes, the Hulk was green (usually with purple pants) and Spider-Man was mostly red and blue. You didn't know if Spider-Man was white or Black. When the Hulk showed up, nobody said, "Sure, he looks green. But I bet that when he calms down, he whitens up good."

That meant, as a kid, I could easily envision being Spider-Man or the Hulk. Everybody knew Superman was white. Everybody knew Batman was white. And those were the big four superheroes when I was a kid. And yes, there were a few Black superheroes around when I was a kid, but nobody really cared about them. They were side dishes to the main-course superheroes. There was Black Lightning, Black Vulcan, the Black Panther . . . Notice anything? Yep, when I was a kid it seemed like every Black superhero had to have the word "Black" in their name. Like it wasn't enough that they *were* Black. It wasn't enough that their *skin* was Black. There was seemingly some sort of contractual obligation to put the word

"Black" in their superhero name. (Bill Cosby made fun of this idea on his cartoon *Fat Albert and the Cosby Kids* by naming their favorite superhero the Brown Hornet.) Later, when I grew up, I discovered a Black hero named Blue Marvel, but the only way he got away with not using "Black" in his name was to cover his face so you couldn't see his skin. And there is a story in the comic book that once President Kennedy discovers that the Blue Marvel is actually Black, he asks him to retire, because I guess a president having an affair with Marilyn Monroe is one thing, but a BLACK SUPERHERO? ARE YOU CRAZY?

Creating Black superheroes with the word "Black" in their names was a way for America to once again normalize whiteness. It wasn't "*White* Superman" or "*White* Batman" or "*White* Green Lantern." Because "white" is normal. White doesn't need to be mentioned. But "Black," on the other hand, needs to be announced. To me, it made the superheroes sound less intimidating, less powerful, less normal than their white counterparts. I think some of that had to do with my own feelings at the time about being Black.

I was growing up in post-'60s Civil Rights–era America. I had been taught that Martin Luther King Jr. had ended racism one day when he and his friends took a long walk. But something didn't feel right about that. If racism was over, why was mom always referring to white people as "crackers"? Early on in my stand-up act, I had a joke where I said that I was eleven years old before I realized that a cracker was also a delicious snack. I was joking, but just barely. The best kind of joke. And that's what these "Black *Black*" superhero names felt like: a joke.

Think of the absolute ludicrousness of a superhero putting his own race in his superhero name. You can choose ANY NAME. And you choose something with "Black" in it? The whole idea of taking on a superhero name is to protect your secret identity, AND IN YOUR ALIAS YOU ARE GIVING OUT CLUES TO WHO YOU ARE??? It would be like if instead of Clark Kent just naming himself Super-man, he called himself "Superman . . . you know . . . from Small-ville." Putting "Black" in the name just felt corny to me when I was a kid. And that corniness made it obvious that these characters were being created by people who weren't Black. It went so far that there was actually a white superhero named Goliath, and when his powers ended up in a Black guy, the Black guy's superhero name was Black Goliath. I have no words for how dumb that is. WHY WOULD THAT BLACK GUY DO THAT TO HIMSELF? Am I supposed to imagine him saying to himself, *Nobody would ever believe that I'm Goliath. I'd better go by Black Goliath . . . because I have low superhero self-esteem.*

It may not seem as ridiculous to you. But think about it with a more famous superhero.

"Don't worry, Lex Luthor. Regular Superman isn't here. He sent Black Superman instead. We don't have to fight him. Just call the cops. They'll take care of him for us. They'll arrest him for loitering."

And yes, there were Black superheroes who didn't have the word "Black" in their names—Falcon, Cyborg, Power Man—and there was even a Black Green Lantern who was just named Green Lantern, not Black Green Lantern or Dark Green Lantern . . . or even Pine Green Lantern. But that didn't seem better. Everybody knew that the *real* Green Lantern was (white) Hal Jordan. (Black) John Stewart (yes, the Black Green Lantern's name was John Stewart) was just holding the position until Hal showed back up . . . which Hal always did. And Cyborg didn't really count because his *cyborginess* made it such that he didn't really have a secret identity anymore. He had half a robot face. Good luck convincing anybody that you're *not* Cyborg with that going on.

"What do you mean, you think I'm Cyborg? You're being ridiculous, I don't look anything like Cyborg! . . . Anyway, I gotta go change my eye battery and reboot my face's operating system."

And Falcon . . . Sigh . . . Falcon is one of those superheroes of many different races, including white, who just has the general feeling of a comic book writer saying to his boss, "WHAT? The new superhero is due tomorrow? Ummm . . . No . . . I totally have something to show you! It's going to be great. I'm just going to get in my brand-new Ford Falcon and go home and get my brand-new superhero . . . Wait a second! I GOT IT!" Heroes like Falcon—whether they were meant to or not—felt like they were designed to purposefully give the Black heroes shitty superpowers.

Falcon's big powers were that he had the powers of a falcon . . . Also he could talk to falcons. Falcon was like Aquaman but much less impressive. At least Aquaman had a blue whale for backup. Falcon only had one bird hanging out with him. His powers are so ridiculous that when they put the character in the *Avengers* movie, they just gave him some robot wings and left the "falcon powers" behind. Rightfully so.

And Power Man started out as the superhero version of the star of a Blaxploitation film dressed like an extra from *The Pirates of Penzance*. He had blue pants, swashbuckler boots, a bright yellow puffy shirt, metal wristbands, and a weird metal headband. Eventually he gave all that nonsense up, and now he just wears regular clothes and goes by the much better name Luke Cage (exploding out of a Netflix box near you!).

So when I was a kid, as much as I paid *some* attention to these Black heroes, I rode hard with Spider-Man and the Hulk. All I had to do was picture my face under all that red and blue fabric of Spider-Man and under Hulk's green skin. It was easier than calling myself "Black Batman" or trying to get excited by a Black superhero with the powers of a gnat—*Gnat-Man*! *Like Ant-Man, but even smaller!*

And this is important. This is about representation. For some reason, white people in America are perfectly comfortable with the idea of people of color just contorting their imaginations such that we can imagine ourselves as white heroes, but white people generally aren't OK with imagining themselves as Black heroes. Every time there's talk of a new actor taking on the role of James Bond and Idris Elba's name comes up, white people freak out: "HOW CAN A BLACK MAN BE JAMES BOND???" Meanwhile Hollywood *regularly* takes characters of color and turns them white whenever it wants. In the movie *Prince of Persia*, the prince (and most everybody else) was white. In the movie *Gods of Egypt*, the gods were not Egyptian. I guess their godly status had caused them to transcend the Egyptian plane . . . and skin tone.

And while we're on the subject, I'm not even sure that I want Idris to play James Bond. Because I don't know if I even want a Black James Bond. Well, truth be told, I'm not that excited about the white James Bond. Seems a little rapey and way too homicidal-maniac-y to me. I'm a fan of Idris bringing his own action hero to the big screen. One that he can turn into whatever he wants. It's not enough to have Black James Bond. We need new heroes. We need new heroes who can build their own legends and not be walking in white characters' footsteps.

Enter *Doc McStuffins*.

The need for Black heroes has become increasingly clear to me since I've had my oldest daughter, Sami. Like me, she was born with the TV gene. She can sit and watch TV for hours. Like it's an Olympic event and she's trying to set a new world record in the five-year-old division. I'm so proud. But it was important to me, as I saw her fall in love with TV the same way I had, that she have heroes who look like her. Not just Black versions of white heroes, not just Black heroes who seem like diminished versions of white heroes, and certainly not just white heroes who require my daughter to always twist and contort her imagination to put herself in those white shoes. I want my daughter to have her own Black *girl* (yup, I'm aiming for the stars here) heroes.

And that's where *Doc McStuffins* has come to the rescue.

When Sami was around two years old, she was just starting to really dig into TV. I had hooked her through *Sesame Street*, the gateway show to good children's television. *Sesame Street* had been there for me and was there for my daughter. And thanks to YouTube, many of the same exact segments were there for Sami. It gives me great pleasure that Sami knows how to count to twelve using the same jazzy Ella Fitzgerald–esque manner that I learned, thanks to *Sesame Street*. But around the time Sami turned two, a new sheriff showed up in town, and just like in *Blazing Saddles*, this sheriff was Black . . . and not really a sheriff. She was better than a sheriff. She was a doctor. Dottie, aka "Doc," McStuffins. Doc McStuffins is to TV what Shirley Chisholm was to Congress or what producer Shonda Rhimes was to primetime television or what

Oprah was to daytime talk shows . . . or what Oprah was to book clubs . . . or what Oprah was to a billion dollars. Doc McStuffins is a Black woman in a space not normally welcome to (and certainly never dominated by) Black women. Which is even more impressive when you realize that she's only seven years old.

OK, I'm getting ahead of myself.

Doc is a cartoon character who is the star of a show named after herself on Disney Junior. And Disney Junior is ethering the game right now. (That's probably not a sentence that's written that often.) Look, I'd love to be one of those people who is too righteous to support a corporation, or one of those people who can't trust anything that comes from corporate America, but I can't. And believe me, I wish I could. It would get me invited to much cooler parties in Oakland. I am totally suspicious of corporate America, but honestly, I'm also the person who, when I'm hungry in an airport and can't figure out if I'm going to eat at the "sad sandwich" place, where the premade sandwiches are wrapped in plastic and the lettuce often tastes like it gave up and took its own life and the bread tastes like buttered shoe leather, or the "Asian fusion" place, where the orange chicken has been there so long that it should be called *oranged* chicken, looks up and sees the golden arches, and like the five-year-old I used to be, runs frantically toward it, screaming, "YAY! McDONALD'S!!!" So I ain't afraid of Disney.

Yes, Disney has heavily contributed to "princess culture" in America's young girls. *Snow White and the Seven Dwarfs* was the first of many mighty blows to get young girls to think that "princess" was a job, the same way young boys wanted to be firemen, astronauts, and cowboys. Disney clearly recognizes that they should expand the definition of what girls can do, and which girls can do it. After decades of white princesses, they finally added a Black one, Tiana; a Chinese one, Mulan; an Arab one, Jasmine; a Native American one, Pocahontas; and recently a Latina one, Elena. Well, maybe Elena—while she is a Latina princess, she hasn't actually made the cut as an official Disney Princess on the list of princesses on the Disney Princess website. I'll keep updating my browser as you read and see if anything changes. Maybe she's on probation. Not a great look for Disney to just sort of, kind of add a Latina princess, when so many Latinos in America are also having so many problems being officially added to this country.

But since Sami's been around, Disney has expanded the list of jobs a little girl can have to include sheriffs (OK, technically Sheriff Callie from *Sheriff Callie's Wild West* is a cat, but she is a female cat), undersea explorers on *The Octonauts* (hell, Tweak, a rabbit, is even the ship's *female* mechanic), and, yes, even astronauts. *Miles from Tomorrowland* not only features a mixed-race family (Asian and white), but the captain of the ship is *THE MOM*!!! It may sound like I am making too much out of all this, but the only way you can allow a kid to truly dream is if you expand their idea of what is currently possible. A kid who has nothing, sees nothing, and is taught nothing can only dream of breakfast. They can only hope to get to the next moment successfully. I want more than that for my kids . . . just like my mom wanted more than that for me. And I want *them* to want more than that too.

And *Doc McStuffins* went way further to expand Sami's world than I ever could have imagined. And the show—and Sami's and later my daughter Juno's reaction to it—blows my whole childhood dream of "Maybe I could be Spider-Man or the Hulk" completely out of the water.

———

Doc McStuffins is about a seven-year-old Black girl. That basically makes the title character the Diahann Carroll of children's TV. Diahann Carroll was the first African-American woman to be the star of a TV show . . . who wasn't playing a maid. Diahann's show was a sitcom called *Julia*. It ran from 1968 to 1971 (which is the equivalent of twenty-one seasons of twenty-first-century white television). Julia was a single mom . . . because of course. And since then not enough has changed in grown-up real-life TV, especially if you subtract shows produced by Shonda Rhimes. And kids' TV is even worse as far as meaningful diversity and inclusion. How many children's TV shows other than *Doc McStuffins* have a Black female lead character? Hint: The answer is "not nearly enough."

In the show, Doc McStuffins is a doctor for her stuffed animals and toys. And that may sound merely adorable to you, but I'm raising a pair of powerful Black girls who will one day be powerful Black women. And *Doc McStuffins* is the reason that my four-year-old could say the words "stethoscope," "otoscope," and "sphygmomanometer" when she was two years old. I had to use Google just to figure out how to spell "sphygmomanometer." Being a doctor is Doc's job. Doc diagnoses, fills out a chart (the Big Book of Boo Boos), and heals. She does everything from replacing dirty bandages to full-on surgery. Doc also encourages her patients to brush their teeth, wear helmets on bicycles, and be good friends. And she makes house calls. By any measure, Doc McStuffins is a more reliable and trustworthy TV doctor than Dr. Oz. And she's not even real.

And then there are Doc's parents. On the show, Doc's mom is an actual doctor. Which means young kids don't have to wait until they're old enough to watch *Grey's Anatomy* to see a Black female doctor on television. And it means that for my daughters, a Black female doctor is no big deal, as it shouldn't be. The show even has interstitials with actual Black female doctors to prove that the idea of a Black female doctor isn't just for cartoons. *Did I just blow your mind? No? Keep reading.*

Next, we have Doc's dad. What's his job? Well, actually, I'm not sure exactly what he does. I'm pretty sure he's a stay-at-home dad, which is also revolutionary for multiple reasons. (Mom works. Dad's at home taking care of the kids. And again, these are Black people!) But what Dad mostly does is hang out in the kitchen chopping vegetables and offering them to Doc and her friends—vegetables that he seems to grow in his garden!!! *Now did I blow your mind?*

And then there are Doc's patients. The toys. Now, yes, there is the argument that the toys are the real show here. Doc has a room full of toys, and her friends are always bringing new toys over, and every toy is a marketing opportunity for the Big D! (And, yes, Disney does take many of these opportunities. But I ain't mad at 'em.) See, the toys that Doc attends to are her friends as well. They all come to life and talk with the help of Doc's magic stethoscope.

Yup, I said "magic stethoscope." Now, at first when I watched the show, it was a *Calvin and Hobbes* situation. We, the audience, didn't know if the stethoscope was really magic or if Doc just had a vivid imagination. But over time it has become clear that the stethoscope's magic is very real. And it is also clear that the toys really are living a life of their own when Doc's not around. When Doc walks into a room and presses the bell of her stethoscope, it emits a melody that is as ubiquitous in my house as the "YEE-HAW!" of the Duke boys was in my mom's house when I was a kid. And when that noise rings out, every toy in the room comes to life. And I mean every toy: stuffed animals, dolls, action figures, remote control cars, soccer balls, xylophones. And each toy serves a role in helping teach kids how to communicate with real-life doctors and the world around them in general. Among Doc's dozens of toy friends, there's a toy with asthma, a toy in a wheelchair, and even a toy that Doc teaches how to respond to inappropriate touching. Yes, that happens in a kids' cartoon. And it happens with a song. And like any good mystical amulet, Doc's stethoscope's powers grow. In the third season it suddenly becomes a time machine and takes Doc and the gang back to nineteenth-century London to meet a young Florence Nightingale. And later we learn that Doc received the stethoscope from her grandma. So not only is #BlackGirlMagic real, but #BlackGrandmaMagic is real too. And any TV show that is going to teach my daughters to respect the mystical power of old Black ladies has a permanent spot in my DVR.

The show's objective is to get kids to be more comfortable speaking up for themselves and to not be afraid to get help when they need it. But wait, there's more! There was the episode about a big storm that was coming. Hallie the Hippo and Chilly the Snowman are separated from Doc and the other toys, and they get scared. *I swear I wasn't crying. I just had bad allergies that day.* And at the beginning of the episode, Professor Hootsburgh just happens to mention in passing, "As the earth gets warmer and warmer, big storms get bigger and bigger." Yup, *Doc McStuffins* just told kids about climate change. *OK, now your mind is definitely blown!*

And no matter what the theme of each episode is, they all are inherently about inclusion and acceptance. There's an episode that is basically about people with curly hair accepting that it won't ever be long and flowing. In my house of mixed daughters, that hit us right where we live. *I swear, I wasn't crying that time either. Again, these damn allergies!* Recently, the show has released some episodes about taking care of pets, and in the process it's gotten meta, which is to say that some of the characters now occasionally seem aware of the show's conceits (the songs, the magic stethoscope). Which means my kids will appreciate metahumor years before I did. And another episode about the parents of a friend of Doc's contains the takeaway that the parents are two moms. *BOOM!*

And through every episode, Doc is there handling everything. She is the boss. She is the Olivia Pope of children's television. *Doc McStuffins* is not only one of the best shows on television, it's also one of the most important shows in the history of television. And my two daughters watch it thinking it is awesome, but more importantly, they think it is normal. A Black female doctor is no big deal. And it should be no big deal for children of all races. But it is. And the proof is that it took TV a *lot* longer to have *Doc McStuffins* than it did for TV to have a seven-foot-tall green monster. And as much as I love the Hulk, Doc is way more important. Because one day I might get to play the Hulk in a movie or TV show (with lots of makeup . . . and even more steroids). But my daughters *can actually be* Black doctors. I know they can. Because they've already seen that it's possible.

CHAPTER 2

My Awkward Blackness

So it turns out I'm a "Blerd," aka "Black nerd." And unbeknownst to me, I have been one for years. I only found out about my Blerd status in the past few years. I didn't choose it. It chose me. Well, actually, it sort of rose up around me while I wasn't looking. Kind of the same way that "cisgender" did. I first heard both of those words when I was making my late-night talk show, *Totally Biased*. "Cisgender" was taught to me by Guy Branum, one of the comics who wrote for the show. Guy had come out of the same San Francisco scene that I had come out of, but several years later, so I didn't really know him that well. I did hire a bunch of comics who I was friends with to write for the show, and several of them suggested Guy in the second season. Guy immediately made an impact on the show. He was hilarious, gay, and had a law degree from UC Berkeley, which meant Guy covered a lot of areas I wanted the show to be covering. I wanted *Totally Biased* to be funny and inclusive, but I also wanted it to be smart. TV generally only cares about the funny part. While FX was very supportive of what I wanted the show to be, internally at the show there were voices pulling it in another direction. "Just be funny!" I didn't know how to do that. I had purposefully hired friends who were smart and funny and who had different perspectives from me.

Hari Kondabolu, Nato Green, and Janine Brito were all great comics and three of my best friends in comedy. Hari is a Brooklyn-based, Queens-born, Indian-American comedian with a master's degree in human rights from . . . (wait for it) the London School of Economics. You know . . . just like most comics! Nato Green is a San Francisco native, old-school lefty, white, Jewish union organizer who also happened to grow up in San Francisco during another of SF's many golden ages of comedy. The Patton Oswalt, Marc Maron, Dana Gould, Margaret Cho era. How could Nato not want to be a comedian when all those legends were just walking around the streets of San Francisco? Janine was also a San Francisco comic. I liked her the first time I saw her onstage. I started calling her my comedy daughter. This was before I had my own real-life daughters. Janine is half Cuban, all lesbian, and she has a degree in business from Washington University in St. Louis. We had veteran TV writers in the room too, who could help us rein in all the "We're gonna change the world!" energy when we needed to focus on the deadlines.

And right between those two poles was Dwayne Kennedy. Dwayne is a stand-up comic and folk hero from the Chicago comedy scene. Nobody really knows how long Dwayne has been on the scene, but everybody has stories of working with him, from Chris Rock to the brand-new open-mic guy who started last night in Chicago. And everybody has the same impression of Dwayne:

he's funnier than all of us, and it doesn't make sense that he's not famous. Dwayne is like the apocryphal playground legend from basketball. He has had a couple shots. He's played in the league several times (he's been on *Letterman* and Comedy Central), but his best games happened when no cameras were around. And if he reads this, he'll probably laugh and say, "Yeah, bub. You right." Much of the reason that Dwayne hasn't had the career that seemed to be just waiting for him is that Dwayne is a conscious iconoclast. Dwayne has only recently come around to this whole "using a computer" fad that swept the nation in the 1980s.

I met Dwayne at the No Exit Café in Chicago, where I started doing open mics. He came in and did a joke about what it would have been like to be Jesus Christ's bitter brother, Steve Christ. He leveled the place, absolutely killed, and then immediately got offstage. Dwayne was a truth-teller in the spirit of Richard Pryor, Dave Chappelle, Lenny Bruce, and Chris Rock, but like all those dudes, Dwayne also just wanted to be funny. He often straddled the line between "earnest" and "just effin' funny" of any big picture discussions in the writers' room.

A lot has been written about "the writers' room" in recent years. And in my little experience with them, they definitely do tend to be places where straight white men can let their hair down and just be comfortable being themselves. (Finally!) And honestly, I don't know that we need more of those rooms, especially when they just got back their favorite room to do that in: the White House. When writers' rooms have any diversity at all, it is often hard-fought for and often pushed back against, because of one word: "experience." People want to go with "experience" over the unknown-ness of a new writer. And that is especially true when those writers are *not* white men. Writers who are not that funny—or worse, lazy—get job after job because . . . well, because their résumé has a lot of jobs on it. That means that in most writers' rooms that have any diversity, there is just one woman or one person darker than mayonnaise. Which means that person has the pressure to either speak up when their issues come up and then look like "Here comes the diversity hire chiming in just to bum us out," or that person has the pressure to shut up, so they don't look like they are trying to bum people out.

Even on the first season of *Totally Biased*, Janine was the only writer in the room who was a woman. That meant every time there was some news story involving women, there would be a subtle head tilt of the room toward Janine. And this would happen no matter what the news story was. Basically we were all saying, "Hey, Janine! What does the fairer sex think about this?" And Janine, who was usually wearing some form of men's-style blazer, a button-up shirt, and a tie, would sometimes say, "If you're looking at me to give the 'lady perspective,' then we're screwed." None of the men in the room had to hold "the men's perspective." We were allowed to just be ourselves. I knew that look on Janine's face. I gave similar looks throughout my life, when I was expected to represent Black-ness when I knew that I was the wrong Black guy to do it. And this show was making me feel that as one of the few Black hosts ever in late-night TV, I was expected to represent a lot more than just myself.

While I didn't know what to do about my problem, I was pretty sure that the show could do a better job with diversity. So the second season we hired two more writers who were women—Eliza Skinner and Aparna Nancherla. Aparna is South Asian–American, so now also Hari wasn't the only South Asian–American in the room. And we also hired Guy. Immediately all the new writers had an impact. Guy and Janine came up with a perfect segment for him called "No More Mr. Nice Gay." In the first one, he tore apart a story about NFL players and homophobia. It was beautiful. I could have done many of the same jokes myself, but they were much more powerful coming from a guy who had a stake in the game. That's why representation is not just opportune but also essential.

On camera, Guy was a force of nature. But off camera, Guy was the perfect guy to help slowly and methodically lead me to a new understanding of gender. He explained to me that you are "cisgender" when whatever gender people *think you are* is the same gender that you *know you are*. So since I feel like a man and people treat me like a man, then I am a cisgender man. It was confusing at first, because I was trying to figure out where sexuality came into it. But it doesn't. That's a whole different thing, Guy explained. In other words, Anderson Cooper looks like "a man" (or whatever society says a man "should" look like) and Anderson Cooper identifies himself as a man, so Anderson Cooper is a cisgender man. And none of that has anything to do with his being gay. The concept of cisgender is a way to denormalize something that is thought of as "normal," because *there is no normal*. Not in gender. And not in race. I had definitely grown up feeling like I was not a "normal Black boy." And that's where "blerd" came to the rescue. I only wish that it had shown up twenty years sooner.

I found out that I was a Blerd when I was reading an article by Eric Deggans, an entertainment writer for NPR who is also a Blerd. In the article he referred to me as this new generation of Black people who are cool with being nerdy, unlike the stereotype of Black people. Now, even though I had never heard this word before, when I read it I thought to myself, "Oh, is that what I've been this whole time? Awesome! Let's go with that!"

Growing up as an only child who was left to march to the beat of his own drum, I just thought I was not into the right (Black) stuff. The TV was my best friend, and I just sort of watched whatever looked interesting to me at the time. And this was the era of five, maybe six, channels, and these channels weren't going to spend a ton—if anything—on original programming. So my TV was awash in reruns. Mostly 1960s- and 1970s-era reruns. It was an all-you-can-eat buffet of one of America's greatest art forms: situation comedies! I ate a steady diet of *The Brady Bunch, Sanford and Son, Good Times, I Dream of Jeannie, Bewitched* (aka boring *I Dream of Jeannie*), *Soap, Wonder Woman, What's Happening!!, The Partridge Family, The Jeffersons, Gilligan's Island, The Monkees,* and eventually *Diff'rent Strokes* and *The Facts of Life* when they were around long enough to go to syndication heaven. It was a wide range of shows with diverse casts, although they were definitely divided into "Black shows" and "white shows." *Good Times, What's Happening!!,* and *Sanford and Son* featured white people as mostly a threat from the outside . . . or as a punch line (the white cop from *Sanford and Son*). In the 1970s, Black people were still regularly referring to "the Man" as a catch-all for white supremacy, white privilege, and racism in general. So even when white people weren't on the show physically, their presence was still there.

But on white shows like *The Brady Bunch, The Partridge Family, The Monkees,* and the rest, not only were Black people not onscreen, we were not a factor at all. Sure, every now and again a Black face would pop up, but that was it. They popped up and immediately popped right back down again. I have to give *Gilligan's Island* some credit, though. When Black people finally showed up, there were like ten of them at once . . . because it was *the Harlem Globetrotters*.

The shows that made it into the 1980s did a better job. George Jefferson basically came on TV every week to tell the white man to kiss his rich Black ass. It was kind of like—what if Ben Carson had a spine? *Diff'rent Strokes* created a weird trope that other shows and movies followed: white people getting Black kids through strange circumstances. But as much as Gary Coleman became an easy target for lazy comedians and others to make fun of, his character of Arnold Jackson was like a three-foot George Jefferson often telling his white dad to kiss his ass . . . but in more adorable language.

But looking back, these shows were all the same to me at the time. I knew I loved *Good Times,* but I also knew I loved *The Brady Bunch.* I never thought to pick. Eventually, I found that people regularly wanted me to pick between Black stuff and white stuff. I just like stuff. I'm a stuff-ist.

Me and my mom always loved watching TV together. And Friday night in the late '70s and into the early '80s was the greatest prime-time lineup of television of all time period. On CBS, they had *The Incredible Hulk, The Dukes of Hazzard,* and finally *Dallas.* These were two of the whitest shows on television and definitely the greenest show on television. If I watched *Dallas* now, I'd be like, "Where are the people of color? I've been to Dallas" . . . but I wasn't thinking that critically back then, and my mom loved watching those ridiculous story lines featuring rich white people who couldn't stop screwing up their lives. I loved knowing I was watching grown-up TV. And my mom loved watching me watch *The Incredible Hulk*. Like I said, she even cut up some of my old clothes (including a Julian Bond for president T-shirt I had that had gotten too small) so that I could properly Hulk-out the two times an episode the producers could afford for David Banner to do it. But there was a problem in the middle of this awesome TV sandwich. It was called *The Dukes of Hazzard*.

Part of my love of *The Dukes of Hazzard* was that I'd spent all that time in Alabama, so the Southern-ness of it felt familiar to me. Also I loved cartoons, and it was kind of like a cartoon, even though it was not at all a cartoon. The portrayals on the show were super over-the-top, and it was super campy, and the car was always bright orange and didn't have a scratch on it, and it had doors that didn't open. They were in fact welded shut. I was one of the kids who wanted to crawl through the car window to get into our car. But my mom never let me do it. Also the *Hazzard* car could basically jump over anything in its way. At least as long as somebody had left a ramp—or something that could easily be used as a ramp—nearby. And somebody always did. Or at least twice a show somebody did.

I feel like my generation was the first one that was raised to look at the world through what would later be called a post-racial lens. I feel like school taught me that racism was an issue solved by Martin Luther King Jr. . . . all by himself . . . nobody else was there. Not even his wife, Coretta Scott King. He was a solo act, according to my history books. So I wasn't wondering where the Black people were on *The Dukes of Hazzard*, because MLK had fixed all that bad, sad, no-good racism. So this show, even though it was set in "Hazzard County, Georgia," a place where there would be boatfuls of Black people, only had like one

Black dentist, according to my memory of watching it. I remember thinking to myself, "He must be a really good dentist!"

Looking back, I cringe. What was my mom thinking? She was smart enough to know that banning me from watching it would only create more mystery around it. But as someone who lived through the Civil Rights era, as someone who had grown up in Indiana during the heyday of whites-only drinking fountains and Black sections in the balconies of movie theaters, I have no idea how she was strong enough to sit there and *watch me* watch that show. What was going through her mind as every week I watched these two rednecks get into wacky hijinks? And then what was she thinking when I would sometimes get excited and scream out, "YAY! The General Lee saved the day!!!" Yup, that was the name of the car: the General Lee. Racism is deep. And great at creating brand loyalty.

When I was about four, me and my mother moved to Boston. I went to a couple different schools there and eventually settled at the Park School, which is a very northeast private school where there was only one other Black kid in my class, Dana Jackson, who I would define as like, "I met Will Smith when I was in elementary school!" because Dana Jackson was a light-skinned, tall, good-looking Black dude. Later, when I saw Will Smith for the first time, I thought, Oh, he's like Dana Jackson. A super-confident, handsome kid . . . He was just one of those kids who, at eleven years old, for some reason, had abs. I was friendly with him, but we weren't the best of friends; we were just the only two Black kids in our class.

The only physical activity I was interested in was martial arts. And the only reason I liked that was because every weekend I gorged myself on Black Belt Sunday. Every city I lived in when I was a kid had some form of this. Black Belt Sunday or Kung Fu Saturday . . . These were programs that showed cheaply produced B-movies imported from Hong Kong that featured maximum butt-kicking. I loooooooved these movies. They were about duty and morals and the underdog winning the day. Things that all resonated with me as a Black kid growing up in America. But let's be real. They were also about kicking mofos upside the head when mofos stepped out of the mofo'ing line. My favorite movies were the Bruce Lee movies. Well, at least I thought they were showing Bruce Lee movies. When I became a teenager and video stores became all the rage, I found out that Bruce Lee actually only made four movies in his lifetime, and, more surprisingly, I found out that I hadn't seen any of them. I had fallen in love with the knockoffs, the aptly titled "Bruceploitation" flicks that flooded out after Bruce Lee's early death.

When I finally discovered the real deal, I forever swore off the imitators and only watched the authentic Bruce. Which meant I watched those four movies over and over and over and over again. *Enter the Dragon, Return of the Dragon, The Chinese Connection, Fists of Fury*—you could drop me in the middle of any of those movies and I would know all the dialogue and the moves. From there I started taking weekend karate classes, then tae kwon do classes, and then, finally (and most awesomely), after I moved to Chicago, when I was in high school, I began studying Wing Chun kung fu, the style that Bruce Lee had started with in Hong Kong when he was a teenager, like I was at the time. Clearly I was going to grow up to be the next Bruce Lee.

I felt a real connection to Bruce. Bruce Lee had become my hero and, in a way, my surrogate dad. My and my dad's relationship was good, but we didn't talk that often. I could pop in a Bruce

Lee movie anytime I wanted. In addition to being a student of martial arts, Bruce was also a student of philosophy. I memorized my favorite quotes from the books he wrote during his brief lifetime. My favorite one was, "Absorb what is useful, discard what is useless, and add what is specifically your own." That became my mantra. It was Bruce giving me permission to live my own life without worrying about what other people thought. Bruce was preparing me for my future as a leading Blerd.

My walls were covered in Bruce Lee posters. (Still would be if I thought it would fit in with my and Melissa's decorating scheme.) This was the '80s, when finding Bruce Lee stuff meant going to Chinatown and doing a deep dive in the tourist traps. At that point he hadn't been taken fully into the bosom of mainstream pop culture. A few years ago, I saw a Bruce T-shirt at Target; I was horrified that his image was in such a crass store, and I bought it immediately. To this day I wish I had bought two. But back in the '80s, the only Bruce Lee shirt I had was a thin white T-shirt with a cheap iron-on transfer. I felt like I was the only Bruce Lee fan left in the world, but I also felt cooler because of it. That was the true beginning of my pride in being an outsider.

And I wasn't just an outsider to pop culture. At the same time, while I was digging into *Black Belt* magazine and *Inside Kung Fu* magazine, it seemed like every other Black person in the world was inventing rap music and hip-hop culture. I didn't miss it entirely. If "Rapper's Delight" comes on, I'll get as giddy as anybody, but it didn't resonate with me like it seemed to resonate with every other Black person my age. To this day I get a little skittish when I find myself in a position where people assume that I am a fan of hip-hop. Black people, white people, all people have done this to me. "J. Cole's new album is good."

"Ummm . . . sure . . . You betcha it is!" I'm not free of rap music in my life at all; I just treat it like I do all my other interests in my life. I don't like any whole thing. I like individual things. I really love one thing in particular to the exclusion of all other things that are even similar. Heavy metal? Depends. Metallica? YES!

So do I listen to every rap album released? Nope. But did I squeal like a kid on Christmas morning when I saw Run the Jewels had dropped their new album days before it was supposed to be released? Yup. I may have even let a little pee out.

Many years ago (I'm guessing in the '90s; you'll see why that's my guess soon), I was waiting to board a plane, and a younger Black dude sat down next to me in the way that says without words, "I'm happy to see a Black dude my age around here!" And then he said the words that I had at that time learned to dread from a Black person around my age: "What are you listening to?" I slowly peeled off my headphones and said, "Umm . . . Pearl . . . Jam." He responded, confused, "Are they a hip-hop group?" Me: "Um . . . No." I kind of wanted to say, "Sorry. I'm a weirdo. Please don't tell the other Black people." He responded, "Can I check it out?" I was shocked. I said, "Sure." And I handed over my headphones, but he used his own instead. Even though we shared a race, we didn't need to share earwax. He listened for a little bit, and finally took them off and said, "Not my thing, but it's cool anyway." I felt something approaching ultimate relief. *I wasn't as strange as I thought!* . . . Just kidding. None of that happened. Well at least everything only happened up until I said "Pearl Jam." Then the conversation was over. Then we sat in silence until one of us needed to board our flight. In the 1990s, being a Black person who does not listen to hip-hop as his music of choice *by definition* makes you an outsider.

———

Me and my mom moved A LOT! Palo Alto, Indianapolis, Boston, and sometimes there would be moves within each city. By the time we got to Chicago in 1984, I was completely sick of moving, and I kind of snapped. I hadn't wanted to leave Boston. We had been there several years. I had been in the same school for a couple years. I could feel myself getting my bearings. Then in 1984 my mom quit her day job as an editor at a textbook company, where her job was to diversify stories in English textbooks. (I don't know if that was the job she was hired for, but you can bet that was the job she did.) But then out of the blue, we up and moved to Chicago. She says that after living in hyper-parochial Boston—where white people often said things like, "My family came over on the *Mayflower*," as a way to prove their worth, which was made even worse by some of the Black people saying as much as, "My family was purchased by people who came over on the *Mayflower*"—she was ready for a change. And when she saw Harold Washington become Chicago's first Black mayor, and thereby Black America's mayor, she knew that the place to be was Chicago.

But in a way, it was a surprising choice, since, being from Indianapolis, my mom had grown up with a nurtured mistrust and dislike of Chicago. Since Chicago is only a three-hour drive from Indy, Indy is always losing its best and brightest and bravest to Chicago, and instead of figuring out what they could do to stop the brain drain, Naptown residents just hated on Chicago: "Chicago is too big. Too dangerous. Too fast." In my travels around America, living and doing stand-up comedy, I've found this is kind of a thing all over the country. The not-so-big city hates the not-so-far-away big city. Mobile, Alabama, kind of hates Atlanta. Portland, Oregon, absolutely knows that it's better than Seattle, Washington. Philly hates New York City. Sacramento definitely has a chip on its shoulder about San Francisco. And San Francisco condescends to Los Angeles. And for the most part these are one-way rivalries. When I later moved to San Francisco, I was surprised to find out that audiences there hissed (literally hissed) whenever a comedian said the words "Los Angeles."

"I just came back from Los Angeles."

"HISS!"

Or: "I'm visiting from Los Angeles."

"HISS!"

"My mom died last night in Los Angeles."

"Awwww . . . HISSSSS! She deserved it!"

Meanwhile, if you bring up San Francisco to Los Angeles, LA is like, "Love San Fran! The weather's great! A beautiful city! Love visiting there."

That's all true, but then they always go too far . . .

"I should move there."

They always say that. They never do "move there." It's their way of saying that San Francisco is cute. The same way grown men call little boys "big guy."

But in the end, I'm sure some of this nurtured Indianapolis–Chicago hater-ism was a part of my mom's decision to move to Chicago. My mom has that kind of spirit. Tell her she can't do something and she does it. But not to prove you wrong. She does it to prove it to herself. So if Indianapolis is scared of Chicago, then my mom has to go try to take Chicago down.

Chicago in 1984 was on the verge of being the place the world wanted to be. Not only was Harold Washington in place, but Michael Jordan and Oprah were making plans to take over Chicago, and later the galaxy. And Chicago's own Reverend Jesse Jackson was in the middle of running for president. (A Black president??? Come on!) And as much as people have, in retrospect, tried to turn his run for presidency into a joke, at the time it felt real. Not that he could really be president, but that he could really be taken seriously. I stand by this statement: No Jesse Jackson running for president, no President Barack Obama.

But none of that mattered to me. I hated Chicago. Hated it. I hated my new school, a classic large Chicago public school. I had just come from a classic—and classically small—New England private school. And even if I wasn't as popular as Dana Jackson, at least everybody knew my name. In my new school in Chicago, I felt invisible. The one good thing that came out of going to that school is that I met my future best friend Jason Smith, a skinny white Jewish kid, before re-meeting him in high school after I moved back to Chicago. I say "re-meeting" because we weren't even friends at this school. That's how fucked up I felt. I didn't even recognize my best friend, one of the loves of my life, the first time I met him. Sorry, Jason.

So I called an audible. I forced a trade to my dad's house (well, actually my stepmom's house since that's where he lived) in Mobile, Alabama. I had spent every summer there since childhood. I didn't really love it, but it did feel familiar, which is something I desperately craved at that point. I was in seventh grade, a year and a half from entering high school. I wanted to feel normal and not like a freak. Mobile was the wrong place for that. I remember that literally the night I got there, I went to "my room" (minus the Bruce Lee posters and minus my mom, who was at the time my first best friend) and I started to wonder if I had done the right thing. I loved my dad. I wanted that dad/son stuff that I had seen in reruns of *The Courtship of Eddie's Father*. And we occasionally had that, but it wasn't enough. I often felt like I wasn't the son he wanted. Not athletic, not cool. I felt like not much of anything really. And, Dad, I know you are reading this right now. And I want you to know that I *know* absolutely that you are proud of me and that you love me and would do anything for me. It was just hard for me to see that back then.

I stayed there for two and a half years before me and my mom began planning my return to her. I didn't care what city she lived in at that point. It was two and a half years of going from being an only child to being expected to become a part of my dad's new nuclear family. Two and a half years of hearing (and knowing) that I was not living up to my potential in school. Two and a half years of my dad wanting me to play basketball, because he knew I was going to be tall like him. Two and a half years of not getting much outward affection. Now, that may not sound like much, but it was a big deal for me as a guy who grew up with my mom's constant words and physical expressions of love . . . Because of my mom, I'm powered by hugs.

When I moved back to Chicago without my dad's blessing, it was hard on him. I know it was. I didn't care at the time. I just needed my mommy. I was a sophomore in high school enrolled at the University of Chicago Laboratory High School. I re-met Jason by recognizing him from years before, so I sat next to him at lunch one day. He soon after told me that when I sat down, he thought to himself, "I know that I know him from middle school, but why does he think I want him to sit here?"

That feeling didn't last long. We were fast—and are forever— friends. It was an odd coupling from the very beginning. He was a long-haired Deadhead. I would get haircuts every few months. And when I did, I would just get it cut off. Not bald but close. I've always hated haircuts. But I lived during the era of Kid 'n Play flattops, Bobby Brown's Gumby cut, back when Ice Cube had Jheri curls, and NBA players would get the entire team roster photo cut into the backs of their heads. Meanwhile I was walking around looking either like week one of boot camp or— when my Afro grew out—an African exchange student. (It was the late '80s, and Afros hadn't come back yet.) Jason had found himself in high school, but I was clearly still trying to figure myself out.

Me and Jason bonded over our seemingly equal outsider-ness. He was the son of a University of Chicago professor dad and an award-winning piano teacher mother. He lived in a house stacked high with books and filled with classical music. He had a sister, but he seemed like an only child like me, because his sister was a few years older and never seemed to be home. We would go to his house, disappear into his room, and he would chain-smoke Marlboro Reds. And he would blow the smoke out the window so as to not affect my asthma. Jason had a cynical exterior, the kind that made high school teachers stutter when they realized he was smarter than them, and they knew that *he knew it*. But he was really a sweetheart. And I could use all the sweetness he (or anyone else) had because I came back from

Alabama feeling broken. This was symbolized by the fact that I went to Mobile as Kamau and I came back as Walter. When I got to Mobile, I was twelve, feeling beaten down by Chicago and not excited to look like a weirdo with a weird name, which is crazy considering that being Black with an untraditional name was no big story in and of itself. Black people are a nation of Kobes, Dwyanes, Jameises, and LeBrons. But I just didn't want to be noticed. I was suddenly ashamed of my very traditional and very Kenyan name. For the first time in my life, I didn't want to feel special. I didn't want to be an individual. It wasn't until I was nineteen that I reclaimed "Kamau."

But back to high school for now. My music education started when I moved back to Chicago with my other best friend in high school, Rob Nasatir, less skinny than Jason but still a white Jewish kid. Rob was the school musician. He was a singer and a guitar and saxophone player. And he had a dad who had a high-end stereo system. I would spend hours in Rob's house listening to music. And Rob's taste was all over the map and adventurous. So the music I got into wasn't the beginner's level. It was all advanced level. Stuff like Miles Davis's *Bitches Brew*, John Coltrane's *Sun Ship*, and Jimi Hendrix—but only *Band of Gypsys*–era Hendrix. Rob and Jason are also the people who explained to me that Jimi Hendrix was Black. Before them I didn't know. Awkward. Rob also listened to everything Bob Dylan, Frank Zappa, Kate Bush, Todd Rundgren, and more stuff to make a liberal college radio audience stay home instead of going to the frat party. I didn't fully appreciate it until years later, but Rob basically assured me that I would always have an adventurous musical palate. But it also meant that since Rob didn't listen to much rap, I didn't listen to much rap. But that was a much bigger deal for me than for him.

One night we went to Rose Records in the suburbs of Chicago. Rob bought a bunch of cassettes from the new releases section. When we got in the car to head to the movies, Rob popped a cassette in. The sounds that came from his car speakers lifted me up and called me to attention. It sounded like somebody had taken the sounds inside my head and turned them into music. It was screaming guitar, funky bass, syncopated drums, and soulful rock vocals. It was the band Living Colour. They were four Black dudes from New York who played rock-and-roll but with a modern and super-Black twist. (The twist being mostly that people loved to forget that Black people invented rock-and-roll.) They wore bright colors and had dreadlocks and braids. I was in love. They immediately became my favorite band. Their songs rock hard but were filled with Black images and political messages. Songs like "Pride," "Time's Up," and "Information Overload." Kind of like if Public Enemy had a guitar player, and it was Jimi Hendrix. A few years later when I went to college I grew my hair long on top so I could grow dreadlocks like Living Colour's guitar player/leader Vernon Reid. It was a disaster, but it was also the first time I saw Blackness in the world that fit me. It was glorious.

But that was later. In high school it was me, Rob, Jason, and Jon Norton. (I added a third nice Jewish boy.) They had all known each other most of their lives due to growing up together in the small, tight-knit Jewish community of the Hyde Park neighborhood on the South Side of Chicago. Hyde Park was a neighborhood that really only existed because of the University of Chicago. It was surrounded on three sides by the South Side of Chicago—the *Good Times* version of Chicago—mostly Black, inner-city neighborhoods with all the challenges that go along with that. Hyde Park might have also been mostly Black, but it didn't feel like it. It felt downright suburban in comparison. It was a sometimes strained existence between the two areas. When the movie theater in Hyde Park expanded and became the only really good movie theater for miles and miles, the white and solidly upper-middle-class people who ruled Hyde Park bristled at all the new (BLACK) people coming into the neighborhood and causing trouble. Of course sometimes there was trouble, but the difference is when white kids cause trouble, it is dismissed as teenage hormones running amok. But when Black and Brown kids cause trouble, we get tried as adults by a jury of our (WHITE) peers. One night a fight broke out during a midnight showing of Spike Lee's *Do the Right Thing.* I was there with my three good Jewish boys. The fight happened at the very beginning of the movie, right as Public Enemy's "Fight the Power" began and just as Rosie Perez introduced herself and her hips to America. It was such a bombastic moment on film that the real-life fight couldn't really top it. The fight sorta felt like part of the movie. This was when the news was more than happy to talk about "Black people fighting at Black movie openings." And this was the golden era of Black film: *Do the Right Thing, New Jack City,* later *Menace II Society* and *Boyz n the Hood.* I remember everybody standing up during the fight so they could see better. But most of us weren't trying to see the fight. We were trying to see the movie. I was trying to see Rosie's hips.

Looking back it is crazy to me that I grew up during such a classic era of Blackness and I was mostly not engaged in it. It made me feel like I wasn't doing "being Black" correctly. I didn't listen to the right music, still didn't have the right haircut, and I certainly didn't have the right clothes. I wasn't wearing parachute pants, and I didn't feel like I needed Jordan sneakers. I mean, don't get me wrong. I wasn't running from all things Black. My mom's book collection looked like a room at a Black museum, or like the Schomburg Center for Research in Black Culture in New York City. And I was watching *Soul Train* on Sundays like every other Black person I knew. And I watched *The Cosby Show* (damn you, Bill) and *A Different World*. And I felt like those two shows seemed more like my life OR like a life that was adjacent to my life, unlike the other images of Black people we all saw. Even though the family on *The Cosby Show* was rich (and my family was not), their life didn't feel unattainable to me. And their Blackness matched mine better. Cliff and Clair were just like, "We're just people who are Black, living our lives! Sometimes Black things happen. Sometimes they don't. But we're not always defending ourselves. We don't feel under attack." With all the stories swirling around Bill Cosby, it is still hard to let go of all the memories of watching *The Cosby Show*. Thank Black Jesus that *Black-ish* showed up in the nick of time to reboot Black peoples' systems.

I was also watching a ton of *Saturday Night Live*. It premiered in 1975, when I was just two years old, but with the help of reruns, I feel like I was there for the first cast of *Saturday Night Live*. My mom would let me stay up to watch it from as young as I can remember. I recall when Eddie Murphy showed up and worked his way up from featured player to cast member to star who hosts the show while he's still on the show. I remember Bill Murray, I remember Chevy Chase on the news, Gilda Radner doing Roseanne Roseannadanna. So while other kids were play-ing sports and running around outside, I was inside and all about comedy. I would have had *Saturday Night Live* trading cards if they'd existed.

I was also still going to martial arts classes, and because Wing Chun wasn't a popular style at the time, I was hanging out with adults. I loved it, but I wasn't around people my age. I knew that was weird. By the time I graduated from high school, I felt embarrassed about the things I liked. Not so embarrassed that I stopped liking them, but if people asked me what kind of music I listened to, I'd be like, "Uh, you know, I watch a lot of TV." Now you can get away with saying, "I don't listen to music! I watch TV!" and people will think, "Of course! It's peak television!" But back then it wasn't like that.

As I got older, comedy began to define my life. Once I started doing open mics in Chicago in 1994, my entire life revolved around comedy. That happens to most comics. It is such a slog and such an unlikely dream that you have to go all in. You can't just a little bit be a comedian and expect to be even a little bit successful. All your friends end up being comedians too. And some of those friends are people who you wouldn't have been friends with if it wasn't for comedy.

Kevin Avery is definitely one of those friends. Kevin is a come-dian I met when I moved from Chicago to the Bay Area, to live with my girlfriend Catherine in 1997. Me and Kevin have similar backgrounds. We are both Black dudes around the same age who have major love for our Blackness but also always felt slightly out-side of what people think we should be doing with our Blackness. Although Kevin's a huge fan of rap, of Black R&B music, he's also a huge sci-fi geek. When he was in high school and college, being a Black dude who loved Black music and sci-fi was not something people did. I'm not sure that we would have ever gotten over our differences if it were not for the work of one man: Denzel Washington. We bonded often about how he is the greatest actor of all time period. Don't believe me? I'll prove it soon. Now, thanks to the Internet, us Blerds can connect with people all over the planet.

I'm totally jealous of young Black people in high school now. If you feel like you are the only one, you can go online and find out that not only are you *NOT* the only one, but you ain't that unique at all. Wait. Now that I think about it . . . is this new way better?

Awkward Thoughts
about Sports

One of the first toys I remember having as a little kid was a stuffed Raggedy Andy doll. But it wasn't any ordinary Raggedy Andy doll. It was a *Black* Raggedy Andy doll. I have no idea where my mom got it from. It must have been handmade, but not by my mom. My mom, as you can imagine, doesn't have those oft-discussed *magical Black-woman hands* that can make a seventeen-layer casserole or a three-piece suit. And if she did, it would more likely be a three-piece dashiki. When I was growing up, the closest my mom ever came to making a casserole was to pour a can of baked beans *into* a casserole dish, and then she'd drop some hot dogs on top of the beans. Put it all in the oven. Voilà! Beanie weenies! At the time it was my favorite thing she "made." Now, when I think back on it, my stomach hurts. And if I dropped beanie weenies in front of my kids now, the Berkeley Department of Non-organic Foods and Yoga Mat Hygiene Research would show up at my door and take my kids from me. My wife would eat it . . . out of extreme kindness, and also so she could have an *eww* story the next time her mom, her twin sisters, and she get together.

"It was just a can of beans . . . No, *baked beans* . . . and hot dogs . . . No, *that's it*! Don't bring it up when you see him. You know how Kamau is. If you make fun of it, he'll bring it to Thanksgiving."

But back then I loved it. I was also well aware that the qualities that made my mom the greatest mom of all time period had nothing to do with the word "homemaker." They were more in line with the word "change-maker." Is that a word? I'm just going to go ahead and say that it's a word.

And my Black Raggedy Andy doll was a part of that change. My mom didn't want me to be awash in the whitewash of kids' toys. And back before I was born in 1973, being engulfed in white-kid toys was just called being engulfed in toys. But my era is when it began to change . . . slowly.

I feel like I grew up in the era of "HEY! Why can't we make some toys that look like Black people? Why do peach crayons say 'flesh' on them? Why is there only one color of Band-Aids: Midwestern White Person with a Light Tan?"

There had been a few Black toys before 1973. But much like superhero names, they were mostly just the Black version of white toys. The first Black Barbie was actually named Colored Francie. Yes, that was her *official* name. This was because all Mattel did to create Colored Francie was to take their existing (white) Francie dolls (one of Barbie's many less popular friends, of course) and put some blackface on them. But why did they pick Francie to get the Al Jolson treatment? I'm guessing that one day in the boardroom some Mattel executive said . . .

"Which one of Barbie's less popular friends is the least popular . . . saleswise? Francie? Cool, let's paint her brown and call her Nigg— . . . umm . . . Jiggab— . . . umm . . . Colored Francie!"

And I guess instead of just giving this "new" doll her *own* name, the people at Mattel thought it would be more efficient to just slap her "new" race on the front of her old name. How many disappointed kids woke up on Christmas morning to discover this doll under the tree?

"I know you wanted Francie. This IS Francie . . . Sorta . . . But honey, all they had left was *this* Francie . . . Don't cry . . . No. She's not 'broken.' She looks exactly the same as *regular* Francie! It's just her skin that's different . . . and her job opportunities. What was I supposed to do? *She was on sale!!!*"

Incredibly, it wasn't until 2009 that Mattel made a Black Barbie doll that had her own (Black) features. Yup, you could get a Black-Berry before you could get a Black Barbie. And then in 2016 Mattel broke the Internet by creating a limited-edition Ava DuVernay Barbie. If you want to pick up one, you can buy it off a reseller for the reasonable price of $470, at least as of this writing. I guess that's because while (white) Barbie's résumé is several pages thick, featuring varied and impressive careers like astronaut, US president, officer in the US Army, NASCAR driver, paleontologist, yoga instructor, McDonald's cashier, and princess—*because of course princess*—Barbie didn't direct an award-winning film about Martin Luther King Jr. So Ava got a doll, but I'm sure Auteur Barbie is on her way. I'm guessing she'll direct those Jennifer Aniston films where even though everything in her character's life is going great, she's just not happy.

But way back in 1973, even a white toy dipped in chocolate was rare. So my mom had to have either paid someone to make my Black Raggedy Andy *or* she stumbled across it at some NAACP flea market . . . or Baptist church bazaar. Or maybe my mom found it in some sort of black-and-white, stapled-together, Xeroxed Kwanzaa Katalogue on the back of a bus headed to Washington, DC, to reenact the March on Washington. Either way, Black Raggedy Andy was mine.

And his name was Muhammad Ali. And I have no idea why.

OK. That's not entirely true. I have *some* idea why, but I have no idea when he was named Muhammad Ali or whose idea it was. My mom says it was my idea. Which seems weird to me, because I can't imagine knowing who Muhammad Ali was as a two- or three-year-old kid. Although, thinking about my four-year-old daughter, Sami, I was surprised the day that Donald Trump came on the TV, and she said, "I don't like his rules." In one sentence she totally distilled the worst part about Donald Trump. He has horrible rules. When she said that, I immediately knew there was no way I was going to be able to explain to her why I was crying and laughing at the same time, so instead I just took us both out for ice cream. So apparently, when I was a kid, I liked Muhammad Ali's rules enough to name my favorite doll after him.

It also speaks to the ubiquity of Muhammad Ali in Black people's homes in that era of America. And this was the mid-'70s Muhammad Ali. While Muhammad Ali had shook up the world in 1964, when he upset Sonny Liston in Miami and became the youngest heavyweight boxing champion of all time, by the mid-'70s, Ali's great victories were behind him. He was no longer engaged in epic contests of will that held all of America's attention and all of Black America's hopes and dreams. He was just fighting regular old boxers . . . and occasionally a pro wrestler or two (and he almost fought NBA Hall of Famer Wilt Chamberlain, until Wilt wisely pulled out). But while the *man* Muhammad Ali was beginning to fade (and, as it was later discovered, already suffering from Parkinson's), the *legend* of Muhammad Ali was still alive.

We're talking the legend of the young kid from Louisville, Kentucky, with the weirdly Roman-sounding name Cassius Clay. The legend of the kid who had won an Olympic gold medal and then thrown it away due to his hatred of how his country treated his people (or maybe he just lost it—there are other theories). This is the legend of the kid who quickly rose up the heavyweight ranks, offended white America by talking too much shit, and talked himself into a fight with the *original* young Mike Tyson, old Sonny Liston. (At least people think he was old. There was no record of Sonny having ever been born. And he had that classic Black-people skin where maybe he was a hard-looking five. Or maybe he was a youthful seventy.) And Sonny Liston wasn't just boxing scary; Sonny was actually just regular old *scary* scary. In fact, before he became a boxer, Sonny had allegedly been a leg breaker for the mob. Heavyweight boxer probably seemed like an easier gig than leg breaker. At this point in his career, Sonny seemed unbeatable. And then Ali, at that time still going by Clay, incredibly and unbelievably *beat* Sonny Liston. It was one of the greatest upsets in sports history . . . which doesn't sound like much now, because it seems like every couple days we have a NEW GREATEST UPSET IN SPORTS HISTORY! ("THAT PRESEASON NFL GAME WAS ONE OF THE GREATEST UPSETS IN SPORTS HISTORY!")

And after defeating Liston, Clay decided to go for another huge upset when he angered most of white America by declaring himself "The Greatest" while still *in the ring* celebrating his victory over Sonny. At that point in America's history, America (i.e., white people) liked its heavyweight boxers polite and quiet, like Joe Louis or Floyd Patterson. Or it liked them animalistic and quiet, like Sonny Liston. The key component in the equation is that white America liked its heavyweight boxers *quiet*. But Cassius Clay was not quiet. He came into rooms loudly and left rooms even louder. White America was like, "Damn! Why does the new heavyweight champion have to be one of these new nigg— . . . Negroes? This is the worst!" But it wasn't "the worst." Not by a long shot.

Because just when white America thought it couldn't possibly be more offended, Clay declared himself a Muslim and changed his name to Muhammad Ali. (He did so after briefly going by Cassius X, a conscious rapper name that is just sitting there for the taking, conscious rappers!) But Ali wasn't just any old type of Muslim. He specifically declared himself a *Black Muslim*. And as scary as many Americans consider Muslims today, Black Muslims were the mathematic equation of . . .

Muslims × angry Black people + militancy = Black Muslims

America. Wasn't. Ready. History mostly forgets that people were nervous about Martin Luther King's "militant" message of resistance through peace and love until the ultimate Black Muslim, Malcolm Little, aka Detroit Red, aka Malcolm X (and eventually el-Hajj Malik el-Shabazz), showed up and started talking about "by any means necessary!"

White America: "'By *any* means,' you say? . . . Ummm . . . Is Marty King still here? Wasn't he talking about hugging it out? That suddenly sounds pretty good. MARTY, LET'S TAKE A LONG WALK AND TALK ABOUT ALL THIS!"

But even with all that, we often forget that the thing that *made* Muhammad Ali *MUHAMMAD ALI!* was the fact that he gave up three and a half years of his prime earning and athletic career for his religious *and* political beliefs. That is what made him forever a legend. And not just in America but in the entire world. Without that sacrifice, Ali would have been just another great Black heavyweight boxing champion. And boxing history is lousy with them. Not in recent years but up until Lennox Lewis retired in 2004, Black people pretty much had the monopoly on heavyweight champions. So being a Black heavyweight champion did not make Ali unique. Yes, Ali was a great talker and marketer of himself and of his fights, but that would have faded too. What has kept Ali's legend around wasn't that he was Black . . . It was that he was BLAAAAAACK! And he was BLAAAAAACK! at a time when not only could being Black get you killed (like it can today), it could (and did) also get you assassinated. And Ali stepping away from the sport he dominated showed that he walked it like he talked it. And he took that walk for *THREE AND A HALF YEARS*!!!

Now, I'm not trying to imply that no athlete today would do that for something he or she believes in . . . I'm flat-out saying it. No athlete, no entertainer, no person currently writing this book. It's not that no one has that same type of belief or connection to their people or community; it's just that Ali was more committed than any entertainer in history . . . OK, maybe Dick Gregory, who also stepped away from fame and fortune at the height of his career as a stand-up comic, did something similar. But being one of America's most famous comedians isn't close to the power and celebrity that the heavyweight champion of the world has, or had at that time. The heavyweight champion of the world, up through Mike Tyson's reign, was one of the most famous people *in the world*. The pope, Michael Jackson, and Mike Tyson. And not in that order. In the late '80s, I'd go Michael Jackson, Mike Tyson, then the pope. And let's be clear, heavyweight champion is a title that is earned. Pope is just a title you get anointed with if you're good at keeping your mouth shut and if you don't have a problem with "deals well with child molesters" being a necessary skill on your résumé. And the heavyweight champion was regarded as the toughest person in the world. Which adds an extra layer. No matter how famous the pope is, you're not afraid of him kicking your ass.

> Me: "Move, Pope!"
> Pope: "Are you talking to me like that? I'm the pope!"
> Me: "Yup. I'm talking to you."
> Pope: "Oh . . . OK . . . I was just making sure. I'll get right out of your way now. Sorry."

Currently, LeBron James is the most politically woke and famous athlete we have. From wearing an "I Can't Breathe" T-shirt at warm-ups, to taking a team photo with every one of his Miami Heat teammates wearing hoodies in memory of Trayvon Martin, to establishing a foundation to send every poor kid in Akron to college for free (OK, maybe not *every* kid, but more than a thousand), to speaking out against the racist NBA team owner who admitted his racism out loud to his . . . mistress? (I don't really know . . . Did we ever figure out what was going on with Donald Sterling?) . . . LeBron is engaged and turned on and setting an example of how a twenty-first-century Black athlete is supposed to do it. And yet I'm guessing that there is no situation in which he would consider *giving up three years of his prime* for his beliefs. In fact, LeBron basically did the opposite of what Ali did when he decided to make his prime years even better and more fun. He packed up his prime years and took them (and his talents) from Cleveland to the much more prime locale of Miami. I'm not criticizing LeBron, because he's done way more than I have or ever will. And much of what he has done was accomplished through his financial resources. I'm just pointing out that Muhammad Ali set an unreasonable standard for even the most political athlete of our time to live up to. A standard that is so high that it was instantly and forever legendary.

Which is why I think that in my house, when I was a kid, I had a doll named Muhammad Ali. Because Muhammad Ali isn't just a boxer . . . or a celebrity . . . or a pop culture figure . . . He is a standard of ultimate BLAAACKNESS! He is a standard of how in America we need to be more committed to our people and the liberation of our people than we are to ourselves. He is forever an example of what a famous Black person should do to show that commitment to his people and to the cause. Muhammad Ali is bigger than sports in Black households, in Muslim households . . . and now in everybody's households across the planet. But in Black households, Muhammad Ali is right up there with Martin Luther King Jr. and newly minted and safely alive ex–president Barack Obama. The holy triumvirate of Black male achievement. And when Ali died and joined the ancestors, I'm sure Harriet Tubman said, "Come on over here, Muhammad! Take a seat at the VIP table between me and Rosa . . . Have you met Ms. Parks before?"

I cared about Muhammad Ali before I knew what boxing even was. Before I cared about any sports at all. Whether she knew it or not, my mom had created an ironclad context for sports in my brain. I didn't care about sports at all when I was growing up. It mostly seemed boring to me. It took too long and not that much seemed to be happening. I just didn't understand why we were watching it. This certainly frustrated my dad when I visited him. He'd take me to see a college football game in Mobile, and I'd inevitably get bored. I remember when, as a little kid—maybe six or seven—one of the first times I understood how time worked was at a football game.

> Me: "Dad, how much longer is the game going to be?"
>
> Dad: "About an hour and a half."
>
> Me (excited): "Oh yay! . . . Wait . . . Is an hour and a half the same thing as half an hour?"
>
> Dad: "No. An hour and a half is three times longer than half an hour."
>
> Me: "NOOOOOOOOOOOOOOOOOOOO!"

There was almost no sport I was interested in, live or on TV. Football? Nope. Baseball? HELL NO! Tennis? Nope. Golf? See my response to baseball. I never liked playing sports. (Is that even the correct expression? "Playing sports"?) And whenever I did try to watch sports or do some sort of sporting activity (there, that's better), I would just end up approaching it like an embedded journalist who wanted out of the gig, asking the famous questions: Who? What? When? Where? How? And why?

Whose idea was this?

What's the whole point of all this, anyway?

When can we stop?

Where can I stand so the ball won't come to me? BECAUSE GOD FORBID I SHOULD HAVE TO CATCH OR THROW SOMETHING!

Again . . . how long is this going to go?

Why are we doing this?

To this day if I'm walking past a park and a ball rolls to my feet from people playing catch, I seize up and have to try not to panic. Because I don't have any idea how to throw a ball. My dad does, but he never taught me. Not that I would have shown any interest in learning how. But because of that, when a ball rolls to my feet and I realize that I can't pretend I didn't see it, I have to quickly come up with a plan.

"I got it! You know what? It's a nice day. I'll just walk the ball over to you."

But boxing I could watch. Because of Ali. Because Ali had built a story around it for me. I needed a story. Also because of my interest in the martial arts, boxing seemed real to me. I get what's happening here. That guy is trying to beat up that other guy, because of . . . well . . . truly because of money . . . but it's always billed as because of disrespect, honor, the need to prove his manhood, and to combat the desperate circumstances he is trying to rise up from (which is basically money again). But there was a story that hooked me in. Football didn't make any sense to me. One guy is trying to get a ball over an imaginary line while a bunch of other guys try to stop him, and he only gets four chances, but he will most likely only use three chances and then another guy will kick the ball. Also, it takes THREE HOURS! Football was invented to intentionally be complicated so that if you enjoy it a lot you don't feel like you're wasting your time.

"How can I possibly be wasting my time? I know so many obscure rules and facts!"

Now, this is not to say that football doesn't have great stories too. Every sport does. And if you ask me, those stories are what make sports meaningful at all. Without those stories, sports are just weird. *Why can you do that with your body? Why are you trying so hard to get that ball in that hole? There's got to be better things to do. You practice how long? Why?*

But it is in the stories of the people who do the sports where sports come alive. Don't believe me? How do the Olympics get you to care about the most obscure sports around, like the pentathlon and team handball? They run two-minute packages of clips of America's star athlete in that event, that's how! Preferably the clip package is filled with a small hometown, poverty, struggle, sacrifice, and—if NBC is lucky—a little bit of cancer just to really sell it home.

Every sport has compelling stories like these. And without these stories, sports cease to exist. When sports are just about the weird physical achievements, then they start to become irrelevant. Even football—which I just made fun of, which will cause my father-in-law and brother-in-law to read this and make my next Thanksgiving quite awkward (and it's already going to be awkward with me bringing beanie weenies)—has these stories. Jim Brown is thought by many of the people who should know to be the greatest running back of all time. And Jim Brown is thought by even *more* of the people who should know to also be the greatest lacrosse player of all time. Jim Brown was sitting right next to Muhammad Ali during the famous press conference where Ali affirmed that he had no plans to fight in Vietnam unless it was against a heavyweight contender because after all, as he said, "Ain't no Vietcong ever called me 'nigger'!"

The photo of Jim Brown, Bill Russell of the Boston Celtics, Lew Alcindor of UCLA (eventually he would be Kareem Abdul-Jabbar of the Los Angeles Lakers), and several other Black athletes is, in my opinion, one of the greatest photos of all time. It is from 1967, and because of the times it is in black and white. And also because of the times it is totally BLAAACK! Black men standing up for themselves and rallying around other brothers in need. To the uninitiated eye, it is just twelve Black men. All athletic, all young. I'm sure to most white people watching, they looked like a team. They were, in a way. They were, on that day, the starting lineup of Team Black People. That photo is iconic. More iconic than any other photo taken during their athletic careers. And that says a lot because in that photo nobody is scoring a touchdown or knocking out someone. They are all in suits. But they wouldn't have been there that day if not for sports and its ability to separate and elevate people above their circumstances. And once these men found themselves elevated, they did something with that platform. And when you are Black in America, doing something with your platform seems so essential that to *not* do something seems negligent and selfish . . . even when it shouldn't.

And that's part of the reason that I just can't get mad at Lance Armstrong. I know he cheated. I know he was apparently a jerk. Apparently he wins the yellow jersey in jerkdom too. I know that his actions nearly brought down an entire sport. I know he hurt his teammates and their friends and family through his actions and bully tactics. I know all this, but I just can't gin up too much anger about it because HE RAISED MILLIONS OF DOLLARS FOR CANCER RESEARCH! The story of Lance Armstrong is better and more meaningful than the sport. Try to tell those cancer survivors he helped that he ruined the integrity of cycling. Who gives a shit? Are we on this planet to see who can pedal up and down mountains the quickest, or are we on this planet to see what we can do to continue the species, aka HELP EACH OTHER?

I choose the latter every time.

So that's how it was with me. I didn't care about sports through most of high school except for boxing. And then Michael Jordan happened.

Now, to be fair to Michael Jordan, he had already been happening by that time. Michael Jordan . . . Yes, I'm going to say his whole name every time. Calling him Jordan makes me feel like I'm adopting some pseudo sport personality that I don't have. And calling him Michael seems weirdly distancing because the famous Michael is Michael Jackson, of course. So Michael Jordan was drafted by the Chicago Bulls in 1984, when I was eleven years old. That was just after we'd moved to Chicago, and even though I was still mad about leaving Boston and having trouble making friends, it was hard not to get taken up in the Michael Jordan tornado.

It is very popular right now to discuss how apolitical Michael Jordan was during his career. And it makes sense, because he did it to himself with one quote. In response to someone asking him to support the Black candidate running against Jesse Helms in Michael Jordan's home state of North Carolina, Michael Jordan allegedly said that he couldn't do that because "Republicans buy sneakers too." Damn. Sandwiched between Muhammad Ali and LeBron James, it becomes easy to take the teeth away from Michael Jordan the way history tries to take the teeth away from MLK. But looking back it becomes clear . . . MJ isn't the next step after Muhammad Ali. He's the next step after Jackie Robinson. The only way Jackie Robinson was able to integrate Major League Baseball was by not only being a better player than all the other (all white) players but also being a better person than all the other (all white) players. Jackie even had to be a better person than everybody in the crowd, no matter what their race was. And on top of that, Jackie couldn't let America see the toll that it was taking on him to be better than everybody in the world who cared about baseball.

Michael Jordan was more an extension of Jackie Robinson than Muhammad Ali. Except, thanks to Muhammad Ali's fight to win America over without losing his soul, Michael Jordan didn't have to smile his way through his career. He only needed to smile off the court. On the court, he could be described as "an assassin in shorts." On the court, he could be a killer. He could be a career ender. He could be not nice. And all the while, he could demonstrate an athletic excellence that his coach Phil Jackson compared to the Renaissance artist Michelangelo. You didn't have to like or care about basketball at all to be awed by Michael Jordan. The *thing* Michael Jordan had was clear, and it cut through the "I don't follow sports" crowd. Play anyone any of the hundreds of Michael Jordan highlights and see how they handle it.

"I don't follow sports . . . Wait . . . HOW DID HE DO THAT?"

And ultimately that was the political statement of Michael Jordan. He was not trying to be the equal of the white man (or anybody else). He wasn't even trying to be better than everybody else. Michael Jordan was just trying to be better than himself . . . every day.

He reminds me of a math problem from middle school. The question was something like, "Would you rather I give you five dollars today, or would you rather I give you a penny today, two pennies tomorrow, four pennies the next day, and so on. I'll double it every day." Kids usually pick the five bucks because it seems like the obvious choice. Who wants all those pennies? But once your teacher shows you the math, it makes your head explode how quickly doubling a few pennies every day adds up to real money. The lesson of Michael Jordan was exactly the slogan Nike came up with: "Just do it." "It" being the work. If you do the work, it will all add up. Maybe not right away, but eventually it will. And when it starts adding up, you will blow up.

Michael Jordan knew that if he did the work, then one day he would write his name in the stars. Michael Jordan took what so many great Black athletes had done before—athletes like Jesse

Owens, Joe Louis, and even Floyd Patterson. He took the idea that they demonstrated of being perfect on and off the field of play, put his own spin on it, and then he quite literally sold it back to the people who were amazed by his achievements. He sold it back in the form of shoes, T-shirts, shoes, shorts, underwear, Coca-Cola (of course), shoes, a barely watchable movie with Bugs Bunny . . . and more shoes.

Michael Jordan turned his sweat into a billion-dollar brand. And at the same time, Oprah was across town doing the same thing. And while Michael Jordan certainly could have been more outwardly political, his path was about kicking doors open so that others could walk through and do it their own way. And that's how you get an athlete like LeBron James, who can somehow manage to be outwardly political and even take controversial stances without slowing down his path to a billion dollars. It's also how you get Shaquille O'Neal, who became a superstar in the NBA but never let a little thing like professional basketball get in the way of his good time. And it's how you get Kobe Bryant, who basically said, "I like that Michael Jordan career. I think I'll just do the same thing. That'll work, right?" Nope. Not even a little bit.

I believe that, despite what people say about Michael Jordan's lack of political statements during his career, his existence and his effect on the world clears the way for Barack Obama, just like it did for LeBron. I don't think you get Barack Obama without a few Black people who show that they can wedge themselves into (white) America's collective heart without losing themselves (and their Blackness and their love of and from Black people) at the same time. It is perfect that the city that spawned so much amazing Blackness in 1984 would give "birth" to President Barack Obama.

(For more on how turning away from your Blackness can affect you, see: Thomas, Clarence.)

To me, sports are about these big stories. And as a Black man, I am biased to like sports stars who are managing their careers in ways that not only uplift the race but also get the race's back when the race needs it. And if you've read the news regularly, then you know that we regularly do need uplifting and defending.

And that's why, in 2016, I felt compelled to write a piece about the swimmer and most decorated Olympian of all time, Michael Phelps. In the piece I wrote for CNN, I suggested that Michael Phelps should let someone else carry the US flag during the Rio opening ceremony. And I thought that the someone who should do it was Ibtihaj Muhammad, a Black, female, Muslim (hijab-wearing, even) fencer. I thought that would be a much better story for America at this point in history than Michael Phelps. Because, nothing against Michael Phelps—I don't know him well enough to actually have anything against him—but all he seems to be is a swimmer. And not that there's anything wrong with that, but there's not that much that's right about it either. I'm sure Phelps gives money to charity and does nice things for kids. But whatever he does, it ain't raising millions of dollars for cancer research or redefining America's relationship to his racial group. And it certainly ain't anything as bold as being a Black, female, hijab-wearing Muslim fencer.

Am I judging Michael Phelps? Yes. But that's what sports is ultimately about: judgment. I don't judge him as a person. I'm *sports judging* him. That's different from actually judging him. Even LeBron, who I wrote all those nice words about earlier, is someone I sports judge all the time. I think he is, as a man, a great dad and role model. I think, as a basketball player, "YOU'LL NEVER BE AS GREAT AS MICHAEL JORDAN, YOU IMMATURE COACH KILLER!"

Sports judging is fun. I recommend it. It is basically why sports exist. You just have to be careful that you don't confuse sports judgment with real judgment. That would be bad because sports aren't real in the same way that *Game of Thrones* isn't real. You can TV hate characters on *Game of Thrones*, but if you run into the actors in the street and still hate them, then you need some fresh air. The problem in America is that we often confuse fake hate with real hate. I fake hate LeBron because that's how sports work. But if I really hated LeBron, then it would be clear that I was confused about how life works.

I found out from posting my article on CNN that many people are confused about how life works.

In a matter of hours, I received hate mail and hate tweets. (The word "tweet" really takes the sting out of the word "hate." But it was real.) Mostly it was from white people and mostly the message was the same . . .

"HOW DARE YOU SAY THAT AMERICA'S GREATEST OLYMPIAN SHOULD NOT BE ALLOWED TO CARRY THE FLAG? THAT MOOSLEM LADY"—(Most of the tweets didn't say "lady"; I'm being nice)—"DOESN'T DESERVE TO CARRY THE FLAG! SHE HASN'T WON ANYTHING! YOU ALWAYS CALL EVERY WHITE PERSON RACIST, BUT YOU'RE THE REAL RACIST! LOL! #MAKEAMERICA GREATAGAIN #PooEmoji"

First of all, winning the most gold medals does not automatically make you the best Olympian. It may put you in the running. But the best Olympians are the ones who mean the most. Again, it's the whole need for sports to have a good story. I can think of five

Olympians and Olympic teams off the top of my head who are greater than Michael Phelps. (Remember we're talking *sports judgment* here.)

- Jesse Owens in 1936, who basically shoved Hitler's Aryan race up his ass.
- The 1980 US hockey team, which defeated the Russians. That may be legitimately the biggest upset in sports history. If that upset had happened today, they would have immediately made the Americans go pee in cups.
- The 1992 Dream Team, because of Michael Jordan and ten other Hall of Famers. I'd rather watch Dream Team practices than Michael Phelps's gold-medal-winning races.
- That one runner in the Olympics who collapsed in the middle of the race and his dad walked out on the track and helped him limp across the finish line. I have no idea what year that was or what country that runner was from, but even thinking about it is making me want to call my dad and tell him that I love him. Also, who's cutting onions?

Simone Manuel in 2016 was the first Black person to win a gold medal in swimming. IN SWIMMING! Do you know how huge that is? Do you know how hard that had to be on her friends and family? Every family reunion, church service, or cookout that Simone missed where they had to tell people that she wasn't there because she was swimming? And that she had a chance to go to the Olympics? None of that is on the Things Black People Regularly Do bingo card. They might as well have told people she was building a rocket to the moon in the garage.

All of them and many other Olympians are greater than Michael Phelps. But as I found out after I posted my article, not everybody agrees with me.

In the next few days after the article was published, it got worse and worse. Eventually I became the target of the week for the "alt-right." "Alt-right" is a term I thought I wouldn't have to get used to, but here we are. Every few years, angry white men rebrand themselves as a way to disguise their racism. In my lifetime they have been called the alt-right, the Tea Party, the "silent majority." And when they can't come up with a new name to change to, they usually just go, "Aww, screw it! Let's just call ourselves the Ku Klux Klan again!" Well, on this week I became the target of all the diet KKK's rage. I was all over their blogs, vlogs, podcasts, and even a low-level right-wing "news channel." A channel that makes Fox News look like Disney Junior. Even more than a week later I was getting messages saying things like, "How dare you say Michael Phelps shouldn't carry the flag in the opening ceremonies?" And occasionally I'd respond, "DUUUUUUUDE! It was over a week ago. Go outside and get some fresh air!"

Clearly the point was lost in their need for a liberal to hate. My point was, and still is, that I would have been legitimately proud of him for giving up his position to Ibtihaj Muhammad. I knew that if he had, it would have been much bigger than that one moment. It would have been a symbol for our country at a time when we were mostly known for one of the most contentious, controversial, scandal-ridden, hateful, xenophobic, jingoistic, and just generally unlikeable presidential elections in recent memory. And maybe it could have been a moment of pause for people who thought that America's best symbol is a white dude who has it all. Maybe it could have shifted some ideas around and then Donald Trump could be back hosting *The Appren-tice*, where we all know he really would rather be.

Muhammad carrying the flag would have been nearly a one-stop inclusion shop. Muhammad is an African-American, hijab-wearing Muslim woman who is also a world-class fencer. Those are all groups that could always use some more love, acceptance, and respect from this country. (And yes, I'm including fencers in this group.) If Muhammad had carried the flag, that moment (and Muhammad herself) would have grown into legend. We're talking about something much bigger than just the Olympics.

And Michael Phelps, by giving up his spot, would have been ce-mented in history the same way Australian runner Peter Norman is cemented in Olympic history as the white guy standing stock-still next to Tommie Smith and John Carlos in the 1968 Olympics in Mexico City. As Smith and Carlos stood with their fists in the air, Norman (very actively) didn't get in the way. And he even encour-aged the moment by suggesting that John Carlos wear Tommie Smith's left glove when Carlos discovered that he had forgotten his gloves at the Olympic Village. Michael could have been the Peter Norman of the 2016 Olympics. That would have been a great story. And it would have been bigger than all the medals he won.

Also it certainly wouldn't have hurt that Ibtihaj Muhammad's last name is the same as the first name of Muhammad Ali. Ali had his own history-making opening ceremony moment. The image of Ali lighting the torch in Atlanta in 1996 was what this moment could have been as well—another important symbol of America attempt-ing to bury its hatred of "the other."

But it didn't happen. Yet, luckily, somebody got the message, because during the closing ceremony, the flag was carried by one of my picks for greatest Olympian, Simone Biles, a young Black woman who had won four Olympic medals in gymnastics and was being called by many the greatest gymnast of all time. I was happy for Simone, America, and my daughters that Simone was representing America in that moment. I was also happy for Michael Phelps that he was not in the spotlight in that moment. I thought to myself, *Good for him. Allowing himself to melt back into the crowd.* Later I found out that Phelps wasn't even still in Rio at that point. He had taken his treasure chest of gold and gone home.

Did he leave because he wanted to go home? Or did he leave because he knew his presence would distract people from the better sports story?

CHAPTER 3

My Awkward Start in Stand-Up Comedy

Dropping out of college was the first time I felt like a real grown-up failure. *I may have just broken everything.* I'd graduated from one of the most exclusive and best private schools in the country. About a million years after I was there President Obama's daughters would go there. In high school I was always the student who could have done better if he'd tried harder. My dad was always right about that. By the end of my senior year, I had a B-minus average in a school filled with kids getting so much college credit that they walked into college as associate professors. I was just looking for a college that I could get into. I wanted a big city. Midsize, not too large. And also someplace where I'd still be able to do martial arts. Back in the day, you did this by buying books so you could research colleges. When I found the University of Pennsylvania, I thought, *That's a good-sized school. It's in a city!* Only later did I realize it is an Ivy League school. Maybe I'll be unique there. I bet they don't have a lot of B-minus students!

I decided to apply for early decision. My college counselor said, "I don't know about that . . . Maybe you should look at other places . . . ," but I did it anyway. The day I got in, I brought in the letter, and she said, "I knew you could do it!" and I said, in my head, *"No, you didn't."* I realized then that people in positions of authority don't always know everything. And sometimes they know nothing. And at seventeen, I already felt like there was a racialized component to it.

I was proud that I'd been accepted, and it took all the pressure off the rest of the year. I saw my friends feeling nervous while waiting for college acceptances in April, but the last six months of my high school experience were chill because I'd already gotten in. Jason's last six months were chill too. He didn't bother applying anywhere.

Once I got to school in the fall, I decided to become an East Asian studies major. *Because I like Bruce Lee! And maybe I'll be a martial arts teacher. I'll learn Chinese, and maybe take some Chinese philosophy courses.* OR *MAYBE I'LL BE A SPY BECAUSE . . . I have no idea why.* But then I started taking an intro to Mandarin language class where most of the other students in the class were Chinese-American kids looking for an easy A. And then I took a Japanese history class, and then I realized, *I don't care about any of this.* And I also really didn't care about my other classes. I barely got through the year. I went home, and I spent the summer dreading the return to Penn. There was nothing I enjoyed about it. I made some good friends, but the school felt wrong. It was super preprofessional. I should have gone to, say, Oberlin or Reed. I should have gone someplace where it was all, "We don't even have grades! We just have feelings. How do you feel like you did in this class?" At Penn, if you didn't want to be a doctor or lawyer or a nurse or in high-end finance or a guy who runs for president because he's bored of his reality TV show (Trump, Penn '68), then you were out of place there.

I went back for my sophomore year, looking for a community. Maybe in the arts community, but there wasn't much there. I had come from a small private school, where I hadn't hung out with other Black kids. I'd hung out with a Jewish Deadhead and a Jewish guitar player. Between freshman and sophomore years at Penn, I'd applied to the W. E. B. Du Bois house, where many of the Black students lived. I realized I needed to be around more Black people. I was readying *The Autobiography of Malcolm X*, mostly . . . no, entirely because the movie was about to come out. The book was changing my life as I turned each page. I decided I was going to make a change in my life—I was going to live with my people, in the W. E. B. Du Bois house.

I got in to the Du Bois house, but I'd also applied for, and gotten, a work-study job in the dorm that I'd lived in my freshman year. I couldn't do both. I knew that I was at a crossroads with this decision. *I can hang out with Black people, or I can take this job . . . I need this job.* That meant I had to live in the dorm again. Looking back, I wonder if living in the W. E. B. Du Bois house could have created a community that would have caused me to stay at Penn. Not that I didn't have a community, but it would have been different.

As the semester went on, I was struggling. I went home for Christmas and I told my mom I couldn't do it. That it wasn't working. I went back to school, and I withdrew. But I still had a couple of weeks on campus before I went home, and I found I'd strangely become the popular, funny guy. It was the first time in my life that I'd been the funny guy. I would sleep late, hang out in a friend's room that was sort of like a lounge. He had a double room but he was living there by himself. I would just talk with him and whoever wandered through. There was no pressure to go to class, and there was nothing else to do but sit around and be funny. I think I'd been funny before, but this was the first time I had seen people regularly laugh OUT LOUD at things I said. And not just good friends of mine like Jason and Rob. A lot of these people were strangers.

Comedy was something I'd wanted to do since I was a kid, but I didn't know how to do it. There was no Internet then. Me, Jason, and Rob talked about comedy a lot, and Jason knew I wanted to be a comedian. We'd talk about Frank Zappa a lot, because Jason wanted to talk about Frank Zappa. We'd talk about Bruce Lee, because I wanted to talk about Bruce Lee. We were best friends because we'd jump into whatever the other was interested in, from Bruce Lee to Frank Zappa to the Grateful Dead to comedy. Plus, me and Jason were funny all the time. But my sophomore year at Penn was the first time I'd really been funny around people who didn't know me well; the first time I really actually tried to be funny; and the first time I heard people say I was funny and introduce me as, "This is Kamau; he's hilarious!"

There was a white guy named Seth down the hall. Seth was the prototypical '90s white guy who was really into rap music. He was the one who actually introduced *me* to the music of Public Enemy. I had heard of them before, but he sat me down to listen to their new CD, *Apocalypse 91 . . . The Enemy Strikes Back*. (The album was great, but I was of course most impressed by "Bring the Noise," the song they did with the heavy metal band

Anthrax. I basically ran to the least "Black" thing on one of the Blackest albums of all time period.) One day, Seth looked at me after I had said something that he laughed at, and he said, "Kamau, have you ever thought about being a stand-up comedian?" and I said, "Yeah, I don't know . . . ," but inside, I was thinking, *YES, EVERY DAY!* and mentally jumping up and hugging him. But I was still too cool to say it out loud.

When I dropped out it was spring of 1992. I got home and I was depressed. I don't know if it was clinical because I never checked. But I was sleeping all day and accomplishing nothing. My mom let me have a mourning period, but my dad was super pissed. I'd been going to an Ivy League school, something he hadn't been able to do at my age. My father wanted me to do what he couldn't. He was in Alabama, but I could feel his presence. I didn't have any friends at home in Chicago. Jason was—I think—in Rhode Island for some reason. Rob was in college at the Berklee College of Music in Boston. It was the lowest I'd ever been in my life up to that point. At the same time, I was burrowing deeper into bed, the LA riots happened in the wake of the cops who beat Rodney King nearly to death getting away with no major charges. MTV was covering it, and I remember Corey Glover, the singer from Living Colour, talking about the riots and racism in America. And I just thought, *The world is truly an awful place, and I want no part of this. I have no idea what happens next . . . Maybe nothing happens next.*

My mom told me I had to get a job, and this was in the olden days, so I looked in the classified section of the *Reader,* the free weekly paper in Chicago. I got a job at a place called Condoms Now, where I had to answer the phone, "Save the human race! Condoms Now." It was on Division Street north of downtown.

This is the nightclub district where people from out of town *think* Chicagoans party. It was surrounded by dozens of bars, and the condom store stayed open until three or four in the morning because it was trying to match the bar hours. I was nineteen, surrounded by this nightclub culture and bars I couldn't go into. There were girls in short skirts, and beefy dudes who looked like they wanted to fight everybody, and non-beefy dudes who looked like they wanted to be beefy dudes. I was still a virgin who had never had a girlfriend. I was intrigued but still thought, *This is scary. And this is not my scene.*

The guy who owned the condom shop wanted it to be like a nightclub. He wanted it to be a cool spot where people came to hang out. And he was always (and regularly successfully) picking up on customers. All my life, I'd had guys around me who talked about having sex but weren't actually having much or any sex. And all of a sudden there was this guy who owned the condom store who was actually having all the sex he could handle. I often thought he had opened this shop so he could get a discount on condoms. He became a weird sort of half-mentor to me. He'd introduce me to women and get me into the bars after hours. I was like his nineteen-year-old virginal mascot. I was having this fun, weird, but wasted life.

At the same time, my mother enrolled me in classes at Second City, which is where I slowly got the courage to start trying stand-up. When I finally did stand-up for the first time, I told my dad, and it was the biggest laugh I got out of him for yeeeeeeears. He told me later that when he told the rest of our family that I was doing stand-up, they couldn't believe it either. I had been so quiet as a kid. But he also told my cousin Nora, who I had grown up with and who later became the award-winning writer, and she said, "Oh yeah, Kamau's always been funny." And he said, "Kamau's funny?" I was funny with her because I felt comfortable with her.

Before I started doing stand-up, Jason had moved back to Chicago. He was in fact responsible for me starting to do stand-up comedy. He had heard of an open mic at a café near his apartment. We went and watched the open mic for about a month. The first night we went, it was awful, a truly bad night. That was perfect for me. If everyone had been great that night I would have thought, *I can never do this.* But because the audience was horrible (or really nonexistent) and everybody bombed, I thought to myself, *I can do this as well as they can!* At the end of the month of watching, I finally decided I was going to go up. The next week came . . . and I chickened out. I felt like a failure before I had even begun. Jason assured me that everything would be OK. He never judged my failures. The next week I knew I had to go up, but I needed help getting pumped up for the show. I needed some performance enhancers. About a year before, Jason had loaned me a Rollins Band CD, *The End of Silence*. Rollins Band was the punk rock band that singer Henry Rollins started after the end of the legendary band Black Flag. Rollins Band was much heavier than most of the music I liked at the time. But the album had a song on it called "Low Self Opinion" that I loved. In the song, Henry is screaming at someone with a low self-opinion. And the person Henry is yelling at is clearly Henry himself. I related. I did that all the time. Henry's music also had a lot of humor in it. And because of his big personality, good looks, big muscles, and his ability to spin a quality yarn,

Henry was in the process of becoming an MTV darling. He was a smart, funny, self-actualized dude. When his album *Weight* came out, the single "Liar" was all over alternative rock radio and the video was on MTV all the time. I was listening to that album again and again as I dove deeper into the heavier music. That was also the era of '90s grunge, so I was getting into Soundgarden and Pearl Jam too. Never was a big fan of Nirvana. I was also still into Living Colour, and I had added some other Black rock bands to the mix: Fishbone, Urban Dance Squad, and 24-7 Spyz. When I'd go to their concerts it sometimes felt like there were more Black people onstage than in the audience.

In addition to Second City, I was also going to Columbia College in Chicago. It was a community college with a focus on media arts. If it wasn't a completely open-admission college, it was damn close. I used to joke that their motto was, "Are you finished with high school? . . . But not *really done* with high school? If so, Columbia College is for you!" I took English 101, and the teacher was seriously going over what nouns are. This was a big drop from Penn. And I was thinking, *Holy shit . . . didn't we all have* Schoolhouse Rock? *A noun is a person, place, or thing or . . . something else . . . Oh yeah . . . idea! I'm sorta smart.* Out of sheer snobbery, I didn't turn in the final paper for the class. The teacher told me I was going to get a D if I didn't turn it in. Even in this easy class, I was still finding ways to not live up to my potential. But I didn't turn it in, and when I got the report card I still got an A or a B. I don't remember. But it was clear that the teacher just didn't have it in her to give me a D.

So the week that I was scheduled to try stand-up for the first time . . . one more time, I was in an acting class at Columbia. We had to do monologues from the Sam Shepard play *Fool for Love*. I was assigned an angry, aggressive monologue about a guy who was bad to his lover, who I also think was his sister . . . It was pretty gnarly stuff, and it wasn't really my style. We were each told to find a song that would help us prepare for the monologue, and lip-sync the song in character. The song I chose was the Rollins Band song "Liar" since it was all about a man being shitty to a woman.

In class that day when it was my turn, I put the cassette in the boom box and waited for the music to begin. When it did I was suddenly jumping all over the place and screaming (well, lip-sync screaming), "I'm a LIAR! A LIAR!" and it was fun, and people laughed. It was a good omen for my first performance later.

That night, I listened to "Liar" over and over and over and over again in Jason's car. It gave me the courage to do stand-up that night. My performance that night was not as good as the lip synced one from earlier in the day, but it was good enough. A few of the comics said that I had good stage presence, which I later found out was code for "Your jokes sucked." I kept going to open mics. I also started following Henry's spoken-word career. His ability to step onstage and just talk really informed my later work. I met Henry years later when I lived in San Francisco, well before *Totally Biased*. I told him how "Liar" had helped me do stand-up comedy for the first time, and he said, "Oh, that's nice." I don't know what I expected him to say. "WOW! Wanna go on tour with me and be best friends?" OK, that is what I wanted him to say.

But I already had a best friend, and he was kicking ass at that job. Jason came to every open mic with me for the first two years.

People thought he was my manager because he was a cynical-looking Jewish dude who didn't say much and rarely laughed. Jason had started to work at bookstores, and he had cut his hair short after years of being a long-haired hippie who sometimes didn't wear shoes. And now he was wearing slacks and hard-bottomed shoes. Jason would only laugh at my jokes that no one else laughed at. I decided that if he was the only one laughing then I should just throw that joke away. It took me years to realize that I was doing it wrong, and I flipped it. When Jason (or my mom) was the only one laughing, that meant I should throw all the other jokes away and really work on that joke. They knew me better than everyone else. So they were laughing at the jokes that were the most *me*.

When you start doing the open mic scene it's fun, no matter what city you are in. You feel like you are on a team with the other comics. You're all living on the edge, staying up late on a Tuesday, and going to a diner later to eat pie and/or burritos and talk about your act! Everybody is hilarious, even if they are bombing onstage. And everybody is turned on. *WE'RE DOING IT! We're not living our normal lives! And we're going to be successful in a year! Maybe two at the most!*

And that's what the first two years of open mics were like for me in Chicago. *This is just so much fun!* But by the beginning of the third year, some people had quit. Some people had gotten better. And some people were actually working on the road in clubs. And other people weren't working in clubs, but they were the best on the open-mic scene. And I wasn't in any of those groups. I was on the middle. I could go up onstage and do OK at best. But a lot of the time I bombed. I wasn't interesting to anyone. By the third year, I'd frozen. I wasn't really getting work, although I'd tried.

Sometimes I wondered if I'd just grown up as a comedian in the wrong time. The '70s are my favorite era of stand-up comedy. Not even for any one individual or record in particular, but more for the totality of the era. If the '50s were the conception of the modern era of stand-up with Mort Sahl, Phyllis Diller, and Lenny Bruce, and the '60s were the birth of modern stand-up with Bill Cosby, Bob Newhart, and Joan Rivers, then the '70s were like stand-up comedy's toddler years, when it was just about having a good time, screaming to get attention, and making up its own rules. From Richard Pryor to Freddie Prinze to George Carlin to Steve Martin to Robert Klein, and many others, stand-up comedy was a real thing then. It sold millions of records. It topped the charts. It was played on radio. Comics became pop stars. They sold out arenas and still maintained an air of being slightly dangerous and outside the mainstream, where comedy belongs.

By the '80s, comedy had been fully adopted by showbiz, and just like a six-year-old being sent off to first grade, it now had a shit ton of rules to follow and much of the bold experimentation that comedy was known for was gone. Comedy was a very solid thing to do and had a look, style, and even a uniform: sports coat (occasionally with the sleeves rolled up to say, "Look, I'm professional, but I'm also fun!"), a polo shirt or T-shirt underneath, jeans or relaxed slacks, and tennis shoes. Basically like a tennis coach at a business meeting. Or everybody's fun uncle at a wedding. And all that bold experimentation within comedy's mainstream that existed in the '70s wouldn't really return until the alternative comedy movement of the '90s, spearheaded by Janeane Garofalo, Marc Maron, Patton Oswalt and others.

By the '80s stand-up was so regimented that there was a

well-established career path that was almost like being enrolled in school. Start out as an opener. Get good, which many times meant going on the road. If you aren't already in New York or LA, then move to either New York or LA. Camp out at one of the comedy clubs in whichever city you move to. Get a TV spot on *The Tonight Show*. Then get another one. And another one. And eventually become a star. Turn your act into a sitcom. Star on the sitcom for enough years to get syndication. At some point write a book. (If you don't have an actual book in you, then just write down your act on paper and that will be fine.) Maybe break into movies. Maybe become a bigger star. At some point return to stand-up, even though you probably at some point said you'd never do stand-up ever again.

Of course there are things you can sub out for other things and additional things you can do as well. Like instead of getting on *The Tonight Show*, you could get on *Saturday Night Live*. And sometimes, like in the case of Roseanne Barr, it only takes one *Tonight Show*. Or you could do *Late Night with David Letterman* instead of Carson—although, despite the comedy community's high esteem for Letterman, his show was never the path to fame and fortune that Carson's was. Back in the early 2000s, I was MC'ing a show and was lucky enough to be working with the late and legendary stand-up comedy genius Mitch Hedberg. I intro'ed him just like he asked me to with, "You may have seen him on one of his many appearances on *David Letterman*." Once he hit the stage he retorted, as he would every night we worked together that week, "I think more people have seen me at the store. Kamau should say, 'You may have seen him at the store.'" And then Mitch would take on the character of one of the audience members: "'Oh yeah, I have seen him at the store . . . He likes kiwi fruit.'"

————

There was also the cable route. HBO and Showtime. Stand-up comedy was everywhere in the '80s. This eventually oversaturated the market, and by the early '90s, the boom was gone. Not just gone, but gooooooooooone. Stand-up started disappearing from TV except for big-time specials and occasional appearances on talk shows. Major cities that had multiple full-time paying comedy clubs went down to one or two. Small towns that had multiple-night runs of comedy shows went down to one-nighters. When I moved to the Bay Area in 1997, comics who had been around during the boom still regularly told the tales of the '80s. It was usually after shows, when the club was empty of patrons and it was just the working comics who were allowed to stay after closing and the few new-ish comics who were deemed cool enough to be there too.

The bartenders would let us keep drinking (99 percent of the time for free—which led to more than one drinking problem). And the older comics would get a wistful and faraway look in their eyes and utter some version of "In the '80s, you could work all year round, multiple shows a night, and never leave the Bay Area." And to be clear, they were talking about getting paid to work. The putting-food-on-the-table-and-paying-rent work. And these weren't all headliners. Many of these comics were feature acts who went on before the headliners, so they weren't getting paid the most money. But there was enough money being made in the '80s that feature acts could make a living, something that is impossible now unless you have some sort of mom's basement/living-out-of-your-car situation. And forget having kids or wanting to save money. There's a dwindling middle class in comedy just like there is a dwindling middle class in America. A comic's best financial plan is very similar to that of a person who works at McDonald's: lottery tickets. The only difference is that a comedian's lottery ticket comes in the form of auditions for film and television. Auditions are like playing the lottery, except you have to explain why you picked your numbers and why you thought they were good numbers before they tell you that you didn't win anything.

So it was in the middle of this gone, gone, goooooooone period, in 1994, that a twenty-one-year-old condom store employee named Walter Kamau Bell decided to start his career. Onstage he called himself "W. Kamau Bell" because it sounded more dramatic and he had seen A. Whitney Brown use his first initial on *Saturday Night Live* in the '80s. That was a terrible year for me to start doing stand-up, but at least I had help. I had become really close friends with Dwayne Kennedy, the godfather of Chicago comedy. The second time me and Jason saw him perform, Jason approached him to meet him. Later Jason told me that he did that because he could tell Dwayne was somebody I needed to know. Dwayne was a little bit older, although I still don't know how much older, and he was a great mentor to me for reasons I still don't understand. Comics normally only hang out with people they think are funny. And I wasn't funny. OK, maybe I was funny offstage, but onstage . . . Nope. And this was a bad time to not be funny. It was the total nadir of the comedy bust. The mainstream clubs were closing. There wasn't a place to get better, and I could feel a profound lack of buzz or interest. I felt like I'd been held back a year. I was friends with another comic named Cayne Collier who had been doing stand-up since he was fifteen. We were the same age. I was jealous he had started so much earlier than me. Cayne was a natural leader, and the guy who everybody thought was going to be someone someday. That guy exists in every comedy town. The guy who people knew was going to make it . . . but didn't. I was the guy who nobody ever thought was going to make it but keeps trying to.

Back then I had a studio apartment that cost about $370 a month, but I thought, *I can't continue to pay that much money.* So I moved into Cayne's apartment and slept in the living room for $285 a month, and I regret that decision to this day—why didn't I just stay in my own stupid apartment and pay $370 a month? Like with the W. E. B. Du Bois house, maybe something would have happened in Chicago if I had stayed living on my own.

Onstage I was making no headway at all. I was a Black comic in the white club scene. I would talk about racism, and the audience would just pull back. A lot of Black comics would successfully do jokes about racism, but something about the way I did it wasn't connecting. So I started not talking about racism, but then I was telling jokes that I didn't care about at all. Student loan jokes and jokes about the year and a half of Mandarin I had taken at Penn, which was just an excuse to say "funny sounding" words. Just silliness that I wasn't invested in, but because I could get a couple of them to work I would keep doing them. My big closing joke at the time—which is hard to even talk about now—was about how guys' sexual fantasy is for a beautiful woman to say, "I want you to take me home and make love to me ALL NIGHT LONG." But how my sexual fantasy was for a woman to say, "I want you to take me home and . . . JUST DO YOUR BEST!

JUST TRY REAL HARD." That was the first joke I wrote that ever got a real hard laugh, and it became my closer. So one thing, at least, was going well onstage. Two things, once I wrote the joke about the blow-up doll. So in other words *nothing* was going well onstage.

More and more through my time in comedy, I was realizing the difference between Black and white comedy circles, and that I didn't really fit into either one. It was the same problem I was having with "Black music" and "white music." I was again not fitting in. Which sucked because Chicago definitely has a history of Black comedy, and it would have been great if I had felt that I could fit into it. There was a club at the time called All Jokes Aside, which was the first full-time Black comedy club in Chicago. I would watch Black comics on TV and I would go see Black comics playing the white rooms, and I was very aware that they were speaking a language that I wasn't speaking. This was around the same time that hip-hop was really grabbing the nation by the throat. There was a nightclub called the Cue Club, and one day a week was called Heckler's Heaven, which ended up being a very Black night. It was a night when the audience was encouraged to heckle performers. It was run by a Black comic, and the whole idea was that if the performers were heckled by the audience, they had to get off the stage, and the audience would throw rubber chickens at them to get them off the stage. I would go there and think, *This is awful. I don't want any part of this. I don't want to perform here.* It made my stomach hurt just to watch the show.

Around the same time, a new club opened up in Chicago. It was on the North Side of Chicago, which means it was not a Black comedy club. Dwayne got me a guest set one night. I was going to do seven minutes in a real show at a comedy club to try to impress the owners and get work. I was excited. I also wasn't really ready, and I knew it, but I thought I might be able to pull it off if I hit it hard and was confident. (I didn't realize that I was confusing "confidence" with "bravado." A mistake all men make more than once in our lives.) I went with Dwayne to the club. It was packed, and all the comics were hanging out in the back watching the show. I was super nervous. This was around the time when Rodney King was back in the news. It was a couple years after the LA riots, and he had been pulled over by cops again. These cops didn't beat him, though, so things were looking up for Rodney. I decided that I wanted to open my set with it, but there was a small problem . . . I didn't have a joke about it. These days I do this regularly: if something's happening in the news, I'll open with a joke about it. But these days I actually take the time to make sure I have a joke.

But I should have known that the stakes were too high to be fooling around on this show. There's a pretty hard and fast rule in comedy: Don't do new material when you are trying to get a job or impress someone. Before I went on, I was going back and forth between doing something about Rodney King and just sticking to my old jokes. But I think I also knew my "old jokes" weren't that great either. Meanwhile the comedy club was feral. The MC was onstage giving out prizes and tickets to get people excited about the new club opening. Classic mainstream comedy club stuff. Some clubs never seemed to think that stand-up comedy is enough to please an audience, so there were raffles, a ticket giveaway, and trivia contests. "And let's sing 'Happy Birthday' in case anyone in here has ever had a birthday ever in life!" And even though this club was on the North Side, there were a lot of Black people there that night. The room had way more energy than I was used to dealing with in empty coffee shops. Next thing I heard was the MC asking a trivia question: "What's the name of the pink Power Ranger?" A Black woman excitedly exclaimed that she knew the answer. She won the tickets. I thought that was funny: *Black people—we don't know our history, but we know who the Pink Power Ranger is!* I decided it would be funny to say that when I got up onstage.

They introduced me and I went up. I had that "new comic" smell. I began with, "Black people, we don't know our history, but we know who the pink Power Ranger is!" and the crowd turned on me *immediately*. They booed. And they were right to boo. It wasn't a joke. It was just a snarky statement for no reason. An attack on someone for no reason at all. This woman was probably a mom. That's probably why she knew who the Pink Power Ranger was; she was a good mom. I understand that now. I can name all of the animals on the Disney Junior show *Octonauts*, because I'm a good dad. Here we go! Kwazii, Captain Barnacles, Tweak, Tunip, Dashi, Shellington, Peso, and Professor Inkling. Just because I know that doesn't mean that I don't know that Madam C. J. Walker is America's first female self-made millionaire of any race. That night at the club when I made fun of that woman, I was an asshole . . . a young, insensitive idiot.

While I was getting booed, I decided to downshift into some classic WKB material to dig myself out of that hole. Maybe a good time to talk about blow-up dolls? Nope. I went with my new half-baked topical joke. "Rodney King was in the news . . ." Ten seconds later I had been booed off the stage, in front of all the biggest comics on the scene who were all there to check out the new club.

One comic said to me, "Well, sometimes you eat the bear, sometimes the bear eats you." It was a terrible feeling, and if it happened today, I would have just left. But I was there with Dwayne, and he was still hanging out. The comics who didn't know me did the only thing they could do. They avoided me like I was radioactive. And I stood there, trying to figure out where to go and what to do . . . and how to stand so I didn't look like I just bombed my face off. I was hoping that maybe it wasn't as bad as I thought. But it was. If you're friends with comics, they'll joke around with you when you bomb. But my only friend there was Dwayne. And Dwayne was talking to other comics. I was just standing in the back of the club, steeping in failure juice, feeling like I had made a bad choice with this comedy thing.

And while we are talking about getting booed off the stage, as much as people think that happens a lot, it doesn't happen that often. Most comics can survive bombing for a whole set. Knowing how to bomb successfully is part of the gig. You can't always just run away. At the very least the club needs you to fill your time. There aren't comics in cages backstage waiting to go on in case of emergency. Sure, there are comics hanging out. And many a comic has been thrown up onstage when the club has had a need for another comic for various reasons. But the type of bombing that I did that night is pretty rare. The feeling of that bombing is rushing back to me right now as I type this. That had been my shot! There was no other club in town where I had any-thing close to a shot at getting up. For all intents and purposes, I was retired.

Being in my twenties was not helpful for my comedy develop-ment because I had nothing going on to talk about. It wasn't un-til I got to my thirties that I had real material. It was only when I got older that I found the right things to talk about and the right way to talk about those things. But one of the best things about being a young comic is going out to watch as many stand-up shows as you can. You are hungry for knowledge. It doesn't matter if you like the comics on the show or have even heard of them. If you aren't onstage then you should be in a club watching other professionals onstage. One night me and Cayne went to All Jokes Aside to see one of Cayne's favorite comedians, a young Black dude named Dave Chappelle. At the time I was twenty-one and I later found out that he was twenty.

Me and Cayne arrived and were seated in the center of the room. We wondered why they put us there. The show started, and one by one, comics (all of them Black) came onstage. And they were all killing. And it was hilarious. But it wasn't a style of comedy that I felt I could pull off. It was raw, dirty, filled with references to rap songs I didn't know and talk of a Black experi-ence that I didn't have growing up. At this point I was watching Janeane Garofalo and Marc Maron, and I was starting to really get into Bill Hicks. All three of them do black comedy but not Black comedy.

This was the *Def Comedy Jam* era on television. HBO's *Def*

Comedy Jam became famous when Bernie Mac, on an early episode, had to follow a comic who had just bombed. Bernie stepped onstage, surveyed the crowd, and proclaimed, "I'm not scared of you motherfuckers," and it killed. The audience was fully on board with Bernie that night . . . and for the rest of his career until he died. But there was a problem. *I was scared of those motherfuckers.* That's the energy of *Def Jam*—you need to be combative. There's nothing about comedy that made me want to be in a combative state. It was the same energy that resulted in throwing rubber chickens. And I think it comes from Black people's experience in this country, having to defend ourselves at all times. Having to be loud in situations where other people might not be loud, because if we aren't loud there's no chance of getting our share. If you're loud you still might not get your share, but you might get more than they'd give you otherwise. And when you're told to be quiet all the time, or to obey, or to shut up, when you're finally in a place that's yours, you can let it all out.

America's favorite pastime isn't baseball. It's telling Black people to behave . . . even when we aren't doing anything wrong. So I get it, when we're in a room with a lot of other Black people . . . and that room is run by Black people . . . and no one's telling us to "behave"—then we make sure that we have a good time. And ain't nobody got time for an unfunny comedian. But back then at All Jokes Aside, I saw Black comedians up there with this aggressive style. I thought, *That's not how I want to do it.* I don't want to go onstage and feel like I have to tame you or beat you back. I've been doing comedy long enough now that I can handle those situations . . . mostly, but I still don't go to those venues that often. I don't seek them out. I got into comedy to share my weird thoughts and seek connection. I can handle hard crowds of all races, but I don't want to deal with it. Some comics get excited dealing with it. But it's still not my thing.

So me and Cayne are at All Jokes Aside, and Dave Chappelle comes onstage. He's skinny. He looks sixteen. And his energy seems way too relaxed for the room. I'd seen him on HBO's *Comic Relief*. This was the first time I'd seen him in real life. And while nearly every other comic onstage that night had made jokes about me and Cayne that were all some approximation of "What's this Black guy doing here with this white guy?" (We finally figured out that was why they had seated us in the center of the club. We were target practice for the comics), Chappelle didn't do that. He came up in Black clubs and white clubs and clubs where everybody hung out in Washington, DC. So it was not a big deal to him that a Black guy and white guy were together. He was just onstage to do his jokes. And me and Cayne are loving him. He's killing us, but in the room he's doing just all right. So much so that people are getting up and going to the bathroom while he's talking. He commented on it: "So many people are going to the bathroom, I must be the bran muffin of comedy." We thought that was hilarious. We were two of the few in the audience who did. After the show we talked to him. It was easy. He was standing by himself, like I had been on the night of the Pink Power Ranger. He clearly realized that he hadn't succeeded with the crowd, even though we thought he'd been awesome. He asked if there was a nightclub he could go to in town, and I wasn't the nightclub type, but I mentioned a place that constantly had ads on the radio. He asked if they let people in who aren't twenty-one yet, and that's when I realized he was only twenty. I thought, *I couldn't have done as well as he did here, and he's younger than me.* And then he disappeared into the night.

Years later in San Francisco, I would spend a lot of time with Chappelle . . . OK, it was really only *near* Chappelle. The Punch Line was one of his favorite clubs in the country. And I tried to be there whenever he performed. It had only been a few years since All Jokes Aside, but by the late '90s, even though he wasn't famous, he was packing the clubs. People knew he was a future legend. I was in the room when he told people he had just finished making a movie about weed (*Half Baked*). And I was there one night when a KKK member went onstage and hurled insults at the audience. It was hilarious, because we could see his Black hands under his white sheets. Later we all realized that we were there during an early tryout of Clayton Bigsby, the blind Black KKK member that Dave played on the debut episode of his behemoth of a sketch show, *Chappelle's Show.*

Once he returned from South Africa after he left the show and Comedy Central, me and Kevin were very established comics in town so we got to open for him a bunch of times. But I wouldn't say that we were friends with him. There was a lot of competition for that by then. And me and Kevin didn't want to try to push our way into the greenroom to see if we could buddy up. Dave would show up in San Francisco unannounced, and the Punch Line would basically book as many shows as he wanted to do. Sometimes they would bump other headliners for Dave. Sometimes they would just book ten p.m. and midnight shows for Dave. Because he always went long onstage, sometimes the midnight shows wouldn't start until two a.m. I saw Dave do two- and three-hour shows regularly. Once I saw him do four hours and fifty-nine minutes. (He didn't want to do five hours because he heard that was the record, and he didn't want to break it.) At one point I got to go on the road with him and do a few cities in the Midwest. Dave always made sure I got paid more than it said in my contract. And he told me that I was funny. That period when he came back from South Africa was the best comedy I have ever seen in my life. And it's all in the ether. Oh, it was recorded. Dave recorded all of it, but who knows if any of it ever sees the light of day. And take it from me, even if you do hear any of it or see any of it, it won't be the same as being in the room. Like the difference between watching someone cook on TV and actually eating the food. The former is fun, but so not the point.

But at All Jokes Aside in 1994, I was just a customer who had paid to see Dave Chapelle. Because I didn't work that club they didn't know me (or Cayne), so we couldn't get in for free since we were comics. And I certainly didn't tell them that I was a comic. Which was weird, because wasn't I supposed to want to be in that room? Shouldn't I have wanted to be a part of that scene? I didn't. And that sucked because the "white" spaces weren't that accepting of me either.

And that's how it continued until I moved to San Francisco. I needed a place with opportunity where I could grow, and I had heard that San Francisco was known for encouraging difference. I was realizing that I might just actually be different. I realized, *I've got to make my own space.*

Awkward Thoughts
about Denzel Washington

When me and Kevin Avery met as baby comedians on the San Francisco scene in 1997, we were not instant friends. Even though we had a somewhat similar upbringing: Black dudes raised during the hip-hop era who both listened to more than our fair share of music that wasn't hip-hop. My tastes skewed more Fishbone, Rage Against the Machine, and Living Colour, and Kevin was more into Fiona Apple, Jason Mraz, and movie soundtracks. And Kevin, unlike me, was a big rap fan. And he actually had a run in a boy band.

Me and Kevin were also the product of private school educations. But while I had spent some time in public schools when I moved around from city to city to city . . . to city, Kevin was one of those kids who lived in the same area his whole life and whose parents were still married, and he described them as "happy." So weird. And we both had that thing where we had spent much of our youth around mostly white people (prolly because of all that private school). It was like there was an episode of the TV show *Chopped*, where instead of making three courses of food, they were making two Black guys. Me and Kevin were made up of a lot of the same ingredients, but the seasoning was different. Kevin had big, bold, classic flavors. And I was the Black guy where the judge would turn to the chef who made me and say, "Why do you use so much cumin in this? I don't think cumin goes in this."

And I think that was the problem—at least I know it was from my end. We had a lot in common, clearly, but we were doing our "Black" differently. And also there weren't a lot of Black guys on the mainstream SF comedy club scene at this point, so we both had a little bit of "Who's this dude? Doesn't he know they only have one spot available? And I want it?" That's the kind of thing that doesn't happen so much between white guys in comedy clubs, because they are like wallpaper; they are everywhere. But it does happen with people of color and with women. You either bond together because you know you will need each other to survive or you run as far as you can in the other direction, because you would hate for people to think there are too many of you in the room at one time. So me and Kevin initially weren't friends, but if I'm honest about it, I had a way bigger chip on my shoulder than he did. Mine was bigger because I was jealous of him. Onstage and offstage, Kevin was super popular and outgoing. Offstage Kevin played it cool and low-key. I was none of those things and I wanted to be. I always said his model for behavior was George Clooney.

Onstage though, Kevin was different. Onstage, he was very physical and loud. Kevin had no problem making himself look goofy for the laugh, because he knew he wasn't a goofy person. Kevin talked about his problems dating, movies, and being a Black guy who had grown up around white people. And he was a killer. Crowds loved him. I may not have liked him, but I certainly didn't want to follow him. And that made me more jealous. Meanwhile, I was just onstage panning for jokes. I would talk about race and racism, but I would also just veer into Kevin's lane talking about dating and movies. There wasn't a through line or a consistent point of view. And I was just sort of ambling around the stage with no purpose or direction. Kevin owned the stage. I was renting the stage . . . nightly . . . and I often didn't have the full rent (i.e., I bombed).

Around 1999, he took me on the road with him on a series of one-nighters in Nevada. I was really surprised when he asked me. We were friendly enough but we were still not friends. I'm not sure if he was offering an olive branch or if he just didn't want to take this trip through the hinterlands of Nevada on two-lane highways through the deserted desert alone. These were horrible shows and the money was worse. This was the definition of "paying your dues." You do a gig in front of twelve people, then do an eight-hour drive to the next one and repeat the cycle. We performed in towns like Lovelock, Eely, and Battle Mountain. The parts of Nevada that are nowhere near Vegas. You're not even playing hotel casinos. You're playing motel casinos and truck stops with slot machines. Places that looked like they were the original model for the Boar's Nest from *The Dukes of Hazzard* or the next bar that Patrick Swayze's character Dalton from *Road House* was headed to clean up. And this is when I started to learn that there was more than one America. It didn't feel like the same country that I lived in. It felt like the past. Not like the 1960s, but at best it felt like 1978. Every place we walked into, the people would turn to us and look at us like, "You *must* be the comedians. Because if you are not, then you two fellers are very, very lost." *Insert the sound of a gun being cocked . . . in my imagination.*

And many of my jokes weren't landing. Even though ostensibly we all watch the same TV and movies, their relationship to it is different. I had a joke that was one of my big pieces about all the Godzilla movie billboards that had taken over the city. They were everywhere . . . at least they were everywhere in San Francisco and Oakland. Those billboards were nowhere in the post-apocalyptic hellscape that was Nevada. And my joke crashed before it even took off. Out there it seemed like Godzilla was a folktale.

Kevin was only paying me about fifty dollars a set, but he wasn't making much money either, and it was just fun to do. We were doing these awful gigs, and that bonded us as friends, as those gigs are made to do. We returned from the trip as friends, and we eventually started writing together, working on screenplays together, and hanging out all the time. And people started seeing us as a duo. People were saying, "It'sKevinAndKamau!" Then he became my roommate. And one subject kept recurring throughout all our conversations. That subject is the greatness of Denzel Washington. Me and Kevin both discovered that we were huge Denzel fans, even though we came to him through different paths. Kevin would be watching *Crimson Tide* over and over in his room, and I'd be watching *Malcolm X* over and over in my room. And in the adjoining hallway we'd come together and say: "He's the greatest actor of all time! WHY DON'T MORE PEOPLE KNOW THIS? WHY DON'T MORE PEOPLE TALK ABOUT THIS?"

Kevin was more of a fan of Denzel's big Hollywood roles. I think *Crimson Tide* is great, but it's not even in my personal top ten. I was more of a fan of his—as Denzel himself describes it—"biography man" roles. Roles like *Malcolm X*, *Hurricane*, *Glory*; the whole "Black man has to save his own ass and his people's asses because he can't count on these crackers to do nothing." We would talk about Denzel all the time, and Keri, our manager (yup, eventually I just decided I should go with his manager too. Also she was the only one interested), would say, "You should do something with this." But we didn't know what.

But when *Totally Biased* got canceled in late 2013, Earwolf, the podcast company, was looking for ideas. And I pitched an idea without Kevin even knowing about it. I called him and said, "Hey, man, I think I got us a podcast."

And that's how our podcast *Denzel Washington Is the Greatest Actor of All Time Period* was born. The original goal of *DWITGAOATP* was to review all Denzel Washington movies in alphabetical order, and each week, we'd prove over time that Denzel Washington is the greatest actor of all time . . . period. We'd also break down his Denzelishness. And we'd have guests who were either superfans like us, or who had actually worked with Denzel. Usually those who had worked with Denzel were also superfans. The podcast is still all of those things at its core, but it has also opened up into a discussion about diversity in Hollywood that always swings on Denzel. And our discussion was happening at the same time April Reign started the hashtag #OscarsSoWhite, which helped inform our discussion. (And I believe her hashtag actually pushed the Oscars and Hollywood to do better.) We also had episodes where we just felt compelled to talk about movies Denzel wasn't in but were important to the Black experience. Films like *Creed*, *Purple Rain*, and *Straight Outta Compton*. We call it "Black People Homework." We started celebrating working Black actresses (WBAs), because in a large percentage of his movies, Denzel has a Black wife. And these are women who would be getting more work if Hollywood wasn't so sexist . . . and racist . . . and shortsighted.

At some point at the beginning of the podcast, Ava DuVernay started following me on Twitter. I figured every Black person in Hollywood likes Denzel Washington, right? She did, and in fact she had been a publicist on one of the greatest hidden gems in Denzel's filmography, a proud little B-movie thriller named *Out of Time*. So I invited her on the podcast, and even though she didn't officially come on—she was just on the phone in her office, and Kevin wasn't even in the episode—it sort of announced the podcast to the world. "THEY HAVE AVA DUVERNAY ON THAT STUPID THING?" Previously when I'd tweeted about the podcast and mentioned it on Facebook, even my fans weren't interested. But shortly after, we had a woman named Liz volunteer to run our Twitter profile. A guy in Russia named Igor built a website for us. We had this small nerd *and* Blerd community. And then about a year into the podcast, we got Spike Lee. We were sitting in a room talking to Spike Lee, and I just thought, *Mission accomplished.* Me and Kevin—two dudes who just a few years before thought maybe, just maybe, showbiz wasn't going to work out for them after all—got to sit with Spike Lee for an hour and talk about Denzel Washington! It was glorious. And it just keeps going. The show has a culture of its own. The fans are called "Denzealots." Superfans often get a nickname based on Denzel's movies. Liz is our "Woman on Fire" (*Man on Fire*). Igor, who lives in St. Petersburg, is affectionately called "the Russians" in tribute to Denzel's movie *The Equalizer.*

The show's success has allowed me to connect with people who I may not have connected with otherwise, like Issa Rae, the creator, writer, and star of *Insecure*; actor Joe Morton, from *Scandal*; and actor and activist Jesse Williams, from *Grey's Anatomy.* The podcast has also allowed me to embarrass myself in front of people like Jesse Williams, who I referred to as "Jesse L. Williams." His middle name does not start with the letter *L*, although a quick Google search reveals that Google believes that it does. (I felt vindicated when, months later, BET called him that too.) On another occasion, in attempting to quote a "famous" line from *Training Day*, I just blurted out to Issa Rae, "I didn't know you liked to get wet." Awk-ward. And classic Kamau.

Awkward Thoughts about Denzel Washington

But why Denzel? Simply, he's on the top of the list of famous men, along with Bruce Lee, Michael Jordan, and Henry Rollins, who have been my mentors whether they know it or not. Since I mostly grew up in a single-parent home with my mom, I pieced together ideal male role models from my pop-culture heroes. I eventually learned about manhood, pride, and dancing to the beat of my own drum from these dudes.

It was my mom who first introduced me to Denzel's work. When I was growing up, my mother always said she had to support anything a Black person was in because there weren't enough Black people in media. Then, around the '90s, she said, "I don't have to do that anymore, because there's enough stuff out there, and some of it is horrible." In 1984, we went to see *A Soldier's Story*, a movie that features a young Denzel Washington. It was some of my original "Black People Homework," along with the mini-series *Roots*. In the movie Denzel starts out as someone you shouldn't worry about, but by the end (spoiler alert) he basically becomes the villain. You realize, watching Denzel, that if he weren't as good an actor as he is, then the whole movie falls apart. You have to believe that even though he starts out as someone you don't worry about at all, he is capable of being the bad guy. He was. For more on that see *Training Day*. Seriously, why haven't you seen *Training Day*?

Denzel was also in *St. Elsewhere*. He wasn't the focus of the ensemble cast, but Denzel basically invented the modern-era "TV Black doctor." You know who I'm talking about. Black Doctor is one of the best at what he does. But he's got a chip on his shoulder, and at times that holds him back from people getting close to him. Oh, Black Doctor! It's Eriq La Salle's character on *E.R.* and Isaiah Washington's character on *Grey's Anatomy*. When Denzel was on *St.*

Elsewhere, Black people were like, "Let's keep an eye on this young Denzel Washington!" Then he played Steve Biko in *Cry Freedom* and then Quinn in *The Mighty Quinn*, the first movie to let him be the sex symbol that he clearly was. Next he did *Glory*, and that single tear he cried, while getting whipped by a white man, turned him into a legend . . . also he won one of those Academy Award thingies for it. It was just Best Supporting, but at least the industry was starting to see what Black folk already knew.

It became clear that Denzel only took roles he could defend. I took that to heart in my career. It's obviously very important to Denzel that the work he's putting out in the world doesn't make it harder for another Black person. Early in his career, he never played the thug or the criminal. And even when he played the role of a bad cop in *Training Day*, it was so deep into his career of being the man above reproach (*Malcolm X*, *Cry Freedom*, *The Preacher's Wife*, *Remember the Titans*) that it became a meta-performance. We all watched *Training Day*, saying to ourselves not "I can't believe Detective Alonzo Harris is being so mean!" but "I can't believe Denzel Washington is being so mean! He was Malcolm X! And Biko! HE WAS IN A MOVIE WITH JULIA ROBERTS, FOR GOD'S SAKE!!!"

There's a ton of controversy in the Black community about *Training Day,* because THAT'S THE MOVIE THAT WON HIM A BEST ACTOR OSCAR?! Of course, the bad cop who abuses Black people is OSCAR WORTHY! Want to have some fun? Bring up *Training Day* at a Black family gathering and watch the sparks fly.

I didn't see *Glory* in the theater because I had heard that they all died at the end. I don't need to see that. I avoided it for years. When it came out, I was sixteen, and I was realizing how hard it was to be a Black man in society. *Oh, it's hard to be Black? I didn't know!*

Thanks! I didn't see it until years later. I couldn't take it. It's a great movie, but it still breaks my heart. I still watch movies hoping they'll end differently. I can only watch about 75 percent of *Malcolm X* before I turn it off and pretend it all works out for brother Malcolm. I'm hoping that the next time I watch it, Malcolm will just die of old age. I feel the same way about *Glory. Can't they win this time?*

Everyone on the podcast lists their top five Denzel movies. I'm going to do that now, but you have to realize that the list changes. And everyone's criteria are different. Some people pick their favorite movies that he's in. Other people pick their favorite performances. Other people pick the movies that are the most meaningful to them, which is what I'm doing. There's only one rule. You have to rank them from five to one. I'll explain why I like them, but I'm not defending them.

5. *Out of Time*: And that's why I'm going to start with *Out of Time.* On its surface it is a little late-night cable, B-movie thriller that weirdly stars Denzel Washington. It's crazy that he's in it. The movie should star C. Thomas Howell or a post–tax evasion Wesley Snipes. But much like *Training Day*, it's also a meta-performance. In most of his films we see Denzel as someone who is in control of everything or good at gaining control of everything. And this movie is about someone who is totally out of control of the situation, and it's no one's fault but his. THE WORLD IS AGAINST HIM! And it's fun to watch.

4. *Inside Man*: I love that Denzel and Spike Lee teamed up together and made a mainstream hit movie. And a heist movie—everybody loves a heist movie! But it's also super smart, and because it is Spike and Denzel, there is still

stuff about race and racism in there. There's a scene where a guy in a turban is confused for being a Muslim, but it turns out he's a Sikh. (Interesting, I thought.) And unlike most of his roles, Denzel doesn't look particularly good in the movie. He's basically playing a working-class cop schlub. But he wins at the end. There are so many movies where he's the Black guy from history where he dies. And when you die, even if it is for a good cause, like the liberation of your people, you still basically lose. But in *Inside Man* he gets to win at the end of a movie . . . finally. I have two Spike Lee movies on my list, and there's a reason for that. Spike and Denzel became cultural icons together. (*Mo' Better Blues, Malcolm X, He Got Game.*) *Inside Man* is them taking a victory lap. *Why don't we just make a fun movie?*

3. *The Book of Eli*: This isn't a movie a lot of people like. I'm guessing it is because there's a thorough belief in God narrative in this movie. As a kid who grew up going to church, I'm good with that. But it's also a great action movie. And the guy who did the fight choreography is a student of Bruce Lee's best friend, Dan Inosanto. So when I watched it, I could feel the connection between Bruce Lee and Denzel. The first time I watched it, it made me cry, because it is about a guy on a mission, and a lot of time in my life, I feel like I'm on a mission, as cheesy as it sounds. By the end, I was thinking, *He finally gets to stop being on a mission! Do I ever get to stop being on a mission?* When you're a stand-up comedian, you're charting your own path, and people think you're crazy. People don't get what you're doing. And Denzel says in the movie, "I don't know

where I'm going, I just know that I'm supposed to be going this way." I love that. Me too.

2. *Training Day*: With this film you get Denzel Washington and director Antoine Fuqua, one of Denzel's favorite directors. And you get that great debate: "Was Denzel great in this?" "Of course!" "Should we be happy that his first Best Actor Oscar is for playing a corrupt cop?" "Erm . . ." "Should performers of color be allowed to play the full range of human emotions?" "Absolutely!" "Am I going to stop asking questions and answering them myself?" "I'll think about it."

1. *Malcolm X*: If you don't make *Malcolm X* your number one, you're just trying to be smarter than everybody. You're like the guy at the end of the bar arguing that the Golden State Warriors team that lost in the NBA finals is actually a better team than the Golden State Warriors team that won in the NBA finals. Or the comedy nerd saying, "Well actually, the last season of *Arrested Development* is the best one!" You are just slowing down the possibility of a good conversation. Now be quiet. Adults are trying to talk.

I do think our podcast has, in some ways, elevated Denzel to a different place. At least with some people. It has allowed them to proclaim their Denzel love in a more public way. People in the industry have even started to see if they can convince him to come on the podcast, but I'm totally fine if it never happens. If he doesn't want to do the podcast, I totally accept it. It isn't about Denzel validating the podcast. What's important to me is that people of color embrace and celebrate our heroes.

And it's also important that we celebrate our heroes when they are still around to participate in the celebration. And honestly, me and Kevin know that Denzel isn't really the greatest actor of all time period. That's not provable. But we do know that generally when people talk about the greatest actors ever, it's usually white guys. Actors like DeNiro, Pacino, Brando, DiCaprio. All the actors whose names end in o. So why not Denzel in that conversation? In my lifetime, only Tom Hanks has maintained a level of relevance, critical acclaim, and commercial success over a thirty-year period like Denzel. And even he acknowledges Denzel's greatness. And Denzel is always raising the stakes. At an age when many actors of his level downshift to costarring grandpa roles in mainstream comedy films, Denzel has said no to all of that. Denzel has decided to take on the biggest challenge of his career. He is producing all ten of August Wilson's plays in Wilson's Pittsburgh Cycle. This is legend on legend. How can we not celebrate that?

CHAPTER 4

My Awkward Middle in Stand-Up Comedy

By 2007, I had slowly (very slowly) worked my way up the depth chart on the San Francisco comedy scene, from opener to feature to in-town headliner. The scene had really been everything that I wanted and needed it to be. The two big comedy clubs in SF, Cobb's Comedy Club and the Punch Line, both encouraged and searched for new talent. They both had nights specifically set aside for local comics to work out new stuff. That was very different from how most other comedy clubs around the country worked. Most wanted to please the audience over everything else. Most clubs were just bars with better entertainment. But the bookers of the two SF clubs loved it when comics did weird shit or experimented. Once you were in, you *were in*. They wanted you to try hard and fail big . . . and get funnier. In fact, one early January, the owner of Cobb's Comedy Club, Tom Sawyer, pulled all the local comics aside for a "pep talk." He told us, "I want to see more new shit from you all. I'm tired of watching you all do the same shit over and over. I'm tired of hearing you say, 'I was just doing my "A" shit' [best jokes]. You don't have 'A' shit. If you had 'A' shit, then you wouldn't be here every Monday night. You'd be on HBO. I want to see everybody doing new shit." I heard the message loud and clear. Despite Tom's drill sergeant–style delivery, it was the most exciting thing you could hear as a comic who wants to get better: the club doesn't care if you bomb. Our biggest fear was now our greatest resource. That helped me make the transition to the next rung on the ladder.

But becoming an in-town headliner is the fool's gold of comedy. "In-town headliner" means you are good enough to headline, but only on Sunday through Wednesday. You are not famous enough or "hot" enough to headline Thursday through Saturday. And historically, those are the nights when the money gets made. Being an in-town headliner is like being the second guy off the bench in the NBA: valuable but not notable. There's an award for the sixth man, but there ain't one for the seventh man.

Even though I was headlining, I was still fumbling around, trying to find my voice. How fumble-y, you ask? After more than ten years in stand-up, I had one major TV credit, *Premium Blend* on Comedy Central in 2005, and I thought I was going to get some kind of bump out of it. I had a good set on the show. At that point I still didn't have a manager or agent. But I had a lot of hope for 2005; it felt like things were about to turn around. At the beginning of the year, I had been invited to the prestigious Just for Laughs Festival in Montreal as a part of their New Faces showcase. New Faces was every comic's dream. I just knew that my life and career were about to change and I told Melissa, who I had been dating for two years, as much. But by the time I got to New Faces, I didn't feel like a new face. The other comics from the Bay Area who were going were all in their early or midtwenties. I was thirty-two. I felt weirdly excited and also like I was pretending to fit in.

My big set at Montreal did not go well. I didn't bomb. It was worse—just mediocre. I could give excuses. But the truth is even at thirty-two I just wasn't ready. I didn't have a consistent viewpoint or great jokes. This was all made worse by the fact that my dad and stepmom came. My dad wanted to be there for my big break. He had really come around to supporting me. He still wanted me to make sure I could make a living, but he understood the dream. I talked of quitting after Montreal, but my dad wouldn't have it. I had put too many years in by that point, as far as he was concerned. I needed to give it a little while longer. I'm still not sure where that advice came from, but it really helped a lot. Especially since I was still at a low point. I went into Montreal with no manager or agent. And I came out the same way.

My friend Molly Schminke, who was also the booker at the Punch Line in San Francisco, had sort of started talking about managing me. There was precedent there. Many of the biggest comedy managers in Hollywood had come out of comedy clubs as bookers, managers, and bartenders. And at the Punch Line, Molly was the queen. She ruled the scene. It was up to her who went on and when. In a male-dominated industry, Molly had quickly become a legend. And like a lot of people who ran comedy, she didn't come into it with that intention. She just needed a job, liked comedy, and got a job working the door. She had actually started working the club around the same time I showed up in town in 1997. I didn't realize that until years later, because even when she was only a door person, she seemed like she was in charge of everything. Molly was about five foot nine, but back then she wore platform boots that made her well over six feet. She had long red hair and looked like she had walked out of 1960s-era Haight-Ashbury in San Francisco but by way of Mars. She was above it all literally and figuratively. She was intimidating. But by 2007, me, Molly, and Kevin were old heads on the scene and great friends. She had seen me work my craft over the years. She had also seen my frustration, and I think her wanting to be my manager was her just rolling up her sleeves (actually, she rarely wore sleeves. Sleeves would have covered up her tattoos) to see if she could help her friend. Me and Molly fooled around with the manager thing for a while, but eventually it just lost steam.

So by 2007, I was just working in comedy. Trying to pay the rent, but with no audience draw of any kind. Meaning, if my name was at the top of the marquee, it must be free-ticket night . . . and it must just be a Monday . . . because no one is paying to see me. No agent. No manager. No road work. No prospects. My biggest opportunity that spring was that I was hired to do shows in Okinawa, Japan, for "the troops." I say "the troops" because it is definitely *not* what you are thinking. The USO has a great reputation for taking entertainers overseas to the heart of the fight and giving the young men and women over there a break from all the hectic "I might die soon" feelings. But this wasn't that. This was a local Okinawa promoter who had hooked up with a local San Francisco comedian, and together they booked comics to do a week of gigs at the various (and way more numerous than seemed necessary) military bases on the island. And in case you thought you might have missed a news story or two, no, we are not at war with Okinawa, or anyplace in Japan, or with anybody else in that region (for now). As far as I could tell, the military bases are a remnant of World War II. And they are thought to be well placed just in case something jumps off in that area of the world. Sort of a lazy imperialism.

That was a hellish week for me in Okinawa. Me and Kevin were "co-headlining," which meant we were each contracted to do forty-five minutes to fill the required time of a ninety-minute show. We both knew we had forty-five minutes. But we were both extremely nervous.

I didn't know what Kevin had to worry about, though. Kevin's act was all big and physical and cartoony and instantly relatable as soon as he hit the stage, and my act was . . . Well, at that point, it wasn't all anything, really. It was sort of trying to be edgy and sorta, kinda political, but then there would be these unrelated middle-of-the-road jokes that I put in to try to bridge the gaps to the material that I really wanted to do. My act was a mess, and these troops weren't my target audience.

The local comic who produced the gig kept saying that we were going to get first-class treatment and that the crowds were going to love us. But I got suspicious. Anytime someone says a gig is *too* good, you shouldn't trust them. Usually that means it's good in a very specific way, and I wasn't usually that specific type of comic. So I did some research, just like my mom taught me. I knew that Tom Rhodes, a true "no gig is too perilous or too scary for me" veteran comedy road dog, had done the same gig recently. I emailed him and asked how it was. A simple response came back: "Worst gig ever!" He told me about a fight that had broken out during a show and how there was no security. Now, Tom was the kind of comic who literally played everywhere. All over the world. He was legendary among comics for this. The dude was on the road so much he didn't even have a home address. Seriously, no apartment or anything. He just stayed out on the road. So if Tom thought it was the worst gig ever, he knew what he was talking about. And I knew I might not survive.

I immediately told Kevin the news. We both went into panic mode, dreading what we had gotten ourselves into. The night of the first gig, we developed a strategy: I would go up first, then Kevin would close the show. I wanted the first position so I could get it over with. Kevin wanted the second position so he could watch how I did and adjust from there. We agreed that after the first show, we would flip-flop the order the next night so he didn't have to close every night. Well, the first night, I started OK, but then very quickly got weak. I wasn't bombing per se. I was just playing to the complete indifference of about two hundred mostly male, mostly eighteen- to nineteen-year-old troops. It was as if, after Tom's performance and bad experience, they had been told, "It doesn't matter if you don't like the comedian. You at least have to stay in the room."

They were having conversations with each other and just generally treating me like I was a jukebox playing a song they weren't into, and they were patiently waiting for the next selection, hoping it would be better. I filled my time. And by that, I mean I was onstage for forty-five minutes. I have no idea what I said to get through it. There's an interesting phenomenon in stand-up comedy that I find to be true across the board. If you are killing, like really *murdering* the crowd, then you never get through all the jokes you had planned to do. When audiences are being hit right where they live by a comedian, then they laugh longer. Literally the laughter lasts longer. And as a comic, when you hear that kind of laughter, you do every tag (extra punch line) that you ever thought of for the original joke . . . which makes the joke go longer.

And then there's applause. Beautiful, beautiful (and occasionally annoying) applause. Applause at the end of a punch line takes up even more time. And when you combine the longer laughs, the extra tags, and the applause, you end up getting offstage and saying to anyone in the vicinity, "I didn't even get through half my act!" A humblebrag if there ever was one. In fact, applause is so desired that comics often talk about how they did after performing on a late-night talk show by the number of applause breaks they got.

"How was your *Conan*?"

"Great! I got five applause breaks."

Applause is the french fry you find at the bottom of your onion rings.

Applause is like the first time as a kid when you order a soda pop, and then they say the phrase that pays: "Free refills."

Applause is the double rainbow of comedy.

Applause is that rare second orgasm that follows immediately after the first orgasm. (That's rare, right?)

Applause is Oprah saying to you, "YOU GET A CAR! YOU ALSO GET ANOTHER CAR! YOU ALSO GET ANOTHER CAR! YOU ALSO GET ANOTHER CAR!"

Well, applause was something I didn't experience that first show in Okinawa. That is unless you consider the tepid institutional applause that came after me saying, "That's my time. Good night!" I don't. Because it's not.

At the end of my set that night, I quickly introduced Kevin and got offstage. Kevin looked at me like, "Uh-oh. What am I getting into here?"

Kevin did much better than me, but not great. And by the end of the evening, we both realized we were in for a looooong week. How we were going to handle it might be different, but one thing we definitely agreed on was that we would keep the order the same. I would still go on first every night so I could get it over with, and he would still go on second so he could size everything up. It was definitely bad, but we didn't want to change the order and somehow make it worse.

That week I got through the shows. They got somewhat better because I threw away some of my more political and attempting-to-be-socially-relevant jokes, and dug back into my "back catalog," my older jokes, to find more middle-of-the-road stuff. Not necessarily great jokes, but certainly more relatable. Sex jokes, men-and-women-are-different jokes, jokes about my parents—we all have parents, right? RIGHT? I also opened my set every night trying to do as much local stuff as possible, because I quickly realized that they really loved that more than anything else. So every night I went onstage and riffed as much local stuff as I could . . .

"What's up with your commercials on the base television? Apparently you guys are spending a lot of time shaking babies, and you give your power of attorney to anybody!" You know the phrase "You had to be there"? You *literally* had to be there. In Okinawa . . . on those military bases . . . that "joke" KIIIIIIIILLED!

I spent every day before the shows frantically going over my set list, trying to remember old jokes, trying to write new "jokes" like the one above that would help me fill the time and get laughs. I was trying to make sure that the time I spent with my actual current act was as short as possible. Well, I survived. And when I got home, one question went through my mind over and over again: Is this what I do for a living? The answer came back to me: If this is what comedy is, then I don't want to do this for a living.

When I returned from Okinawa, I took a break from stand-up. No going onstage. No writing. No booking gigs (not that the world was pounding my door down for my services). The one thing I did do was spend a lot of time feeling like a failure. College dropout turned stand-up dropout. I was living in the Sunset District of San Francisco. The Sunset is the neighborhood that gets the crazy-thick depression fog that San Francisco is known for. This was perfect for my mood. I was living in a two-bedroom apartment with two other dudes. But this time at least I wasn't living in the living room. But I was still ten years too old to have someone living in *my* living room, which is where one of those guys lived. About a month into my wilderness period, I got a copy of *Rolling Stone* in the mail. I had subscribed for a few years. Mostly because at that point it was the only way to get any news about the bands I liked, even if that news was little and irregular. Even though this was 2007, the Internet was still working on being the one-stop-everything shop that it is now. My bands, as I've mentioned, were still the same ones: Fishbone, Living Colour, 24-7 Spyz, Urban Dance Squad, Rollins Band, and Rage Against the Machine. And yes, those were not the biggest bands of the day. In fact, most had been broken up for years. And those that hadn't were certainly not on the *Rolling Stone*'s list of top bands of 2007. So when *Rolling Stone* showed up during this wilderness period, I quickly flipped through the magazine looking for any news about my favorites getting the band(s) back together. There was none, but there was something else that caught my eye. In fact, it caught my eye and dragged it across the room and slammed my face into the wall. It was an article on a drag performer named Shirley Q. Liquor.

But Shirley Q. Liquor wasn't just your regular drag performer. (As if there is such a thing.) Yes, Shirley was a man who dressed as a woman for fun and profit. But that man, a Southern white man named Chuck, added very specific elements that helped Shirley stand out from the beautiful and equally bold crowd of others. Chuck added blackface and fright wigs in addition to over-the-top dresses and shoes. And Chuck also added a very thick and cartoonish "Black-cent" to the proceedings. Chuck was a caricature of a stereotype of a lie about Black women. Shirley sang songs and told old and overdone racist jokes. And Shirley was packing in the crowds at the gay bars and nightclubs where she was booked. OK, fine. If that's your thing, enjoy it. It's not how I or anybody I know gets down, but whatevs.

But the horrifying thing about the article was the author's "journalistic" take on it. After describing all of this, the article posed the question "Is this racist?" HUBBA WHAT?

The article interviewed people on both sides—fans of Shirley on one side (yes, some of whom were Black), and on the other side Black academics and activists. I wasn't an academic or activist, but I was firmly on that side. And I was furious. How was *Rolling Stone*—a KNOWN liberal rag—going to ask if, IF, this was racist? It clearly was, no matter how many Black people on Shirley's side of the argument had house negro syndrome. I was furious. If *Rolling Stone* couldn't see this, then what was the hope that the conservatives on the other side of *Rolling Stone* ever would? I did something I had never done before. I wrote a letter. Well, actually, I emailed a letter. And they published it. I felt like I had accomplished something, but I also felt like there was more to do.

I knew if I went onstage at a comedy club and talked about the Shirley Q. Liquor experience, people would have one of two reactions. Either they wouldn't want to take the time to listen to me set up the story (the article, who Shirley was, my reaction)—aka "GET TO THE JOKES!"—or they would think I was lying: "Shirley Q. Liquor? You made that up." And even if they did listen to the setup and believed me, how would they be able to really understand my level of outrage without seeing at least a picture of Shirley?

I was at a dead end again. I was fired up to get back onstage, but I didn't know how to relate to the audience what I wanted them to understand. And then a question popped into my head...

What would you do if you were famous?

Well, that would be easy. I would just perform in front of an audience who loved me. And they would be patient and listen and already be invested. A second question...

Well, what EXACTLY would that look like?

Well, thanks for asking, voice in my head! I'd be in a theater where people paid to see me. And I'd have a screen onstage so I could show them the specific things I was talking about, so the jokes would have context and make sense. Sort of like my version of *The Daily Show with Jon Stewart* but about racism and starring me.

Another question:

Then just do that.

Umm . . . that's not a question.

I don't care. Just do it. Rent a theater. Find a screen. Get a projector for the screen. Figure out how to make the technical side work even though that's not your area. And just do it.

OK.

And I did.

Four months later, I debuted my solo show: *The W. Kamau Bell Curve: Ending Racism in About an Hour.* Not the shortest title in showbiz history but very effective. It got my name out there for the first time in San Francisco. And it was a funny title so people would get that it was a comedy. And it referenced *The Bell Curve,* a thick, supposedly scholarly book that featured a chapter about how Blacks and Latinos are genetically incapable of learning at the rate of Whites and Asians. And that meant that the title of my show also contained a dog whistle to the Blackademics, militants, and their allies who I wanted in the audience but who I *knew* were *never* coming to the comedy club.

So by November 2007, we had done the show twice. We were doing it once a month at the Shelton Theater on Sutter Street. I say "we" because, as should-be president Hillary Clinton wrote, "It takes a village." A whole gang of people volunteered to help me put the *Bell Curve* together. Most of the people who did were members of my Solo Performance Workshop. It was called Solo Performance Workshop because when I started it with my friend Bruce Pachtman, we didn't know we were starting anything. It's been going for more than ten years now.

I had fallen into directing Bruce's solo show after seeing it one evening in 2001. I had met Bruce when he booked a comedy showcase called the Mock Café. It was in a room that was so small that eventually it was turned into an elevator. (Truth. Not fake news.) I was directing Bruce's show in parallel to my not making any headway at the comedy clubs. After his performance one night, Bruce asked for my feedback. Now, that sounds like he really respected me, which he may have at the time, but really he was asking *everybody* for feedback. He was pretty much a one-man band at that point. He had written a hilariously neurotic show about a bad first date turned worse relationship with the awesome title of *Don't Make Me Look Too Psychotic*. Bruce was big on titles. And he taught me to be big on them too. And he also produced his show. People often wonder what a producer does. In my experience, being a producer can mean that you do literally everything all the way down to being in charge of *absolutely nothing*. Bruce was certainly on the doing-everything end of the spectrum at this point. He often told the story about the night he had to run the "ultimate solo show," as he called it. His box-office person/tech-booth operator didn't show up . . . which is often the case when that person is a volunteer. So Bruce sold the tickets at the door, introduced himself onstage, and told the audience to close and then open their eyes when the tech operator of the show would normally have the lights black out. Bruce delighted in this. And all the experience he got from this eventually made him an in-demand producer for small local productions that didn't have big bucks. That meant Bruce often worked way too hard for way too little money.

I think Bruce enjoyed working this way, independent and low to the ground, because I think he felt that he wasn't going to get his shot any other way. That was one thing we definitely had in common. And it bonded us. And we needed something to bond us, because as people—well, maybe mostly us—pointed out, we were an odd pair. Bruce was a middle-aged, East Coast–bred, Jewish bundle of outwardly exhibited nerves and insecurities. (And he would tell you all that himself.) I was none of that. I kept my bundle of insecurities mostly on the inside.

Luckily I had Bruce on my side. Bruce had been a friend for years—he was actually the one who had introduced me to the solo show scene in San Francisco years before. He recommended my directing services to other people. And eventually he set up a class for me to teach. It was a great way to talk to people about the lessons I had learned from years of performing. When I told Bruce about my show idea, he insisted in his gently nudging (but consistently consistent) way, like a termite you can hear in the walls of your house but just can't find, that I had to book more than one show to give a new show a chance. I certainly wasn't ready for a full-on, several-days-a-week-for-several-weeks run of shows. But I knew that if I just did one weekend of shows, it wouldn't give me enough time to make it better. I also knew myself, and I knew I needed time to breathe between performances. So we settled on once a month for four months: October, November, December, and January. And luckily, the Shelton Theater, the San Francisco theater that I taught most of my classes at, had Thursdays available. I knew it was rare to get such a good night to do a semi-regular show.

I got this lucky break because the Shelton had a show that had an open-ended run, but it only wanted Friday and Saturdays. That show was put on by a guy who had a knack for making the kind of theater tourists wanted to see. His first big hit was entitled *Shopping! The Musical*. It was a musical all about . . . shopping. Actors belted out the songs, Broadway-style. They all had voices that were so loud and big that it often sounded like they were trying to do their New York auditions from San Francisco. Whenever I was backstage at the Shelton, I would see the show's set list. It had titles like "Returning a Gift" and "Waiting in Line." I could just imagine a husband and wife from out of town—which could be thirty minutes outside of San Francisco—in line at the ticket booth in Union Square. They would see how expensive the Broadway-famous shows were, like *The Book of Mormon* or *Wicked*. And then they would see a piece of printer paper taped to the ticket window, and it would read, "Shopping! The Musical: $10." And the wife would be like, "OH MY GOD! WE WERE JUST SHOPPING MINUTES AGO! WE HAVE TO GO!"

So thanks to that show, I got to do whatever I wanted on Thursday. And because I had built up lot of goodwill with Matt Shelton, the owner of the theater, by renting his space to teach my class, Matt gave us a good deal. It was made even better by the fact that we were allowed to pay for the nights after the show was over. So I wouldn't have to pay anything out of pocket (unless I sold fewer tickets than the rental costs). Not that I wasn't worried about that—I was . . . a lot—but I knew it was better to be able to pay as late as possible. And I also knew that Thursdays were a great day to do a show. As Dave Attell joked during one of the weeks I worked with him at the Punch Line in San Francisco, "Thursday is Baby Friday."

The first two shows went great. Or at least they went better than anything I had ever done in my career before. Yes, they were both sloppy. Yes, neither one had a real defined ending. And the first show we couldn't figure out how to get the PowerPoint presentation off the edit screen. So people were looking at several of the images at once instead of one at a time. Plus the projector hardly worked. Melissa was in town that first night. At that point she had moved to Riverside, California, to get her MFA in dance, but she came back to support me. That's how we do. We hadn't thought about where to put the projector, so she just held it in her lap. By the end of the evening her legs were sweaty and burning from the projector's heat. She never complained. That's love. But the production had issues on issues upon issues.

But onstage . . . Onstage, I was taking big swings, or at least bigger swings than I had been taking at comedy clubs. I was telling personal stories. New stories. Stories I had never told onstage before and certainly wouldn't have even tried to tell onstage at a comedy club. Comedy club audiences are notoriously fickle when it comes to hearing long stories. It doesn't matter how funny it is at the end; they want the story to be consistently funny all the way through. Not most of the way. All. The. Way.

But this wasn't a comedy club audience. This was a theater audience . . . sort of. Actually, I wasn't really sure what kind of audience this was. It absolutely had your regular theatergoers in it, thanks to Bruce's ever-expanding email list. And by "theatergoers," I mean older white people. The kind of older white people who, when they really enjoy something, very slightly nod their heads in the affirmative. And if they hate something—I mean really, really hate something—then they purse their lips slightly and scrunch up their noses as if they have just smelled a dead body but don't want to be too rude about how bad the smell is. But they were what I needed. Theatergoers have patience. They don't judge the show by the individual moments. They judge the show by the total experience. That is very different from comedy club audiences. "You were funny, but that one joke, BLAH BLAH BLAH . . ."

But the first two *Bell Curve* audiences weren't composed of only theatergoers, or even mostly theatergoers. There was a part of this audience that really did want to laugh out loud, or maybe groan out loud depending on the joke, in the tradition of the comedy club audience. And these people were Black, and Brown, and Asian. And that was all my fault.

When I came up with the idea of doing a solo show about racism, I knew I didn't want to do it the way I had seen it done. And I had seen it done a lot. San Francisco is a national hub of solo performance, and therefore there were people of all shades, sizes, sexualities, and genders spilling out their solo tales onstage. And I had noticed . . . That's not true. I hadn't *just* noticed . . . It had bugged the ever-living shit out of me that every time I saw an obviously ethnic performer do their solo show, the majority (if not all) of the audience was white. Now, there is nothing inherently wrong with a mostly white audience. As hard as it is to get audiences in independent theaters, who the hell is going to complain about whoever shows up? Not me.

But I knew that I wanted something different, and that I wanted a more racially mixed crowd. Because this wasn't about me not wanting white people—it was about me wanting some of everybody. I had done enough shows in front of all-white crowds in my career already, and it always felt less like comedy and more like court testimony. This was especially true if the subject was race and racism. Here's how it usually went in my experience . . .

Black performer says something is racist.

White audience thinks to themselves, "I don't know if that is true."

Black performer experiences the white audience's lack of empathy and trust as more racism, which proves the Black performer's original point.

I knew if I got a critical mass of Black people in the room, then their laughter or response would many times back me up, as if to say, "You're damn right it's true, whitey!" OK, maybe I'm adding the "whitey" part in myself.

At that point, San Francisco was in the throes of Brian Copeland's solo show *Not a Genuine Black Man*. The word on the street (the streets of the solo world, anyway) was that it was sold out every night and was getting standing ovations every night. I sort of knew Brian, but although we are probably only a decade apart in age, I don't think I'm insulting him by saying we feel like we are from different generations. Brian was (and still is) a smooth Black guy. His politics skew conservative. He always felt a little like I would imagine 1960s-era heavyweight champion Floyd Patterson would have been like in real life. Floyd was a proud Black man who wanted to work within the system. Muhammad Ali was a proud Black man who knocked out Floyd Patterson. At the time it was seen as a referendum on Blackness. Because that's what we do with Black people of opposing views. We make it about their Blackness instead of about their individuality.

So when I heard Brian's show was blowing up—for a few weeks, I could quite literally hear his show blowing up from a room right above it that me and Bruce rented at the Marsh theater—I was jealous and I was suspicious of it even though I hadn't seen it.

And when I finally saw Brian's show . . . I was impressed. He did take the mostly white audience on a journey. I thought it might be too feel-good, but it wasn't. He talked about his life. Much of his show was a harrowing story about his family integrating in San Leandro, California. He painted a picture of the past that has become familiar to most of us. The "You don't belong here nigger!" picture. And the effect on the audience was powerful. White people in the Bay Area like to locate racism in the South. Brian was locating racism less than an hour's drive from where we sat. And Brian talked about the racism that he was currently experiencing in his life. Because of his politics someone had told him that he was "not a genuine Black man," which is where he got the title of his show. I had no idea me and Brian had so much in common. Brian's show had unintentionally inspired me. But I knew that I had to do things differently.

I knew I wanted my show to primarily deal with the racism that currently exists in the world. When art sets racism in the past, no matter how good it is, it allows white people in the audience (and others) to say to themselves, "Wow! That racism sure was bad way back then!" It's what happens when people go see *12 Years a Slave*. My response is always, "Yeah, you wanna know another time when racism was bad? Earlier today."

That type of show or movie or book or song doesn't put its audience on the hook. People relax in their seats and feel like once it's over, so are the problems. They don't feel blamed for the problems the main character is dealing with. And I believe if you are talking about race and racism in America, then it should be in 3-D, high-def smell-o-vision. It should be like a Gallagher show where, if you sit in the front, you had better bring a raincoat because you are gonna get some on ya. I wrote *The W. Kamau Bell Curve: Ending Racism in About an Hour* to get some on ya, in hopes that we end racism. Ten years later, I still do the show and I'm still—obviously—just trying.

Back in 2007, though, I needed help getting it up on its feet, so to make sure that I lived up to that standard I brought on Lisa Marie Rollins. Lisa was a transracially adopted, mixed-race PhD student in the African diaspora from UC Berkeley. She was my Black-ademic on staff who could help me reach that audience, and she could also help me make sure my show was good enough once those people showed up. Lisa was a friend and former Solo Performance Workshop student of mine.

When I did my show, I mixed up personal stories, late-night theories, and topical news stories. Hell, the first two shows I opened with an allegory that I had written. All these strands of thought and comedic investigations that seemingly had no place in a comedy club were at home in a theater. I was hard-core experimenting with everything, and I was having a great time on-stage for the first time in a long time.

By the second performance of *The W. Kamau Bell Curve*, things were going well by any small-theater metric. Both shows were sold out. People were buzzing afterward. I was getting local press. I finally had pull quotes for my bio! A comic's dream. But I wasn't satisfied.

The show was clunky. It kind of had a through line of "ending racism," but it didn't always sustain the whole time. People, I felt, were giving it credit for the totality of it and not each and every individual moment, which, as I said, is what I like about theater audiences. But I knew if the show was to have a long life, it needed to get sharper. If the show was like a sculpture, right now you could clearly see it was a statue of a person standing at attention, but it was a long way from Michelangelo's *David*. At this point, you probably couldn't even tell my statue was a man. It was a beautiful mess. And literally the stage was a mess.

Because I was writing up to the moment I went onstage, I had a bunch of notes with me. There were sixteen pieces of printer paper laid across the stage the night of the second show. SIXTEEN! And because I didn't trust my handwriting, this was all done on my computer printer. And since I was writing all the way up until showtime, I would just bring my computer printer to the theater. And let me be clear, I didn't have some sort of sleek and thin portable printer. I had one of the old-school beast printers that was supposed to be taken home, placed gingerly in the spot you wanted, and then NEVER MOVED AGAIN. Like if you sold the house or moved apartments, you would just leave the printer behind. Well, not me. I was loading that baby up every show and taking it on the N-Judah streetcar from my apartment to the theater. Nobody ever accused me of doing things the easy way.

So by the end of the second show, I knew something had to change. I needed structure. I needed streamlining. I NEEDED HELP CARRYING THE PRINTER! Normally that stuff fits under the umbrella of the director. I didn't have a director. Even though I was a budding solo show director, I couldn't imagine handing over my creative reins to another person. I knew that my creative process was hyper-personal, especially with the *Bell Curve*. And I knew my creative process could be bruised very easily. And when it got bruised, it sometimes would just shut down. I couldn't take the chance that I would work with a director who would push the show in a different direction when it was still finding its own direction. And besides, who would be qualified to direct my show? It was this weird hybrid of solo theater and stand-up comedy with a multimedia component. Very different from any other show that was currently running in San Francisco. Well, the answer was right in front of me. And when I found it, it didn't just change my show; it changed the entire way I thought about comedy . . . and my life. And I'm not being dramatic for effect just because this is the end of the chapter.

Awkward Thoughts
about *Creed*

Stop saying that *Creed* is the best *Rocky* movie. You aren't saying that because you believe it's true—you're just trying to sound smart. Yes, *Creed* has universal critical acclaim. And yes, *Creed* also has something better: the universal acclaim of the people (including this "people" who is typing this right now).

And yes, it may just be the best in the franchise. But we don't know that for sure yet. We need time.

Here's what we do know: writer-director Ryan Coogler, cowriter Aaron Covington, actor Michael B. Jordan, and Rocky himself, Sylvester Stallone, have created a film that masterfully adds to the incredible legacy of the *Rocky* franchise. At the same time, *Creed* makes the *Rocky* narrative relevant to twenty-first-century concerns.

I love *Rocky* movies as much as I love Black cinema—and surprise! *Rocky* is now officially a part of Black cinema. Who could've imagined that Coogler would follow up his debut film, *Fruitvale Station,* the best film about racism in 2013; sorry, not sorry, *12 Years a Slave*—with a *Rocky* sequel? It's kind of like if Spike Lee had followed up his debut film, *She's Gotta Have It,* by directing a James Bond film, but with Denzel Washington playing James Bond.

And Coogler does all this without losing any of the voice that made *Fruitvale Station* so important and revelatory—making *Creed* feel bigger in scope than any of the other *Rocky* movies. *Creed* stars Michael B. Jordan as a young Black man who is dealing with many of the issues that affect young Black men in this country today. This is a movie about how Black lives matter without ever using the hashtag.

And the movie does something else that Black people needed right now—well, at least I needed. It puts Phylicia Rashad back in the type of role that made us love her in the first place. As Mary Anne Creed, Rashad, once again, plays the mom you always wanted, even if you already have a good mom. (Having her in the movie feels like a rescue mission really, but that's a whole other article.)

Maybe this newer, Blacker version of a *Rocky* movie shouldn't come as such a surprise. As much as the earlier *Rocky* films have been classified by many (including a young Eddie Murphy in his stand-up comedy film *Raw*) as Italian-American films, they were also very Black. Apollo Creed was always a very authentically Black character; to me, he always felt like the answer to the question "What if Muhammad Ali had memorized Malcolm X's dictionary?" He was an athletic marvel in the ring and as savvy as they come outside of it. In the 1970s, he was the rare Black character in the movie who was clearly way smarter than the lead white character in the movie.

Apollo's indelible mark on the franchise is what makes *Creed* feel like such a natural extension of the narrative, while at the same time taking the franchise down a new path. *Creed* does for the *Rocky* franchise what happens in comic books all the time: it hands the reins over to a new generation of creators. It's like how every few years, some new guns take over the *Spider-Man* comic book, strip it down to the spine and all the essential details, then rebuild the body to connect with new readers. A radioactive spider bite becomes a genetically altered spider bite; a simple "boy genius" transforms into a computer nerd with an internship at the local bio-tech company; and in another universe, Spider-Man goes from white guy Peter Parker to half-Black, half-Latino Miles Morales.

That's what's happened with *Creed*. For the first time, Rocky is the costar and not the star of his own film, with Adonis Creed—the son no one knew Apollo Creed had from an affair—stepping into the center of the cinematic ring. (It helps that Michael B. Jordan, as Adonis, owns the movie from beginning to end.)

What director Coogler accomplishes by remixing the essential story elements is extraordinary. The way the film remakes the iconic scene of Rocky running through the city, for instance, is genius. Like Rocky in previous editions, Adonis lives in Philly, but Adonis's Philly is, rightfully, Blacker, filled with hip-hop, and edgier. The blue-eyed soul of Frank Stallone in the early *Rocky* films is also replaced with the neo-soul of Adonis's neighbor, a singer named Bianca, played by Tessa Thompson as an effervescent, luminous world beater in her own right who has no time for Adonis's "my dad never loved me, so sometimes I act like a jerk" nonsense.

The focus on this and other relationships is in large part why the film works as well as it does—because, despite the sizzle of boxing, the steak of *Rocky* has always been the relationships. Whenever someone goes toe-to-toe with Rocky—whether it's his wife, Adrian (Talia Shire, for the record, is way underrated for her transformative portrayal of Adrian), his opponent Apollo Creed, or his friend Apollo Creed—the movies reach their emotional peak. When those "adversaries" can't match Rocky's dramatic energy, then the movies just become boxing films (see: *Rocky V* and much of *Rocky Balboa*). In *Creed*, though, Michael B. Jordan gives everything he gets from Sylvester Stallone as Rocky . . . and more. It's a beautiful, touching, heart-wrenching dance. (No, I didn't cry; that theater I saw it in must have been dusty or something. Which seems to happen to me quite a lot, hmm . . .)

This touches on another thing that makes this film so exciting to me: Coogler clearly loves the source material. *Creed* is not a reimagining or a reboot; Coogler is an artist who wants to build on the existing universe with love and respect. He uses the iconic *Rocky* song "Gonna Fly Now" perfectly. But he is also an artist who wants to make the franchise more relevant to him and the current era.

Yet as much credit for the success of the film goes to Stallone as it does to Coogler, Covington, Jordan, and Thompson. Stallone—who had written all of the films up to this point and directed all but two of the previous entries—has never put this much of the *Rocky* story in other people's hands. Here, he's even trusted millennials with his baby.

On some level, this shift makes sense; collectively, the six films before *Creed* have been all over the map of genres, making the franchise one of the most malleable in Hollywood. The franchise has been a low-budget movie (*Rocky*). It's been a film that symbolizes (and is a big part of the birth of) Hollywood's never-ending sequel obsession (*Rocky II*). It's been a film featuring maybe the first full-on, big-screen bromance (*Rocky III*), and a film that speaks directly to its times in an effort to make the world a better place (yup, *Rocky IV*). It's been a glorified B movie (*Rocky V*), a sentimental favorite (*Rocky Balboa*), and a touching love story (*Rocky* and *Rocky II*). It's been a prescient predictor of boxing (*Rocky III*, in which Mr. T plays Mike Tyson before there was a Mike Tyson). And it's been a victim of the style of its era, as *Rocky IV* is basically a ninety-minute '80s-style MTV music video.

Awkward Thoughts about *Creed*

It goes without saying that no other American film franchise has had that much tonal difference and cultural relevance. Not *Friday the 13th*. Not *A Nightmare on Elm Street*. And certainly not the seven films of the *Faster, Furiouser, Kill Kill Kill* franchise. And even though the James Bond franchise has a tone that is all over the map, every time they change the tone, they change the Bond. But Stallone has been Rocky from the grimy first film through the over-the-top, Hulk Hogan–wrestling third film to this one, where he tenderly plays Adonis's white "uncle." But, like, whatevs, Rocky has been postracial since before anybody thought to make up that dumb word.

This latest turn weirdly makes sense because Rocky Balboa is Hollywood's most fungible character. You could just as easily see him wander into one of the *Avengers* movies, teaching Ant-Man how to fight, as you could see him wander into a Judd Apatow movie, teaching a Paul Rudd character how to fight. Yes, I know Paul Rudd played Ant-Man. I'm saying Rocky is the Paul Rudd of film characters. Put Rocky anywhere. He'll be great. You could imagine Rocky in a Woody Allen film. You could imagine him in one of those Wayans brothers parody movies. Quentin Tarantino could figure out how to use the Italian Stallion, and so could Spike Lee. So when Rocky Balboa suddenly makes an appearance in the middle of *Creed*'s first act, a movie that has at that point already established itself as a meditation on Black manhood, it just seems right. Who knows more about dealing with the harried cocktail of ego, machismo, and false bravado that makes up modern manhood than Rocky? And if he could turn Apollo Creed from one of cinema's greatest onscreen villains (*Rocky* and *Rocky II*) into one of cinema's most horrific and tragic deaths (*Rocky IV*), then he can deal with Apollo's angry, lost son.

Stallone is the guy to do all this, and he plays the character of Rocky more convincingly and honestly than any actor has played any character in Hollywood history. You can try to put that on the fact that Stallone *is* Rocky—something people tried to say when the first movie premiered—but this simply isn't the case. Sly, the man, is a good-looking, charismatic, intelligent, HGH'ed-up, tale-spinning, quippy movie star. When Sly the actor plays Rocky, he lets that go and allows the character to take him away. Rocky is maybe the only franchise hero in Hollywood history who we have seen get old and frail and still maintain his franchise. To return to the James Bond analogy, every time the actor playing James slows down even slightly, he's tossed onto a pile of wrecked Aston Martins like the expendable commodity he is. But not Rocky. We've seen him go from palooka, to overbloated star athlete, to elder statesman, to broken-down and dead-broke loser, to humble business owner, to . . . Well, you'll have to see the film, if you haven't already, to find out.

So is *Creed* the best of the *Rocky* movies? Maybe. I don't know. What I do know is that whenever I brought up my love of the *Rocky* franchise before this, I had to pretend the films were a "guilty pleasure," even though I knew they weren't. And I'm happy to finally be able to embrace them publicly now.

Yes, I have to stop tears every time Adrian tells Rocky to "win" from her hospital bed in *Rocky II*. And yes, I get goose bumps every time I see Apollo and Rocky hugging on the beach in *Rocky III*, because it reminds me of my own interracial bromance with Jason, my best friend since high school. I have quoted Rocky's speech from the end of *Rocky IV* more times than I feel comfortable mentioning. And even the first scene in the very flawed *Rocky V* guts me every time I see it. I still laugh every time I see Rocky respond, "I don't use them," to a question about investing in condominiums in *Rocky II*. When I need inspiration, I've been known to play "Gonna Fly Now" on a loop on Spotify. And if Survivor's "Eye of the Tiger" comes on, I nod my head enthusiastically—while I pretend I'm doing it ironically if anyone sees me.

I will no longer be ashamed of any of this. And admit it: you've done the same stuff. If you haven't run up a bunch of stairs and thrown your fists up in the air at the top like you have a whole city supporting you, then you haven't really lived. And if you haven't called old white guys you like "Unc," as I'll be doing now after watching *Creed*, you haven't done life right either.

Creed may or may not be the best *Rocky* film ever, but it is exactly what the *Rocky* franchise deserves: a truly great, and culturally relevant, film.

CHAPTER 5

My Awkward Sexism

When I first moved to San Francisco in 1997, I wasn't particularly comfortable—or even familiar—with what we now call the LGBT community. In fact, I was so unfamiliar that I'm pretty sure I didn't know to call it the LGBT community, whereas now I know that LGBT isn't even close to enough initials for that community. If you want to keep it really real, the last I heard, you can go LGBTQQIIAA for Lesbian, Gay, Bisexual, Transgender, Queer, Questioning, Intersex, Interested, Asexual, and, finally—the word where I find myself—Ally. And I know even as I spell all that out, somebody is reading this and going, "How could you leave out [INSERT LABEL I'M EITHER UNFAMILIAR WITH OR TOALLY SPACED OUT ABOUT]?" If you are that person, I just want to let you know that you are right. I'm sorry. I'll do better. Please be patient with me. God, my friends, my family, and my wife, Melissa, aren't through with me yet.

In Chicago, I met Angie, the first gay person who was out to me. But we weren't close, so I can't say she remembers me at all.

At the time I lived on Pine Grove Avenue off Irving Park Road on the North Side. I was blocks from what was colloquially called "Boystown," the gay neighborhood. At night when I biked home through Boystown I felt fear . . . of what exactly? At the time I might have said the neighborhood was packed on weekend nights and there were a lot of clubs and bars, so there were gay men all over the streets. I might have said that it seemed dangerous. Looking back, it was not. I was just afraid of the unfamiliar and then trumped up my fear into something that I could blame on the people I was unfamiliar with. I was ridiculous. Jason, ever my best friend and completely unafraid of confronting me at times like this, told me I was homophobic. I thought he was being dramatic. He wasn't.

I remember how when I moved to the Bay Area, I was almost *looking* for gay-ness. Coming from Chicago, I'd assumed that San Francisco would be gay everywhere, and I remember being shocked that it's really mostly just outwardly and loudly gay in one neighborhood, the Castro. I thought, *It's gonna be gay everywhere,* and I remember sort of steeling myself for it in some way.

And then I got there and realized how normal it is to meet people who are gay but not gay in the way I had imagined it. Now maybe there is an argument that I had been programmed to imagine gay people a certain way, but I have to own that I was a grown person (twenty-four) who was shocked that gay people seemed so "normal." Just "regular gay." And the comedy scene— it's almost like it's way *less* gay than it should be in this city. The San Francisco comedy scene had a couple of gay comics, but it wasn't overwhelmingly gay. A lot of the gay comics performed in their own spaces. They didn't want to be in the mainstream scene, because the mainstream comedy club scene in San Francisco was just as homophobic as a lot of the mainstream comedy club scenes around the country. Not exactly as bad, but you could be in a San Francisco comedy club on a Saturday night with a roomful of people who weren't from San Francisco. The bridge-and-tunnel crowd: they could be coming into town from more conservative towns nearby. People don't realize that without the Bay Area and Los Angeles, the state of California is Texas. Or these people in the club could be tourists, so you're not necessarily performing for the hippest, coolest people in San Francisco. They didn't go to places like comedy clubs.

But by 2007 things were different. I'd been in San Francisco for ten years, and with *The W. Kamau Bell Curve* I was performing for a smarter, hipper crowd. After the second *Bell Curve*, I convened a panel of people who I trusted to sort of give me feedback about the show. This was new territory for me, but I knew I needed help. It was mostly pulled from the community of my Solo Performance Workshop. And therefore it was mostly people who had paid ME for MY opinions of their work. I knew that this could be a recipe for . . . not much. It could possibly just end up in a bunch of "I think you are just awesome, Teacher Kamau!" But I suspected it wouldn't if I picked the right people.

Besides Bruce, there were Coke and Bobby Nakamoto, a married couple from my class. I had directed a full-length show for both Bobby and Coke. And they both had many of the same issues of cultural authenticity as Japanese-Americans that I had had as a Black man. I knew they would have interesting thoughts. Lisa Marie Rollins and Bruce, my producers, were also there. Lisa's boyfriend at the time, Paul, was there too. Paul was not a student, but his band served as the opening act of the first two *Bell Curve* shows. It was my way of bringing an extra draw to the night and also filling the time in case my "about an hour" ended up being thirty-five minutes. That immediately revealed itself to NOT be a problem. If anything, these shows were going too long. First, the band would play longer than agreed to. Then the taking down of the instruments was taking too long, and then I would end up doing over an hour. So the whole evening was ending up over three hours long. The next run I didn't bring the band back. They were great, but I was learning to stand up on my own. Paul was here as a hopefully totally unbiased voice, which I felt was necessary. And finally the last official voice (Melissa was at school at UC Riverside) was Martha Rynberg. Martha was kind of the wild card. She wasn't producing the show. I hadn't directed any of her shows because she didn't have one yet. But she had one thing that assured her a seat—she was clearly my favorite student.

Me and Martha were both only children, but that's pretty much where the similarities ended. Martha was born and raised in Maine, which basically is another way of saying that she is white. Her parents are still married. She is married too, and she and her wife, Mary, had adopted a Black baby a few years before. And they realized that raising a Black baby in the overwhelmingly white, rural state of Maine was not going to work for them and their daughter; they did their research to find a place that would be open, accepting, and loving to a family like theirs, and Oakland won in a landslide. I was only a few years older than Martha, but her life was waaaaay older than mine. She was a full-on wife and mom with real adult responsibilities. I was still a straight dude living in an Inner Sunset two-bedroom apartment with two other straight dudes. My roommates and I definitely were not acting our respective ages. We were all running as fast and as far as we could from "adult responsibilities." How fast and how far you ask? One time, my shelf—that had my entire CD collection on it—collapsed, strewing hundreds of CDs all over the floor of my apartment. There was literally nowhere to stand without stepping on CDs. Well, for about two months, I learned I could jump from my doorway to my bed if I got a good running start. I was thirty-four years old at the time.

So while me and Martha weren't a lot alike outwardly (although we were both tall), we had something inside of us that bonded together like magnets. We just kind of looked at each other all the time like, "I know you," even though we didn't. This is the stuff of romantic comedies and Match.com commercials. But it wasn't like that with us, not by a long shot. It was like I had reunited with my long-lost sister on Oprah or something.

And this was proven to be the nature of our relationship—Martha constantly made fun of me and poked at me during class when I was teaching. This may sound annoying or disrespectful, but it wasn't. It made me like her right away. As someone who was taught by my mom to distrust authority, I respected her lack of "respect" for my title of teacher. Plus, she was a fantastic student. She was a fully embodied performer, and I had often observed in her a gift for insight into other people's work. That last thing is why I invited her that night. Her work was about growing up in Maine as the only child of two parents who didn't seem to understand her and who she didn't understand. Martha had dated her childhood sweetheart through college and eventually broke up with him and came out of the closet. Martha had a lot going on in her head, but on the surface she was just a big goofball. I related to that and resembled most of that. We were instant friends.

So we all assembled at Lisa Marie's West Oakland apartment and ate some food, and then we got down to the task at hand: What did we think about Kamau's new show? I trusted all these people or I wouldn't have invited them, but I did feel a little like I had signed myself up for a firing squad. I had no need to worry. Everybody was mostly filled with praise for the show. Paul, my alleged unbiased voice of the truth, was the most succinct with "I think it's good." And Bruce couldn't stop gushing about the show, like a proud papa. Yes, that night was shaping up as mostly a love fest. I mean yes, there was SOME criticism. Coke felt like I had made it sound like mixed-race kids were better than one-race kids during a bit I was working on. I didn't think I had, but I took her point. But then Martha said out of nowhere, "Well, you know you can't end racism and also make sexism worse."

That sentence stunned me. It caught me completely off-guard. Like a boxer who was out on his feet, I had no idea how to react. I was immediately defensive . . . and fumbling with my words. I felt like surely she had misinterpreted something I said. I made it about her, mostly because I HAD NO IDEA WHAT SHE WAS EVEN TALKING ABOUT!!!

It was like she was a Buddhist monk and she had given me a Zen koan to meditate on. Something like: "What is the sound of a confused straight Black man when confronted with his own sexism?"

Martha didn't back down. And then Lisa Marie jumped on board . . . and then Coke . . . Bruce just looked stunned. And as much as I'm sure I protested, even if it was the weak defense of a tomato-can journeyman boxer who has just had his clock cleaned by a young Mike Tyson, eventually I did shut up and listen. I'd later come to realize that my number one best quality in being an ally is my ability to shut up and listen.

Martha went through my show like a surgeon, very steadily and expertly—but also with enough of a gentle touch as to not spook a cornered straight dude, one of nature's most dangerous animals. She pointed out areas in the *Bell Curve* that contained trace elements of a stand-up comedy act designed to keep the drunks awake on the second Friday night show. Things that I didn't need in my show (or even my act, I would later come to discover). Things that weakened my show's whole overall Up with People, "Kumbaya" vibe.

My "best" defense, I thought, was something like, "Maybe you lefty feminists in this room thought that some of my jokes were sexist, but you should try going to a comedy club sometime! In comedy clubs I'm goddamn bell hooks in comparison!" But Martha's point was that it wasn't enough. It wasn't enough to be the most righteous boy in the boys' club of comedy clubs. She had a (much) higher standard for me.

Martha had an example of what she was talking about straight, oops . . . I mean directly . . . from the *Bell Curve*. I had a piece in the show about the first time I remember feeling like I wasn't as good as white people. The story was about playing the kids' game of doctor.

In the show I talked about how when I was a little kid, I just always kind of knew that I was Black. I don't remember when my mom told me I was Black, but I was sure she did let me know in some way. My mom understood the specific burden and danger of being Black and male in America. She had brothers and grew up in Indiana, which was then the intersection of Ku Street and Klux Klan Avenue. But the first time I associated Blackness with not-as-good-ness was in first grade.

I was going to an elite private school in Boston, which meant I was one of the only Black kids in my class. One day, a few of us were playing doctor. One girl, named Helen, for these purposes, was kissing us boys one by one. (I'm not sure what problem she was diagnosing exactly, but I was aware in my very prepubescent brain that I hoped I had whatever it was.) When she got to me, she stopped. And she made it clear that she didn't want to kiss me. I immediately got mad. It may have been the first time that I was ever pissed in my life. She had kissed each and every other boy sitting there. And now it was my turn. I WANTED MY KISS!

And of course, later I would come to understand that no means no and that her body was her own and that she had the right to change her mind at any time about any sexual activity. But please forgive me if I say that my six-year-old self wasn't quite this mature yet. And since my mom had instilled a huge sense of justice and fairness in me due to her coming up during the middle of the Civil Rights era, I wanted my day in court! I marched over to the teacher and said, "Helen won't play with me!"

Teacher: "Why won't she play with you? What are you two doing?"

What were we doing? . . . Umm . . . That was a hard one to answer. And although I knew exactly what we were doing, even in my prepubescent state I knew that I probably shouldn't share that information with the teacher. So I just said, "Nothing," and then I stomped away, kicking my heels the way I do to this day whenever I get really mad. And even though I didn't know what exactly was going on, I did know two things: all the kids involved in Kissgate were white . . . except for me.

And that was the first time I knew I was Black.

And again, that story doesn't stand up to anything you read about what happened to Black people during the Civil Rights era. And I know for a fact that my worst story of racism, even up through today, is better than the BEST day of being a slave. But I was only six then, and that one moment formed a lot of how I came to see the world from an early age.

Now, of course, I know what some people who hear that story are thinking right now.

"That's just your side of the story. Maybe there was another reason Helen didn't want to kiss you. Maybe you just weren't a cute kid."

And that was the point in the show when I used the full power of my MacBook and the projector I had traded for from a friend. I pulled up the cutest, most cuddly picture of myself from around that age that I had. It was a classic school picture. It was me in a red denim jacket with my chin cocked jauntily to the left and resting in my hand, looking like it should've been the Jackson 6 instead of the Jackson 5. I was cheesing from ear to ear with a smile I couldn't replicate today if I tried to. I'd call it a pre-weight-of-the-world smile that only kids and dogs have access to.

The audience usually melted and laughed and applauded the ridiculous nature of my supposition that it was either Helen's racism or her inability to see my cuteness. At the same time, they got the point that I had internalized it as racism whether it was or not. And that I left room for the "not." Which was exactly the stuff that the *Bell Curve* did best. I was doing the kind of work that I felt like only I could do.

And then, just to top the audience's response, I would yell over their reaction as if they were in agreement with me, "You're right. That little bitch was RACIST!"

And there was the problem that Martha was highlighting.

Martha: "Why do you say 'bitch' there?"

Me: "Because it's funny."

Martha: "Maybe it's funny to you, but it's not funny to me."

Me: "Yeah, well, but every joke isn't funny to everybody."

Martha: "But I'm your friend. Don't you want it to be funny to me . . . and people like me?"

Me: "Yeah, but . . ."

Martha: "Then don't say 'bitch.'"

Me: "But it's funny."

Martha: "Not to me. And every time you say 'bitch,' you are linked to every other man and specifically every other Black man who uses that word as a way to refer to all women, no matter who they are and what they do."

Me: ". . . . . But it's funny."

I STILL thought it was funny if I said "bitch." So I struggled with it, and the next time I did the show, I changed that line to "That little doctor was racist!" And it got the same laugh. It might even have gotten a bigger laugh because I was pretending she was a real doctor. But it certainly didn't lose anything. And that became the point through which I would really start to look at things, and I began writing with the question in mind: Am I stepping on the right toes, here?

Because it's a very easy thing to do in comedy, to make fun of the person you hate—like, blah blah blah, Republicans—but then as a part of making fun of Republicans, suddenly it turns into jokes targeting disabled women at McDonald's. Suddenly you're making fun of people who have nothing to do with the original thing you're talking about, and it both demeans them and diffuses the point you were making. That happens in comedy a lot. It's the reason why midgets are often used as comedy. It's a very easy trope to go to. Some jokes are like a shotgun blast, where a bunch of pellets come out and hit whoever's in the area. That's the point at which I decided, to use a clumsy analogy, to be very target-focused. When I'm talking about something I don't like, I can only include other things I don't like, for the same reasons, in that joke.

It's been a process. I didn't completely learn that lesson that night. But Martha had placed an inescapable idea in my head. An idea that I later learned from a *New Yorker* article written about *Totally Biased* is called "intersectional progressivism." In other words, only step on the toes of the people who you think need their toes stepped on. And more than that, figure out a way to include other people who are also in need of help. Make the bandwagon to freedom as big as possible. And it is my job specifically to make it as funny as possible for all the people I want on the bandwagon.

And long story shortish . . . that is how Martha became my director. For the next two years, we would meet in her kitchen,

sometimes with her daughter there. And I would have my computer on, with a thousand windows open to articles and images.
And I would talk out *Bell Curve* ideas while she asked hard
questions, asked for clarification on my point of view, and said
"YES!" when I hit on a particularly good angle. There was much
laughter and anger (mostly at the outside world), much explaining of pop culture (not Martha's strong suit), and much plotting
to make the world better and more hilarious. These were those
"good times back in the day" that people talk about. And I knew
that was true even when it was happening. Among Martha's first
few edicts: no more sixteen sheets of paper, no more taking the
printer with you; get it in your head before the show or don't do
it. I was allowed—or, more accurately, I negotiated for— two
pages of notes onstage and no more.

Martha also connected this idea back to stand-up comedy
and my act specifically. As I said before, back then I only had the
TV clip from Comedy Central. Martha had never seen my
stand-up act, so I sent the clip to her one day because I wanted
to impress my friend. And the Comedy Central clip was good.
The next time I was in her kitchen working on the *Bell Curve*, I
was excited to hear what she thought about it. Although I knew
it was a great set. After being there for a while, I realized Martha
hadn't brought it up. I knew Martha well enough to know that
was not a great sign. I finally just asked if she had watched it.

Martha: "Yeah."

Me, still excited: "What did you think? Did you like the joke
about my mom? She loves that one. And the one about my
dad is his favorite. And I'm still doing the Obama one . . . "

(Barack Obama had at this point declared his candidacy for president. It was still early days, though. I was hoping that he would do well enough to be Hillary's veep.)

Martha: "Yeah . . . But that Condi joke . . ."

My stomach immediately seized up. I instantly knew what she was talking about. The closing joke in that Comedy Central set was a joke that was ostensibly supposed to be a political joke about Condoleezza Rice being not great . . . OK . . . It was way harsher than that. In the joke I called her evil. But that wasn't where Martha's problem with the bit was.

Martha: "You called her ugly . . . You had a perfectly fine point about you not agreeing with her politics and then you made it personal by calling her ugly. *That's ugly.*"

Martha was one hundred percent correct. I had stopped doing the joke by then. But it was still alive on the Internet. And I had never really confronted myself about it. Martha made me do that right there in her kitchen. She continued.

Martha: "You don't like Bush's politics, but I bet you wouldn't call him ugly. And here's the thing, *she's not ugly.* When you call her ugly, you are just subscribing to a white European version of beauty. And you can't do that. My daughter looks way more like Condoleezza Rice than she does whoever that white woman is on the cover of *Rolling Stone* over there. AND YOU ARE A BLACK MAN WHOSE PARTNER IS A WHITE WOMAN? WHAT ARE YOU DOING?"

Martha was right that day. And she has only gotten more right with every day that has gone by. Every time I think about that joke, I just feel sad. Someday I will have to explain that joke to my two Black daughters. It makes me sick just thinking about.

One day online after Martha had staged my intervention, my cousin Nora, who was still new to publishing then but was becoming known for her writing and her out-loud, new-school Black feminism, posted about me. It was a post filled with compliments. I found it and was proud that she thought enough to write about me. She was becoming a big influencer in her community. In the comments section, a Black woman said something to the effect of "I want to like him, but that Condoleezza Rice joke is a problem." Nora lightly defended me in the comments but also said she was interested in my opinion on why I did it. I replied to both of them the only way I knew and the way I still do when that joke comes up: a full-throated apology. It wasn't one of those non-apology apologies that we have all gotten used to from politicians, celebrities, and Internet trolls who get caught. It was a full apology that tried to put the guilt on me while at the same time tried to assure them that I understood why it was wrong in the first place. I knew I couldn't blame it on my youth, since I was thirty-two at the time. I also wanted to let them know that I was not going to make the same mistake again, but if I did, please feel free to call me out again. This was bigger than stand-up comedy. I was trying to be a stand-up human.

And to Condoleezza Rice, if you are reading this (I'm not sure why you would be, although you and my dad are both from Alabama. I'm betting he's met you), I'm sorry. I had no right to involve my criticism of your work in the George W. Bush administration with anything about you personally. I can't imagine all the things you had to go through as a Black woman from Alabama who has risen to the levels that you have. It was the ultimate cheap shot that reduced your hard work and humanity to sexist and racist nonsense. I have learned my lesson. But that doesn't excuse what I did. Again, I'm sorry.

Awkward Thoughts about Being a Black Male, Six Feet Four Inches Tall in America

I am afraid of the cops. Absolutely petrified of the cops. Now understand, I've never been arrested or held for questioning. I've never been told that I "fit the description." But that doesn't change a thing. I am afraid of cops the way that spiders are afraid of boots. You're walking along, minding your own business, and SQUISH! You're dead.

Simply put, I am afraid of the cops because I am Black. To raise the stakes even further, I am male. And to go all in on this pot of fear, I am six foot four and weigh 250 pounds . . . at least. (I stopped keeping track, which is the next best thing to actually working out.) Michael Brown, the unarmed Ferguson, Missouri, eighteen-year-old shot dead by police in the summer of 2014, was also six foot four. Eric Garner, who was strangled to death by the NYPD, was six foot three. Depending on your perspective, I could be described as a "gentle giant," the way that teachers described Brown and the way that friends described Eric Garner. Or I could be described as a "demon," the way that Officer Darren Wilson described Michael Brown in his grand jury testimony. And just like Eric Garner, I have asthma, so when I hear him say on video, "I can't breathe," as the officer chokes the life out of him for selling loose cigarettes, I can feel it in my chest as I'm sure he did.

I don't engage in any type of behavior that should place me in a cop's crosshairs. I don't live in "one of those neighborhoods" or hang out with a "bad crowd" (unless you count comedians). I am not involved in felonious activity. I'm not bragging. I'm just boring. And I'm not playing the game of "respectability politics" here. Because I know that not being a part of criminal activity is no assurance that you will go home safely after an interaction with a cop. Because "boring" is no assurance of safety when you are Black. What's more boring than shopping at Walmart? That's what John Crawford III was doing when police shot him in the back while he was on his cell phone talking to his girlfriend. What was his crime? He was carrying a gun . . . in Ohio, an open-carry state where people are legally allowed to carry guns . . . openly. Why did he have a gun in Walmart? Because Walmart sells guns. I think he was at the very least thinking about buying the gun. I don't really know, because a customer saw a Black man carrying a gun in the store and called 911. The cops showed up and shot him immediately, without warning, apparently finding him guilty of attempting to practice capitalism. And the thing that really sucks is that it was an air rifle. At most, he was in danger of putting his eye out.

But I don't carry guns (unless it's on TV). And again, the only crimes I'm generally guilty of are jaywalking or not wearing a seat belt in a Lyft. But the fact that I'm not involved in any serious, notable criminal activities doesn't leave me any more confident that I won't be killed or harassed by the police. Because I know better than to think that doing nothing illegal is enough to guarantee that nothing will happen if you have to interact with the police. Chris Lollie was just waiting to pick up his kids from school when someone called the cops because the bench he was sitting on was private property. Lollie didn't end up dead, but the cops did tase and arrest him. Every time I watch the video it crushes me to hear him say, "THAT'S MY KIDS RIGHT THERE!" and "I HAVEN'T DONE ANYTHING WRONG! CAN SOMEONE PLEASE HELP ME!" His voice is elevated and cracking under the pressure, and he is clearly completely confused. By the end he is angry and on the verge of tears. Every time I watch it I'm surprised that he doesn't just break down and cry. But then as a dad, I'm guessing that he was trying to hold it together for his kids. I can't imagine my daughters, Sami and Juno, watching me be tased and arrested. But I feel like maybe I should imagine it so I can be prepared for it if it happens. Like the same way my wife bought an earthquake kit because we live in California. Earthquakes aren't guaranteed to happen when you live in California, but you'd be stupid not to be ready for one. Same principle applies here.

I find myself watching these videos of Black people being harassed/assaulted/killed by the police way too much. Maybe I shouldn't watch them, but I just need to see them. As I was writing this I found another one. Dejuan Yourse is sitting on his mom's porch in Greensboro, North Carolina, which is the reason why moms have porches, so their kids can sit on them. And two cops show up because someone called them when they saw a Black man sitting on a porch in broad daylight. By the end of the video, Yourse has been loaded into a police car with handcuffs on his wrists and ankles. One of the two police officers has punched him in the face at least once. And while the other police officer goes along with the arrest, her energy the whole time is, "Uh oh. We may have gone too far this time." All I could think when I watched it was, *Thank God this brother is still alive!*

I also couldn't help but think of Harvard professor and future postage stamp Henry Louis Gates Jr., who was arrested in his home in Cambridge for the crime of being in his home in Cambridge. He

181

had apparently forced his way into his house when his front door was jammed. As far as I've always known, breaking into your own house was legal. But it is apparently not legal if you are a Black man. Even if you are a Black man who is world-renowned as a leading intellect and all-around nice guy. The cop claimed he was arresting Gates for being disorderly; but who wouldn't act a little out of order when a cop was arresting them for the crime of being at home? I'm guessing the cop just checked "disorderly" on his paperwork because the Civil Rights Act of 1968 forced cops to take the charge of being "uppity" off their arrest records.

The cops in the Dejuan Yourse case were forced to resign. It turns out the female cop was right to think, *Uh oh*. But Henry Louis Gates Jr.'s officer was "disciplined" by being invited to have a beer with the president himself! And it was on the White House lawn of all places, so that all could see what happens when you illegally detain a Black man in America. There it was. Three of the most accomplished human beings on the planet—Skip Gates, President Obama, and Vice President Joe "Never Had a Picture Taken of Me That Couldn't Be Turned into a Meme" Biden—and a random cop. A random cop who stupidly arrested someone for being in his own house. I'm not saying that I don't think that cop should have been allowed to have a beer with the president. I'm just saying that it is an honor that every Black person on the planet should have had the option of partaking in before a random, hothead cop was invited to do it. The Beer Summit, as it was called, was proposed by President Obama as a "teachable moment," a moment when the country could come together and see how racism needed to be learned from and confronted in new ways. Well, if the election of Trump proves anything, it's that the people who needed to learn from that moment weren't watching. And if they were, they were yelling at their TV, "That poor police officer. Having to share beer with some uppity New England Negro, a Kenyan-born Muslim socialist, and Joe Biden! THE HORROR! Be nice to meet Joe Biden, though. He seems fun!"

I've never had the honor of meeting Barack Obama. I have had the honor of meeting Henry Louis Gates Jr.; a few years after the Beer Summit he invited me to be in his documentary, *Many Rivers to Cross*. It was one of the great honors of my life. When I first met him I initially thought about performing a citizen's arrest on him just in case it would automatically mean I would get to have a beer with the president, but I chickened out.

Finding humor in these situations is what I have learned to do. I can't imagine being able to take all this horrible in without processing it with jokes. The jokes don't always come right away, but they come. It's an extreme coping mechanism. I have to cope because so many times these stories involve people who are like me. And I don't just mean that these people are Black. Many times they fit my exact description. I've been endowed with the Triple Crown of being killed for no good reason: big, Black, and male, or BBM.

My whole life, and since the dawn of this country, big Black men have been targeted. It's a reality of life in America that some people are only catching on to now, and many people still seem to refuse to catch on to. I think about this a lot as I move through the world. Mind always racing with possibilities and scenarios. It feels crazy to live that way, but again, it feels stupid to pretend that I don't have to live this way.

One Monday night in 2014, I was thinking about all of this. Earlier that day the news broke that Michael Brown's killer, officer Darren Wilson, was not even going to be indicted for the killing of Brown. The

St. Louis grand jury didn't think the situation even warranted a court trial. Not for murder . . . not for involuntary manslaughter . . . not for ruining Michael's day by not letting him live to see the end of it . . . not nothing. With all the controversy and community outcry that came out of the killing of Michael Brown, to me and to many others, a court trial seemed like the least the grand jury could do. At the very least, go through the ruse of a trial. Black people in America are used to trials of police officers in situations like this leading to nothing. But at least give us that nothing. This was a post–Trayvon Martin, post–Oscar Grant world, post–a-lot-of-dead-Black-people-at-the-hands-of-cops (or in Trayvon's case, at the hands of George Zimmerman, who was treated like a cop). I was deep in thought about this. What the hell was I supposed to do as a Black man? And what the hell was I supposed to do as a comedian? Specifically, as a comedian who talks about dead Black men? And as it sometimes happens when all of this is rolling and roiling through my mind, I couldn't sleep. So I got out of bed and told Melissa I needed to take a walk. Melissa asked, "Are you OK?" I responded, "No . . . I don't know. I . . . just . . . need . . . to walk." This is one of the hazards of being an only child. When the shit hits the fan, you run from the fan. I often need and crave solitude, especially at a time when everything seems lost. I need to be with my thoughts. And I don't want to be interrupted by others. It is a luxury that I had as kid that I wasn't prepared to lose when I got married and had kids. If I don't get some alone time, I lose a sense of myself. But Melissa often saw it as running from hard situations. She may be right, but sometimes I just don't know how to express myself and I just need my own counsel. Even though in situations like this my counselor is just saying, "Fuck," over and over again.

Awkward Thoughts

That night I didn't have a destination. I was just walking. One block turned into three or four. Then I realized it was more than thirty minutes that I had been gone. I must've walked more than a mile. It was around 12:30 a.m. Too late to be on the street in most places, but we lived in Berkeley. Specifically, downtown Berkeley. Blocks from the campus of the University of California, Berkeley. To say that it's sleepy doesn't do it justice. I could hear the sound of my "fucks" bouncing around my head easily and clearly even with the podcast I was listening to going on in my headphones.

I had my hoodie up, because it was cold and it made it easier to listen to the podcast. At some point along the way I decided I needed . . . No, I decided that I deserved some ice cream. By the time I found a late-night convenience store, I had passed a few—in my eye—unsavory characters of all races. One of the great things about living in the Bay Area is that the inclusiveness extends to unsavory people too. Everybody can be someone you should avoid. So as I walked into the store, I took some precautionary actions. For starters, I took the hood down. I took it down even though my Afro had become a flat-fro from being squashed underneath. I didn't touch anything that I wasn't absolutely sure I was going to buy. (Just as my mom had taught me when I was eight years old.) I kept my hands out of my pockets, with palms clearly visible, so the clerk behind the counter could easily see that I wasn't shoving things in or—maybe more importantly—about to pull something out of my pockets. And as soon as I decided on an It's-It ice-cream sandwich, I went directly to the counter and gingerly placed my selection down, again keeping my palms visible and only making the movements I needed to get the money out of my wallet.

All seemed to be going well. But I was so preoccupied with not seeming unsavory, myself, that when the clerk said, "Two twenty-five," I thought he said, "One twenty-five." As he wordlessly stared at the two bucks I had given him without looking me in the eye, I realized my error and simultaneously felt a tiny jolt of adrenaline.

"Uh oh!" I thought. "He's going to think I'm pulling some sort of scam!" I envisioned him getting loud: "WHAT ARE YOU UP TO HERE?" Then I imagined myself trying to calm him down . . .

He misunderstands and pulls out a gun. I run out of the store. He calls the cops. Since this is a "good neighborhood" they show up quickly. They cut me off as I'm running home. They leap out of their car, guns drawn. I start to truly panic: "YOU DON'T UNDERSTAND! IT WAS A MISTAKE!" I put my arms up in the air. At this point I realize I'm holding the It's-It ice-cream sandwich, which I never paid for. I wave my hands frantically and say, "I DIDN'T MEAN TO STEAL THIS!" The cops take in all my hand waving, crazy talk, and BBM-ness and then, POP! POP! POP! POP! POP! POP! POP! I'm dead.

The next day, it comes out that earlier that night I'd had a fight with my wife . . . and that in the wake of Robin Williams's suicide, I had written a blog post about comedians and depression . . . and that in my stand-up act I have jokes that are critical of police. The media reports that when I was in high school I was an assistant instructor at a kung-fu school. Headline: "Black Comedian, a Martial-Arts Expert Who Hated Cops, Fought with His Wife, and Was Clinically Depressed, Demonically Steals Frozen Treat from Local Muslim Merchant Who Is Thought to Be a Member of ISIS."

That all went through my head—in about a second. And I was just trying to buy ice cream. And again, I don't live in a socio-economically deprived neighborhood. I haven't been denied a good education by my local government. I don't generally feel trapped by my circumstances. (Well, at least I don't feel trapped by my physical circumstances. My brain is always setting traps for me.) But I definitely feel every bit of my six-foot-four-inch, 250-pound body, and every bit of my Black skin. And lest you think I am exaggerating in the above scenario, know that it contains elements of the deaths of Michael Brown, Oscar Grant, Kajieme Powell, Eric Garner, and others.

The fact is that being a BBM has consequences. Being a BBM is why I smile quickly. It's why I don't usually stand to my full height. It's why my posture is so bad. I slouch and bend instead of lording myself over people. When people haven't seen me for a while, I often hear, "I forgot how tall you are!" I know you did. It's because I'm trying to make you forget. This is what being Black in America has done to me, to others like me, and, in some sense, even to you. It's not that I think I will be killed by a police officer. It's just that if I am, it won't be a surprise.

Being a BBM is why I realized I was so happy to have a daughter. And it is why I was so happy to then have a second daughter. I felt some sense of relief. I didn't want to have to figure out how to talk to them about how to be a Black man in America. I recognize that is an extremely selfish thought to have. I need to be talking to every Black man I know about being a Black man in this country. Now more than ever. But I just honestly didn't feel equipped to handle that if I'd had a son. Don't get me wrong. I would have figured out some way to deal with it, because the stakes are too high to skip it. But I just don't know how to tell someone, "Despite your best efforts to live a life on the straight and narrow path of righteousness, America might still kill you for no reason . . . And here's the scary part . . . America will feel completely justified when you die."

And believe me, I know having Black daughters doesn't mean they are exempt from these experiences. I've seen those videos too. Like the one of the teenage girl at a pool party in McKinney, Texas. A police officer wrestled her to the ground because . . . no reason. She was being a teenager at a pool party, and he didn't like that. And there's the video of the officer in a Columbia, South Carolina, high school, tossing a teenage girl across the classroom for the crime of not listening to him. The video was only a few seconds long, so many people (mostly white) had the convenient out by saying, "How can I judge what happened? The video is so short. I need to know the whole story." I often respond, "OK. Well, our story begins during a thing called the transatlantic slave trade . . . You wanted the whole story, right?"

The officer in South Carolina who tossed the young woman across the classroom as if she were nothing was not convicted or even charged with a crime. In fact, none of the officers I mentioned have even been indicted. That means everything I've described is well within their job description. Which means police in this country have not changed how they interact with Black (and Brown) people. What kind of message does that send to the world? What are Black (and Brown) people supposed to think as we walk the streets and try to live our lives, especially now under an even more profound threat of scrutiny and retribution? And what am I supposed to tell myself when I walk the streets or even just sit in my house? And what am I supposed to tell my daughters?

Fuck.

CHAPTER 6

My Awkward Love of a White Woman

When me and Melissa met, it was that whole ridiculous love-at-first-sight thing. It must have been. Because we have been together ever since. Ever since Sunday, March 30, 2003. (I know that is true . . . because I just Googled it. Thank God our wedding website is still up.) And I say "ridiculous" because I'm not really sure that I believe in the idea of "love at first sight." Or at least I don't believe that "love at first sight" is the only way to find the love of your life. I'm really more of a believer in the *When Harry Met Sally* model. (*WHMS* of course being the greatest romantic comedy of all time period!) You meet somebody. You meet them again. You become friends. You become good friends. They annoy you. But you can't get enough of them, and finally if the two of you determine that your body parts match up and work well together, then you start dating. Me and Melissa didn't do all that. We just saw each other and were like, "Oh . . . There you are! . . . WHERE HAVE YOU BEEN?"

Also, because I didn't grow up with my parents together or

with really a ton of married people around me, I always feel like I'm not totally sure what exactly goes on in this whole marriage thing. Melissa comes from a family that's lousy with marriages and great at marriages. Her parents are the classic high school sweethearts who decided to turn pro once they graduated. Whereas with me, my mom was married twice before my dad, and my dad was married twice after her. To be fair, his marriage to my stepmom is still going strong after more than thirty years. But much like how Deadheads feel about every keyboard player in the Grateful Dead after Pigpen, my stepmom always seems newish to me. But marriage was nowhere in my mind when I first saw Melissa. Because when I first saw Melissa all that was going through my mind was, "DAAAAAAAAAAAAMN!"

My dating history has been less than legendary. I went on one date in high school. It was with a super popular girl. I think it only happened because our parents were friends (the way Black parents often bond at private schools), so we were around each other a good bit. I wasn't super *unpopular*. I was just not a factor in school at all. At. All. She, who will remain nameless, was a friendly, smart person who glowed from the inside. In my mind I was going to be her Dwayne Wayne to my Whitley Gilbert. And I was so nervous the next day that I literally (yup, literally) didn't say one word to her. And not in a cool, mysterious way. It was more like in a future-serial-killer way. Years later—after we had both gotten married and had kids—we had a chance to talk about it; she told me that she thought I was mean. I appreciated the feedback. And I tried to explain that I understood why she thought that. I didn't explain that I wasn't mean. I was just so afraid of screwing it up that somehow I convinced myself that not talking to her at all and even walking the opposite direction when I saw her in the hall was the best "approach" to a new relationship. And that's not all. Wait, there's more! There was another time in high school when I mailed handwritten poems to a girl to declare my "love." She was way, way, waaaaaay above my high school station. I'm guessing that she was the prom queen, if my high school did that. (I have no idea. I didn't go to prom. I went to the movies . . . with Jason and Rob.) She handled the creepy package the best way possible . . . by telling me that I should be a writer and by also telling me "No" in clear yet remarkably gentle terms for a teenage girl who had just received a pile of furiously scrawled love notes from a dude who got her address from who knows where. (The school had a book with everybody's addresses. I'm guessing that has changed in the years since. Maybe thanks to me.) And even though that all happened a long, long time ago in a city far, far away from where I sit now, even knowing that you are reading this right now makes me want to move to the hills and live all by myself, surviving off whatever I can figure out how to grow off the land . . . which would be nothing.

By the time I went to college in Philadelphia. . . . and then dropped out, I was still nearly completely inexperienced with women. So after high school, I knew I needed to make some big changes. I actually decided to make a concerted effort to have some friends who were women. I knew instinctively that I needed to at least be around them and get comfortable, if I was ever going to have chance to maybe, you know . . . date one.

Angie was one of my first attempts at making friends with a woman. It sounds so stupid even as I type this, but this was a big deal for me. I was a twenty-one-year-old college dropout (twice by that point). I had met Angie at Ben & Jerry's, and then she helped me get my next job working with her at a video store, Nationwide Video. (It had three locations, all in Chicago.) Angie was easy for me to be friends with. She was easygoing and darkly hilarious. And because she was a lesbian, I had no nerves about talking to her. There was no fear of sexual tension. We weren't great friends, but I knew she liked me. She had helped me get a better job after all.

During this time I was starting to do comedy. And even though I was not very good at all, it was helping with my confidence and also making me feel like I was a part of something. Like I had a secret mission. (Mostly because I knew I sucked and I didn't want anybody to come see me.) That "new me" must have started to make an impact. One day one of my coworkers, Gigi, told me, "There are two people here who have crushes on you." I thought, "WHAT? . . . *TWO PEOPLE?* . . . *THAT'S TWO MORE THAN I NEED!*" This was something I wasn't used to hearing.

Gigi said, "Do you want me to tell you who they are?"

"Yes, of course I do!"

Gigi replied, "Well, I can tell you one, but the other person isn't sure she wants you to know yet."

Me in my head: "WHO GIVES A SHIT, LADY? JUST TELL ME THE ONE WHO WANTS ME TO KNOW. TIME'S A-WASTING! WE'RE BURNING DAYLIGHT!!!!"

Me in real life: "Cool. Whatever . . ."

The one who was fine with me knowing was Catherine. We went on a date as soon as possible, which turned into dating for three years. We moved to California together. I was twenty-one, and she was six years older, which, weirdly, was almost the same age difference between my mom and my dad. She was a white public-school teacher of Irish descent. Catherine was a really good person who loved her job, which was an incredibly hard job. Not her public school job in particular, but teaching is a hard job, being an elementary school teacher is a harder job, being an elementary school teacher in a public school that is underfunded and understaffed is an even harder job, and then getting paid so little that you have to take a part-time job working at a video store so you can pay your rent *and* keep up with your student loans makes Sisyphus seem like a hipster working on his screen-play in a coffee shop.

We were together from the time we went on that first date. And pretty quickly I moved into her place, which seemed like a better move than sleeping on a pull-out couch in the living room of the apartment I was living in with three other comedians (including Dwayne Kennedy, who later I would hire for *Totally Biased*). After two years of doing stand-up mostly in coffee shops and bars (there was only one full-time comedy club in Chicago at that point. It was Zanies, and I had done one or two sets there without anything close to success), I told Catherine I had to move to a scene where there was more opportunity and also a place where I could feel freer to grow. I had read a bunch of books about the history of stand-up comedy, and every one of them made the San Francisco scene sound magical. I figured I could move there for a couple of years, and then once I was setting the world on fire, LA would beg me to come down and take its money. That didn't happen then. And it still hasn't happened. Catherine said she wanted to come with me. And we moved out to Oakland together. Well, honestly, she moved us out to Oakland. She had all the adult stuff. She knew how to call a moving company. She knew how to both find a new apartment and how to get the lights turned on. Without her I probably would have moved, but it would have been some sort of sleeping at a bus station situation while I got my shit together that I'm guessing would have ended up with me reenacting the real-life version of hard-to-watch heroin scenes from the movie *Requiem for a Dream*. Hopefully I would at least get to be the Marlon Wayans character. I don't know if Catherine knows how important she was to that move. She probably does, but I'm guessing that she doesn't know that I know. Hopefully, you are reading this, Catherine. Thank you.

After about a year, it was clear things weren't working. I was wanting to be out doing comedy and hanging out with my new comic friends. She was getting closer to wanting to settle down and have a family. After a year, Catherine had a great job but hadn't really established her life out there, and I was always going off to do comedy . . . or see comedy . . . or hang out with comedians. In my mind, I had to choose between my relationship and comedy. I chose comedy.

So we broke up, and very soon after, I met Lynn. By this point I was twenty-five, and Lynn was younger than me by a few years. Lynn was Vietnamese and Southern Californian. We met at our job at a Berkeley school supplies store. Where Catherine had felt like the first person in my life who had really liked me and pursued me, Lynn was the first person I really liked and pursued . . . successfully. I didn't know I had it in me before that. She's attractive. I want to date her. *Wait, I got her?*

I flirted hard-core with Lynn for a month, and when things were finally officially over with Catherine, I asked Lynn out. And later that day we were making out in front of a church down the street from where we worked. The first few months were the kind of relationship that songs are written about—but like Prince songs. It was amazing and very TV-MA. After that, things pulled apart, as usually happens. It became super on-again, off-again for the next two years. Everyone has to have a relationship where you look back and think, *That person is crazy!* And for me and Lynn, we are EACH that person. We were two people who were holding tightly to each other because we felt like we didn't belong on this earth and needed someone, but we were the wrong people to cling to. It was the kind of relationship where we'd break up, and people would say, "Good For you! You're much better without him/her," and the next week we'd be back together, and our people would say, "Oh . . . Good. For . . . you both? I guess." I know I screwed up by moving in with her super quickly. The place I found after Catherine was not livable long-term. I wormed my way into Lynn's apartment. I was a punk. And I'm sure it totally screwed up our time together. I should have grown up and handled my business differently. Sorry, Lynn.

One thing about Lynn, though, that was markedly different from Catherine was her approach to race and racism. Catherine was goodhearted and had been a schoolteacher working in the Chicago public schools. She was basically living that *Dangerous*

Minds life of a white woman with hope, trying hard to use the minimal resources the school system provided to teach kids who needed the maximum resources. (I've known a lot of public school teachers in my life, and I've seen how all of them end up using their paycheck to subsidize their kids' education. It's gross that the system doesn't have their backs.) When I was dating Catherine, I was starting to talk about race and racism in my act. I wasn't that funny yet, which meant that sometimes it either sounded like weak diatribes or petty criticisms of white people. And after we moved to Oakland, I had a bunch of free time before I found a job. I had also read Richard Pryor's autobiography, *Pryor Convictions*, so I think I was trying on some level to replicate the mystical mixture of the Bay Area that I read he put together when he moved out there. No, not crack and alcohol and fire. That was his Southern California mixture. When he moved to the Bay Area he had apparently begun reading a lot of books to help him understand his feelings about Black liberation. I started regularly going to a used bookstore on Grand Avenue in Oakland. I bought *Roots,* a collection of Alex Haley's interviews from *Playboy* magazine, *The Autobiography of Malcolm X* (that I was rereading), *Soul on Ice,* and others I hadn't read in any of my schools. Catherine noticed that there were suddenly all these Black books around, and I just remember there was a feeling in the air of Catherine being like, "Oh, are you going to be doing this now?" It wasn't necessarily said out loud, but I just remember being conscious of where the books were in the house. But I kept going with all the reading; after all, if you're going to be doing *this*, Oakland, birthplace of the Black Panthers, is a great place to do *this*.

But onstage I felt like I couldn't *lean into* (yeah, I know) trying new material about race and racism because it made it weird at home. But when I started dating Lynn, things were immediately different. Lynn had the classic story of a person of color who goes to a suburban school with mostly white students, and the mostly white students had given her four years of simultaneously treating her like a white person (racist jokes and never taking into account that as a Vietnamese-American she might have a different experience from theirs that could be helpful in their understanding of the world at large) and also like she was weird because of the food she ate or the second language she spoke. Lynn moved to the Bay Area and was deeply committed to letting the white man have it, while at the same time, due to her upbringing, she was also deeply committed to Radiohead being the greatest band of all time period. I thought the dissonance was hilarious, but I also thought it was awesome.

I loved Lynn. She was very freeing and fun. Her sister was in grad school and also lived in Oakland and was dating another academic. It seemed like everybody I was hanging out with was an activist or ethnic studies major. And mostly they were all people of color. It was glorious. I was fully living my version of Richard Pryor's experience. They were younger than me but also smarter than me. I started talking about race and racism more directly in my act. Lynn liked it and pushed me to do it more, which made me want to do it even more.

But at the same time, we clearly weren't meant to be. We had all the benefits of a crazy relationship, and all the shitty things about a crazy relationship. Super fun when it's fun, SUPER not fun when it's not fun. Also despite Lynn pushing me to step into my full self as a comedian and more importantly as a Black man, there was a problem. She knew her parents didn't want her to be with a Black man. So when they came into town I had to ske-daddle. One time they stayed for a couple of days and I actually had to get a hotel. This was before the days of pulling up a hotel on your Hotels.com app on your phone, so I didn't know how to get one, especially since I didn't really have a lot of money. I knew me and Catherine had stayed in a cheap hotel when we visited San Francisco before we moved. I went there. It was the kind of hotel that is downtown but is super cheap . . . too cheap. It was depressing to be back there. It was as if my life wasn't moving forward. I stayed there for two days feeling rejected by my girl-friend, but at the same time I knew I was a loser for not having my own place to live. I vowed that if Lynn and I broke up (at that point it was already "if we broke up *again*") I wouldn't ever again date somebody who didn't want me to meet her parents.

Now it was the early 2000s. Me and Lynn were fully done. The last time we really spoke was after 9/11, which makes it a weird marker for my life. "Where were you on 9/11?" "At my house, promising myself that I would never talk to my ex again! . . . Also watching the towers fall on TV." This was my first time truly being single and not immediately running into a new relationship. When I met Melissa I was coming off a really bad stretch of dating. I was excited to be single, but it quickly got out of hand. I didn't know what I was doing. People always think male comedians have a lot of people wanting to hook up with them after shows. And some do, but in my experience most defi-nitely do not. For one reason, comedy clubs are classic date-night venues. Everybody is already with everybody. Two, most comics' acts are far from sexy. You spend a lot of time onstage talking about either how much you suck or how much the world sucks. This doesn't turn most people on. Three, in my observation, the guys who do find a disproportionately high number of hookups after the show would find those in their regular life anyway. And/or they have written an act that is basically a walking personal ad, about how they are single and can't find a date, but also . . . "Here's some stories about me having sex so that you know I do like all that stuff." I'm not mad at those guys. I'm just saying that when people say humor is an aphrodisiac, they don't realize it only really works that way *if you are already attracted to the person.* I bet Idris Elba is hilarious to everyone he meets: man, woman, child, animal, and mineral.

So since I wasn't meeting women at the clubs, I had basically gone on an Internet date bender. The early 2000s were the Jurassic period of Internet dating. There were the beginnings of dedicated dating sites like Yahoo! Personals and Match.com, but a lot of the dating sites were charging money to join them. I was a broke comic. I was going to be lucky if I had money to pay for the date let alone money to pay for access *to* the date, so I went to the back alley of Internet dating . . . Craigslist. Do you need a slightly used, not too stained couch and a relationship? Well, then Craigslist is here for YOU! No disrespect to Craigslist. (Or even to Craig himself. I used to see him in my neighborhood in San Francisco all the time.) Maybe dating on Craiglist is better now. But back then in the still relatively early days of the Internet, it was pretty bleak. Initially all you could do was run an ad with words. It wasn't a dedicated profile. It was just an ad. That meant that like two days after you posted it, it was buried. And the only way they might, *might* find you is if they happened to search for your key words. Good luck with that. Everybody was mostly still enjoying the same "hiking, watching movies, and hanging out." This led to me (and others, I found out) posting multiple ads so you could get more attention. And then it led to me posting multiple ads with multiple perspectives just to try to expand my customer base. Soon it became addictive. It was just sort of a video game where the high score was love . . . Who am I kidding? The high score was usually a drunken make-out in a bar that neither of us had ever been to before just so we were unlikely to run into friends. Cue the romantic violins. Also initially on Craigslist you couldn't post pictures, so you were counting on someone's prose to describe their physical appearance, which is a lot like someone trying to describe a bad smell to you; you need to be there, so you can know why you don't want to be there.

And when there was a picture swap after a few e-mails had been exchanged, the pictures were never good enough to tell you what you needed to know. This was way before camera phones had fully replaced cameras for most people. A lot of the pictures you'd get from people were physical pictures that had been scanned into computers. Pictures where uncles and exes had been cropped out. Scanned on cheap scanners. And this was before we were all so used to getting our picture taken. Now everybody has a way they want their picture.

"Hold the camera at a high angle. Let's move over there where the light is hitting my face. OK, lemme put my right leg forward. Don't shoot directly on. Give me a little angle to the right. OK . . . OK . . . I'm ready for my DMV photo now."

So all these pictures were of people not looking at the camera or caught in the middle of a laugh or with a complete expression-less look on their face. These pictures were the kind that Lennie from *Law & Order* would carry around so he could say, "We're looking for this girl." (And of course the all-time best *Law & Order* cast, with no regard to year is of course Lennie and Ray as the cops, Sam Waterston and Angie Harmon as the DAs.)

By the time I met Melissa, my Internet dating had stopped being fun, and I found myself in a wilderness of horrible. I'm not blaming the people I dated. It just felt sort of destined to fail. Every Craigslist date had become the same: Two people set a date. They both show up for the date. One person would show up thinking, *"I can't believe it's you. You are everything your Craigslist ad said and more. How did I get this lucky? . . . Should we spend the holidays with your family or mine?"* And at the same time the other person would be thinking, "I CAN'T BELIEVE IT'S YOU! *HOW THE HELL ARE YOU GOING TO SEND THAT PICTURE OUT WHEN YOU KNOW IT ONLY VAGUELY LOOKS LIKE YOU NOW? IF THE PERSON IN THAT PICTURE COMMITTED A CRIME THEY WOUDN'T EVEN BRING YOU IN FOR QUESTIONING. THAT'S HOW LITTLE THAT PICTURE LOOKS LIKE YOU. AND WHAT'S THAT SMELL? IS THAT YOU? I'M GOING TO GO TO THE BATHROOM AND SEE IF THE WINDOWS ARE BIG ENOUGH TO CRAWL OUT OF."* One person would be super sad, and the other person would be super excited. And if you were excited, you knew the other person was super sad. It never matched up. And I was on both ends of that equation. It got to the point where if I realized that I was excited to see the person then I also knew immediately, *"Aw man! I'm the loser here. Dammit!"*

My last Craigslist date was the worst version of this. It was clear that we both thought the other one sucked. But we were trying to honor the social contract by spending a "date's worth of time" together. And as we were both sitting at a coffee shop wondering how long that is—two hours? Three hours? How about an hour? That's fine, right? Forty-five minutes is definitely too short . . . right?—a friend of the woman's walked up to say hi. We were both happy that new blood was being injected into this experience, and then when the friend left to catch the bus, we both got sad again. That's when the woman who I was on the date with said, "I live near her! I could give her a ride home." I was like, "Really?" I immediately jumped up and ran onto the bus. I pushed my way past the other passengers until I got to the friend, who understandably had a confused look on her face when she saw me, the dude who had just been on a date with her friend. Before she could even say anything, I blurted out, "SHE CAN GIVE YOU A RIDE HOME!" The friend responded, "Oh. OK." We got off the bus. They left. We didn't even have to say the date was over.

I was done with Craigslist. And just like the movie says you are supposed to do, I met Melissa the next week. It was 2003, two years after I finally broke up with Lynn. My friend Bruce, who had helped me develop the *Bell Curve*, introduced me to Jill, who was a woman in her fifties developing a one-person show about her crazy life (kinda like most people who write a one-person show . . . It's either that or cancer). Jill told me about a dance and art history student named Melissa Hudson who was going to do the lights and sound. In my mind, I was picturing an eighteen- or nineteen-year-old coed. Melissa had been hearing about me, assuming I was Jill's age. I'd been picturing a kid, and she was picturing a fifty-year-old man. So we had this moment of looking at each other and thinking, *Oh, you're not what I expected.*

We spent the whole day working together. She was actually twenty-three, but I guessed at the time she was twenty-eight—I was thirty at the time, which was key because I had told myself that I could only date women who were my age. I was immediately attracted to her. She had long, dark brown hair, was a dancer, athletically built, and she was tall—around five foot nine—and carried herself even taller. There was something about her that reminded me of Wonder Woman. She looked like she could both throw and take a punch. And she could; I later found out that she was a black belt in Tang Soo Do, a Korean martial art that was popularized by Chuck Norris. We had fun early on, staging mock battles between us, since I had studied Wing Chun kung fu, Bruce Lee's original martial art. We often "re-created" the scene from Bruce Lee's third film, *Way of the Dragon,* where Chuck and Bruce fought. (Do I have to tell you that Bruce won . . . easily? No, I hope not. Take that, Chuck Norris Facts.)

And when I say that Melissa reminded me of Wonder Woman, I'm talking 1970s-era Lynda Carter Wonder Woman, a woman who while, yes, looking completely ridiculous by 2017 standards in her crime-fighting outfit of booty shorts, impossible-to-keep-her-covered-up top, and high-heeled boots, was *clearly capable of kicking ass.* Lynda Carter was broad shouldered, athletic, and looked like she might be descended from Amazons, like the character. This was the '70s, when women in Hollywood could be built like that. Lynda Carter, Pam Grier, Jayne Kennedy, Raquel Welch—and Melissa could have hung out with all of them. And she was in grad school with an undergrad degree in contemporary dance. And even though she was twenty-three, she seemed fully grown-up. I just felt like her whole energy was, "I don't need you . . . but I like you." It was intoxicating. Shortly after we started dating she had parked her car in a lot and lost her ticket as she went to pay. The lot had one of those policies where if you lost your ticket they charged you the full twenty-four-hour fee. And in San Francisco, if I remember correctly, the fee was like one month's rent plus everything in your pockets. I remember being amazed as she calmly paid the outrageous fee without complaint and then went to her car, found the ticket, and went back and got her money refunded. I didn't have experience with my partners being this reasonable in stressful situations. Hell, I didn't have experience with *me* being this reasonable in stressful situations. I was in love. Growing up with my mom, I was attracted to women—and people—who can take care of themselves. You can lean on each other. You're not always being leaned on.

The night we first met we all went out to get Chinese food. I got a phone call saying they needed someone to open at Cobb's Comedy Club that night. Cobb's was one of my two home clubs in San Francisco, the other being the Punch Line. I knew it would be an easy way to impress this woman I had just met. I invited Jill and Melissa to see me perform.

At this point I was confident in my skills to be funny . . . at least for the twenty minutes I was given that night. I knew that Cobb's would see me walk in with these people and give them VIP service. I didn't do this often . . . or hardly ever, so I knew everyone would be on their best behavior to help me impress them. Tom Sawyer, the notoriously hard-ass owner, would give them great seats. Damon and Johnny, the bartenders who had become my friends, bought Melissa and Jill their drinks. During this era, I was one of the local guys. One of the solid local comics the club could depend on to do a good job and help out when needed, from moving chairs for the carpet cleaner to being light-weight security if someone got out of hand. (That just meant standing behind the actual security to create the illusion of more help. Being 6'4" has its privileges.) People genuinely liked me, and Melissa could see that. Later she would often make fun of me by saying, "Everybody loves Kamau!" But really it was im-portant to her that people did like me. She had come out of a relationship where that had not always been true.

The next day, after we worked on Jill's show, Melissa asked me if I needed a ride home. I said yes, even though we weren't going the same direction at all. It was the first time I tried to kiss her, even though she made it clear that she was not going to make her lips available to me on the first day we met. A couple days later, she invited me to see a modern dance show. I of course said yes. Even though I had no interest in seeing a modern dance show. Now I have seen probably several dozen contemporary dance shows. And I can enjoy them. (Some of them don't actually care if you enjoy them. Like a comedian who revels in walking the room.) I'm all about that Robert Moses, Bill T. Jones, and BreadnButter (Melissa's dance company). That night we did what couples in San Francisco are supposed to do on a first date. We had burritos in the Mission. While we were eating, an older Black couple walked in and the woman looked over toward us.

She started talking to the man, and I could tell she was getting agitated. She kept looking at us and getting visibly angrier. I kept tracking them as the lady kept looking more and more upset between taking looks at us. A few minutes later, when their burritos were ready, they quickly left the taqueria, and her husband held her arm and guided her into the car the way a cop puts a suspect in the backseat. By this point I was smiling and almost laughing. That's how I do when things get awkward like that sometimes.

Melissa looked slightly confused. "Is that about us?"

Me: "Yup. I'm guessing she's not happy about us being together."

Melissa: "Really?"

I wasn't totally shocked by this. I had experienced moments like that when I had dated Catherine. (With Lynn, we didn't really have those problems. Something about the fact that we were both people of color made it so that even Black people who didn't like interracial dating thought it was fine. As long as she wasn't white.) And these things do happen, even in the so-called liberal bastion of San Francisco, but Melissa was genuinely shocked. She had dated a Black dude before, but it was in college, and they were both in the theater department so everybody was trying everything in that setting. ("I'm going to do my one-person show where I drink my grandma's blood." "COOL! I'm going to date a Latina and see what my parents say when they see the pictures on Facebook!") Melissa told me later that she realized in that moment that a part of our relationship was going to be about other people's feelings about interracial dating. It opened her eyes. She knew she'd have to decide if she was going to be all-in. She was. Because that is how she do.

After eating and talking about what had happened, we walked to the dance show together. As we were crossing the street, I took a chance and grabbed for her hand. She let me do it. This was already going well. So later, in the middle of the show, when the lights went down between pieces, I leaned over as we were talking and I tried to kiss her. She let me do that too. And we've been together ever since.

Two weeks later, I met her parents. Honestly, I didn't think it was a great idea. But Melissa assured me that this is how it worked in her family. She had an older brother and twin sisters. To me that was so different from my family that it basically sounded like the Duggars (minus the gross stuff). Her family's house was the place where all the friends hung out after school. It was the family where once one of the kids goes on three good dates, the parents ask, "So . . . when are we going to meet him?" I knew there were red flags (and maybe one big 6'4" Black flag) with our relationship. But Melissa made it clear that this was happening. So we all went out to the Stinking Rose, the world's number one garlic restaurant, and had dinner. And I told myself, "This will be fine."

And it was fine. Totally fine. In a "How was your sandwich that you bought from 7-11?" "It was fine" way. Her parents were nice and friendly and I sensed that they were thoroughly unimpressed. I didn't blame them at all. At all. And I really didn't think it had anything to do with me being Black. Well, at least not in the way that makes this story juicy. Think of it from her parents' side of things. Here is their twenty-three-year-old daughter who is in grad school. And she introduces them to a thirty-year-old college dropout, *alleged* stand-up comedian (I say "alleged" because no one believes you are a stand-up comic if they don't know who you are. No matter how famous you happen to be. They always ask for proof. "Really? Where have you performed? When? Are you on TV? Now? Like can I turn on any random TV right now and see you doing stand-up comedy RIGHT NOW?") I'm sure her parents felt like, "How the hell is this guy going to make a living? He's got nothing." And if they weren't thinking that about me, I was certainly thinking that about myself.

But me and Melissa kept dating, and we very quickly became very essential to each other's artistic lives. When I did the *Bell Curve*, she held the projector in her lap. I did lights and sound at her shows and helped stage manage and move chairs and whatever else it took. She used all her dance training to clean up my stage presence. "Stop shuffling your feet so much. Stay rooted while you are talking. It will help the jokes." It did. She ran the box office at many, many of my shows. We were embedded in the most important part of each other's lives. And the best part for me was that nothing I was doing onstage about race and racism threatened her at all. She only offered criticism if she felt like I wasn't making the point effectively, or if she genuinely didn't understand. I showed her an example of what an artist did out in the world. She told me that my example helped her push forward in her dance career. Shortly after we started dating, she dropped out of her graduate program and eventually went back to school to do what she wanted to do: be a dancer and a dance scholar. And now she has her master's in experimental dance choreography and her PhD in critical dance studies. I love referring to us as "Doctor and Mr. Bell." But before all that there were times through the years when I was making money, and times she was. And there were times when we were literally living off her student loans. But she believed I was funny. It was always important to my mom that the person I was with believed in what I was doing, and through Melissa I realized how important it was to me too.

We've been together for fourteen years, which is basically a third of my life. It doesn't feel that long because every day together is like a beautiful new flower blooming. OK. Maybe not that. But seriously, we've been through some shit, and we've been through some ups and downs. And I know who is responsible for most of those "downs." In this relationship it is clear who the crazy one is. This career I've chosen is designed to make the person crazy. It's me. One hundred percent.

But having grown up with my mother as a single parent—who I think did a better job by herself than most two-parent families—I know that the idea of being divorced, and being a single parent, is around. It's in the air. Male comedians talk about how they hate their wives . . . or how they're happy to be divorced and hate their ex-wives. Wives are targets, even if they really love them. It's a male-comedian trope.

During *Totally Biased*, it became clear that the show (and all the tremendous challenges and changes and incomprehensible level of hard work) was destroying me. And in turn it began to destroy my marriage. There was a time when I actually did contemplate divorce. It was in the middle of what should have been the biggest success of my career, but I was allowing it to make me crazy. The pressure and the hours were terrible, and I wasn't healthy. At some point my eyes turned red. A doctor had given eye drops to me, and it turned out I was allergic to them. You can watch *Totally Biased* episodes where my eyes are bloodshot, and at the time I had no idea why. I was barely holding it together.

There was a time when I was living alone at my dad's apartment in New York, and I would just visit Sami every few days. It was a taste of the divorced life. And. I. Hated. It. In one way, there was less pressure. I could just focus on the show. I could come home at night without that pressure to be connected to the family. The pressure to answer questions and check in. I remember thinking, "I can just come home and watch TV! I'm more productive than I've been in a while!" But I hated it. And I am forever grateful to my wife that she waited me out. She let me go through my bullshit and I'm even more grateful that she let me come back. At some point I realized that I refused to let me let a TV show be even partially to blame for my family breaking apart. I didn't care if the show was a hit or not. "Luckily," it wasn't a hit. Stay tuned, true believers!

Awkward Thoughts
about White Guys

I have worked with this white guy three times. Well, I've worked with this white guy at least three times in showbiz. I have met with this white guy. I've been promised things by this white guy. Now, let me be clear: these are three seemingly separate white guys. They have different lives and different names, which I won't be using because that would create the impression that these issues are only related to these three white guys. But as you read I hope you understand that this is a part of much bigger issues. This white guy is everywhere. He is literally unavoidable if you want to succeed in this country. I have worked with him three times in less than four years. And it always begins the same way . . .

He always pitches himself as the "perfect white guy" . . . at least the "perfect white guy" for a Black guy like you. OK, he doesn't say the words "perfect white guy" exactly, but the pitch makes that clear. This white guy has told me in detail that he totally gets me and that he gets what I am doing. And more than that, he gets the elusive "it." The sacred mix of racism, oppression, racial justice, white privilege, sexism, ableism, ageism, homophobia, Islamophobia, transphobia, phobia-phobia, all the phobias—from arachnophobia to zoophobia—that I am railing against. This white guy tells me that he's not like the other white guys. He voted for Barack Obama twice. TWICE! And he reads the *New York Times* . . .

including the articles by Charles Blow. (But not the Roxane Gay ones, because she's a little extreme.) This white guy bought Ta-Nehisi Coates's book *Between the World and Me*. And he's going to read it soon. Very, very soon!

This white guy has even worked with Black comedians before. Famous Black comedians. Black comedians who are *just like me*! Black comedians who are also committed to the cause. In fact, this white guy wrote a lot of those Black guys' "classic" bits. In fact, if only that Black guy had listened to this white guy more, he would have been even funnier. This white guy is so glad to be able to work with me because he knows I "get it" even more than the other famous Black comedians. Together, we are going to team up and get rich . . . Oops, he meant to say, win lots of awards . . . Oops (that ain't it), he *meant* to say, CHANGE THE WORLD! Yeah, that's it. We're going to change the world.

This white guy can relate to me because he's been around Black people his whole career, and/or because he's married/dated [insert nonwhite race here] before, and/or he's actually a member of an ethnic group that is—according to him—adjacent to Black people in the struggle Olympics, and/or this white guy grew up in *Nu Yawk Siddy*, so there's literally no way he can be racist! This white guy is older than me, so of course that means he knows things about the world. He says he can help me avoid the pitfalls and dumb moves that other people before me have made. He is happy to be my mentor . . . OK, not my mentor, if that word rubs me the wrong way, but he will be able to mentor me . . . when I need it. He's happy to do it!

He says he's happy to do it, but when I call him to tell him that Chris Rock has contacted me and wants to see a video of a show that I did that I know this white guy has, this white guy stops me from talking and says, "Well, wait . . . What's my percentage in this?" I re-coil, shocked. We had dealt with money before, but it was money for services rendered. I had paid him for his work before. And I had even set up a deal for him to teach students of mine, which brought him more money, so I wasn't avoiding the money conversation, but I was feeling weird about it suddenly being all quid pro quo: "You let me know what percentage of your career I own, and I'll give you the footage of you that I have sitting on a shelf somewhere collecting dust." I was stunned. And I also immediately knew that we were done working together. I didn't tell him that at the time, which may sound cowardly. But I didn't because I really didn't think I owed him that. We had only been working together for about a year, on and off. And I was pretty far along when I met him. He was Mr. Miyagi, but I wasn't Daniel-san. I had had many mentors in my life at that point and none of them were asking about percentages when I called to tell them Chris Rock had called. They all were just excited. I should also men-tion that the majority of them were not white men. They were Black people, mixed-race people; many of them were women. And my East Bay lesbian friend-collaborator Martha, who had the biggest claim to everything that was working for me at this point, just had a "Let me know if you need me" vibe. I suddenly really appreciated that. And later, I would run to my "in case of emergency" lesbian ac-tivist in a glass case and break the glass.

All my collaborators of various levels knew that if there was a spot for them, I would hold it for them. But at this point there were literally no spots that existed. It was just that Chris had called me with a little interest. The show that I would produce with Chris, *To-tally Biased*, was more than a year away from happening. This was about asking this white guy to help me keep the conversation going. But he turned it into our last conversation ever. His choice, not mine.

But exit that white guy and enter a new white guy. But don't worry. Meet the new white guy, same as the old white guy.

This new (old) white guy is excited about this new project. He is fired up and raring to go. And all he needs for us to succeed on this project is for me to not be so harsh. He doesn't like my new joke about an amusement park based on the Civil Rights era of the 1960s. The whole part about the water slide featuring fire hoses and the petting zoo featuring police attack dogs could leave a bad taste in the mouths of some audience members. (Later, I realize that "some audience members" is code for "white audience members"—i.e., the most coveted audience members and usually the only audience members whose feelings matter.) This white guy wants me to remember that audiences love me because I'm affable and relatable, so I don't want to screw it up with one joke. He wants me to make sure that the joke has a "real punch line" and isn't just a statement designed to make people feel uncomfortable. He reminds me that the white guy I want to say the "mean thing" about is actually not as bad as I think. He reminds me that I don't want to alienate the audience. Flies, sugar, vinegar . . . that sort of thing.

He knows my comedy voice explicitly. Heck, his voice and my voice are almost the exact same. REMEMBER, HE VOTED FOR OBAMA TWICE!!! He is excited that he can finally write for somebody so smart. He tells stories of all the horrible things he has worked on with other comedians. He talks about how dumb the material was, and how working with me is so refreshing, although he often says, "We had a lot of fun, though!"

He lets me know that the kind of writing that is done for this medium is much different from the kind of writing that I do for my-self. He lets me know that some stuff just won't work. He lets me know that I'm lucky that he's there to "help me" by telling me all this. He would hate it if I had to stumble around finding all this out on my own. He tells me that he's got my back. He tells me not to worry about the network. When I say I hadn't been worrying about the network, he says, "Good. Because you shouldn't." Oops, now I'm starting to get a little worried.

He tells me that everything I want to do is possible . . . as long as I'm willing to do it slightly differently. He tells me that some of the things that he is going to ask me to do may seem like they are against my nature but that they will ultimately be good for the show. When I bristle ever so slightly, he tells me, with a heavy, re-signed sigh, that he's seen it all before.

He tells me that he should have had his shot years ago. He tells me that this business is filled with shortsighted number counters who are afraid to do good work. He then immediately tells me about the gig he did recently that is a hip-hop reality show crossed with a Japanese game show hosted by that guy in the YouTube video who fell and crushed his own testicle at his daughter's ballet recital. It got 175 million views. He tells me that the show was absolute shit. But the money was great.*

And then it begins . . .

This white guy pitches an idea. There is a lot of talk in the com-edy world about women not being funny. It is a story that resurfaces every few years. There's always talk about it, but it has come to a head again. Usually it comes from some male comedian who is

---

*I made that up. None of that exists. But you get the point.

allegedly just keeping it real. This time it is from Adam Carolla. But to be clear, it ain't just from Adam Carolla. It's also been from Jerry Lewis—the Adam Carolla of his day. This dumb idea comes from them and many others. And that's just publicly. Privately, I've heard many comics (and many just regular dudes) express this extremely dumb idea over the years. I've heard comics say it. I've heard club owners say it. I've heard comedy bookers say it. I've even heard a female comedy booker say it. Usually it comes out like a proclamation from on high . . . or like a newly discovered yet essential element of the periodic table: "Women . . . just . . . aren't . . . funny."

This is usually followed by a strong shrug of the shoulders and a wry smile that reads as if to say, "How can you argue with my ironclad logic?" Sometimes it comes with a challenge.

"Name me one funny woman . . . And I don't mean kinda funny. I mean *really funny.*"

"OK . . . Tina Fey."

"I'M TALKING STAND-UP COMICS! NOT WRITERS . . . OR ACTRESSES! I DON'T EVEN KNOW WHAT THE FUCK SHE IS. COME ON! Writers aren't the same. I mean somebody who is a touring comedian."

"OK . . . Kathy Griffin."

(Incredulously) "WHAT? DUUUUUUUUUDE! She is noooooooooot funny! At. All."

"What are you talking about? She's got a huge following. She sells out theaters." (Selling out theaters is one of the prime indicators of the truly successful comedian. Selling out basketball arenas was the highest level, until Larry the Cable Guy and then Kevin Hart sold out football stadiums. But back to the ridiculous argument already in progress . . .)

"Just because Kathy Griffin sells out theaters doesn't mean that she's funny. Just because those [insert derogatory word here . . . depending on who in Kathy Griffin's audience this person wants to insult the most—could be women, could be gay dudes] show up to see her, it doesn't mean she's funny."

Ignoring this totally ridiculous argument that just because thousands of people pay to see you be funny doesn't mean that you are funny, I quickly go to a name that I should have started with . . .

"Amy Schumer."

". . . Yeah . . . she's funny . . . but just because she's dirty."

"You mean like Redd Foxx, Dave Attell, Jim Norton—"

"WHAT? YOU'RE SAYING THAT SCHUMER IS AS FUNNY AS THOSE DUDES???"

No, actually I'm not saying that, but I know I can't explain all that, so I just go with the name that always ends this argument . . .

"How about Wanda Sykes?"

"Yeah . . . OK. She's funny . . . She's a killer . . . BUT CHRIS ROCK IS FUNNIER!"

Before you can say the inevitable response of "WHAT THE FUCK DOES THAT HAVE TO DO WITH ANYTHING?" he comes back with . . .

"OK . . . The one female comic you coulda said, if you were really thinking, is Joan Rivers. Joan Rivers was funny! But she's different. She's funny like a guy."

At this point you find a way to excuse yourself from this conversation because you know that if you continue this man-versation, you will forever be trapped in this Gordian knot of male privilege, sexism, and bargain-basement, happy-hour idiocy.

The "women are not funny" argument is one of the most tired and nonsensical arguments since arguments first began with a young Socrates saying, "I beg to differ."

Personally, I know I would not be who I am without the humor of my mom. She can cut you with a word, and then with a look she can stitch you up and send you on your way. Now, that may not sound funny to you, but it is hilarious to watch . . . especially if you aren't directly involved. And my mom wasn't even a (professional) comedian.

My childhood was filled with women on TV who were some of the greatest comedians of all time period. Gilda Radner was one of the tentpoles of the first cast of *Saturday Night Live*. I sucked up all the reruns of *The Carol Burnett Show* that I could. People have forgotten how groundbreaking that show was. It was led by a woman. The content was edgy and satirical. And the costumes bordered on couture. Not that I understood all that at the time. I just knew it was funny. And whether he knows it or not, every time Jimmy Fallon laughs in the middle of a sketch, he was given permission to do that by Carol Burnett. And as a child of the '70s, I watched sitcoms led by funny (and strong) women. Linda Lavin on *Alice*, Bonnie Franklin on *One Day at a Time*, Bea Arthur on *Maude*, the women of *Soap* . . . Florida (Esther Rolle), Willona (Ja'net Dubois), and Thelma (Bern Nadette Stanis) of *Good Times* . . . Dee (Danielle Spencer) and Shirley (Shirley Hemphill) of *What's Happening!!* The fact that I am even feeling compelled to make this list insults the hard work that these women have done.

When I got older I was blown away by Whoopi Goldberg's solo show *Whoopi* on Broadway! She created characters and scenes onstage that extended the most important parts of Richard

Pryor's legacy. Janeane Garofalo showed me that comics could—as the band Nirvana would say—"come as you are." Janeane also showed me that stand-up comics didn't have to create an artifice of showbiz. They could wear what they wanted, talk how they wanted, and, most importantly, talk *about* whatever they wanted. She was my Generation X god. And I realized I had to break up with my then-girlfriend in the middle of watching Janeane's foray into '90s romantic comedies, *The Truth About Cats & Dogs*. I didn't do it right away—like right in the middle of the screening—but it definitely factored into when I did it . . . two years later. (I was a punk.) And Maria Bamford is a singular voice and a genius of such a high level that I wouldn't be surprised at all if she was the first stand-up comic to end up with one of those MacArthur "genius" awards. And even though I had my issues with Sarah Silverman (and all of alt-comedy's "ironic racism") back in the early 2000s, one thing I never said was that she wasn't funny.

And TV was built on the back of Lucille Ball. Moms Mabley is one of the founders of modern stand-up comedy. And if you don't think that Julia Louis-Dreyfus is a first-ballot comedy Hall of Famer, then I don't trust you. Your judgment is completely off as far I'm concerned. I don't trust you to vote in major elections. I don't trust you to be in charge of children. I wouldn't trust you to drive me to the hospital in case of an emergency.

Roseanne Barr not only had a groundbreaking number one sitcom, but she also showed the importance of an artist seizing control of their own destiny. She has written about how the first season of her show featured men in power telling her how to be "Roseanne," and even one man taking credit for creating *Roseanne*, even though *Roseanne* was created by Roseanne Barr in the stand-up act that she wrote that got her the show in the first place. Roseanne wrote that she kept pictures of all the people on the show who had done her wrong, and as the show ascended to its number one spot in the ratings, she fired each of the people who had wronged her and her vision, one by one. At one point that sounded crazy to me, but at this point in my career I know it is essential for survival . . . and to maintain some level of sanity.

And that's just the famous funny women who I've watched. Then there are the many female stand-up comics in my life who I have known personally who just aren't famous . . . yet. Off the top of my head there's Laura House, Laurie Kilmartin, Janine Brito, Aparna Nancherla, Karinda Dobbins, Irene Tu, Marcella Arguello, Elicia Sanchez, and many more—who will inevitably be offended when they see that they aren't listed here.

Now lemme be clear, unlike the semifictional male comic voice that I've created, I'm not limiting the idea of "funny women" to just funny female stand-up comics. I don't care if you "paid your dues in the clubs." That is not essential to you being classified as a comedian to me. I don't care at all if your comedy path didn't lead you to take lonely road trips by yourself to one-nighters in the hinterlands of Amurica, where when you stood onstage as crowds of mostly dudes screamed, "Where's the *real* comic? . . . Take your shirt off!" Many comics think that is essential to being a "real comedian." For my money, it doesn't get funnier than writer Lindy West, and I don't give a shit that she only did *proper* stand-up comedy a few times.

But the real question is—male or female—if you do pay your dues that way, what are you getting in return? For me personally, after a certain point of paying those dues, I decided that all I was getting in return was the loss of my immortal soul. Nine times out of nine, I'd come off the road feeling dead inside, and it wasn't just from the limited food choices on the seemingly endless drive between Battle Mountain, Nevada, and Lovelock, Nevada, where I'd toured with Kevin Avery. And those gigs were way easier on me than they are for many women, because I am a six-foot-four, 250-pound Black man. Nobody was asking me to take my shirt off . . . although there were many, many times that they were asking for another comedian. I hated, HATED, those one-nighters. To me, being a comedian is ultimately about getting in touch with your own comedic voice, and I never understood how I would do that if I was standing in a room filled with people who were not only nothing like me, but who also didn't want to like me.

The thing that is always overlooked by these dudes who say women aren't funny is one indisputable fact: funny is subjective. Very few things are as subjective as funny. Funny is like sexy, and they are kind of related. What turns one person on is hilarious to another person. And vice versa. And you can see all of this at the nexus of clowns. Many people think clowns are hilarious. (Many others think clowns are creepy.) But there is a certain percentage of people who think clowns are sexy. Don't believe me, Google "clown porn" right now. I dare you. And if you don't need to Google that, then it's because it is already saved on your browser. So when these dudes say, "Women aren't funny," they are forgetting a classically important addendum: "to me." They should be saying, "Women aren't funny to me." But they don't say "to me" because if you are a man in America, you are considered the norm. (Remember it's the NBA and the W[omen's]NBA, not the WNBA and the M[en's]NBA.) And if you are a white man in America, then you are also considered the norm.

Even Chris Rock, who I know thinks women are funny because he gave Wanda Sykes her first big gig on his HBO talk show, *The Chris Rock Show*, once at the offices of *Totally Biased* told me and a group of writers, "Put it this way, your funniest uncle is always funnier than your funniest aunt." At the time me and most of the writers (and the entire crew) were still starstruck by him. And Chris isn't one of the greatest comedians of all time for nothing. He is able to craft sentences that cause you to stop in your tracks because of the images that are suddenly and crisply created in your head. When he said, "Your funniest uncle is always funnier than your funniest aunt," the image was so locked in my brain that I was immediately trying to think if I even had a funny uncle or a funny aunt. And by the time I got to the answer in my head of "not really," Chris had assumed my silence (and others') was agreement, and then, with that rhetorical skirmish won, he would move on to the next rhetorical skirmish, which was usually unrelated . . . which made it hard to come back to the last skirmish. ("People go to Five Guys for the burger, but the hot dog is actually what you should get there.") Immediately afterward, I stood around with Hari Kondabolu and Nato Green, two of my friends who I hired to write on *Totally Biased*, all of us frustratedly deconstructing Chris's argument while also contemplating getting hot dogs at Five Guys.

So just to take that argument apart like I should have done with Chris . . .

As I said before, funny is subjective.

1. There are many ways to be funny, so your funny uncle is probably funny because he rips off loud farts during Thanksgiving and/or sticks bread sticks up his nose every

time he goes to Olive Garden and/or he insults his wife every time she leaves the room while she pretends not to notice and/or in her presence refers to her as his "first wife" even though they've been together thirty years.

2. Maybe your aunt is funny in quiet moments with her friends because like many women her age, she was taught to not draw attention to herself. And maybe she also noticed how men of her generation weren't attracted to the women who spoke out of turn and uttered their own opinions out loud. And certainly these types of men weren't attracted to women who were funnier than them. Women have always been funny. They just weren't interested in sharing their jokes with you. Truth in point, my mom is hilarious. She has also been single since 1974.

But one-nighters and *Totally Biased* are both in the past now. (At least I hope they are. I still have nightmares that I have to go back and headline at the Fat Cat in Modesto, California. And I would only go back to *Totally Biased* if the same Eastern Europeans who keep kidnapping Liam Neeson's family in those *Taken* movies kidnapped my family and told me I had to relaunch FXX's late-night cable talk show slate again if I ever wanted to see them alive.) But when that white guy had me in a room, spewing his idea for how to totally destroy the absolutely and insultingly regressive "women aren't funny" idea . . .

"So we do a fake interview. Where you introduce a producer who has just founded a new comedy channel for women. It's called like Beautiful Funny or something. So you bring this guy out—I could play him—and you start asking him questions. Questions like 'Tell me about your new channel.' And I'm like, 'I'm just tired of people thinking that women aren't funny. So I've begun this new network to feature all the funny women out there.' And me and you go back and forth. We'll figure out some jokes. I'll say I brought a clip to show you an example of what we do. And then you throw to the clip. [DRAMATIC PAUSE FOR MAXIMUM COMEDY EFFECT] And the clip is of two women mud wrestling. Just really going at it. But the funny part is that there is a laugh track dubbed over the wrestling."

Silence. Silence from me. From other people in the room. It was like we all spontaneously had a moment of silence for the death of comedy. Now, look, people pitch unfunny jokes in writers' rooms all the time. You have to because that's how you get to the funny stuff. It's like panning for comedy gold. But the problem here is that when you pitch jokes to a show, they should be at least in the realm of possibility of what the show is about.

White guy continued, "The joke is that this producer claims that he is on the side of women, but he really isn't." He laughs at how funny this is.

Yeah, I got the joke. I got it when I was thirteen, fourteen, fifteen, sixteen, seventeen, eighteen, nineteen . . . and right around twenty-five, I kind of stopped getting it. I would still laugh, but I wasn't really feeling it anymore. And now I don't want to get it at all. The thing that I never seemed to be able to explain to this white guy was the simple fact that if I am trying to do comedy that features intersectional humor—which, you'll remember, is humor that only steps on the toes of the oppressor and not the oppressed, humor that only punches up at the big guy and never punches down at the little guy (or girl)—then I can't do a joke that claims to support the idea that women are funny while at the same time is clearly just an excuse to objectify women's bodies. The whole sketch he pitched was clearly just a backdoor way to show women mud wrestling on the show. A kind of low-level way to get people to stop changing the channel, while at the same time he would get to meet these women who we had to hire to mud wrestle on TV. The whole thing was just gross. And it happened at the beginning of the project. I should have put his head on the back of my door then, but I really wanted to give him the benefit of the doubt, even though it was clear he had no idea what I was trying to accomplish and, more than that, he didn't even care. And it sucked because he was supposed to be my right-hand man. And at this point I knew that my right hand couldn't be trusted.

And how this whole comedy-writer thing works, when it does work, is that the producers and writers write in the voice of who-ever is on camera. It can't work if the writers (and especially the producers) don't care to understand who they are writing for. This white guy didn't care at all. Not a bit. And when I attempted to cor-rect his course by inviting him onto mine, he did what white men often do in this situation: he treated me like I was stupid and like I didn't understand. For more, see: the presidential election of 2016.

And the other thing that sucks about this is that it puts me into some puritanical box that I don't fit into. Because when I say I don't want women mud wrestling on my show, it comes off to this white man (and the white men who listen to him) like I'm so whipped by the women in my life that even though I'm heterosexual, my penis ceases to exist on the plain. Like I'm above the simple pleasures of watching two women mud wrestle. And I'm not. I would love nothing more than to write a bit that slyly supports feminism and allows me to watch women mud wrestle. That would be like the sweet and sour sauce of satire. "THIS IS PROGRESSIVE AND I CAN MASTURBATE TO IT! YAY!" But that wasn't happening here with what this white guy had pitched. He hadn't pitched sweet and sour sauce. He had pitched Clamato. You know, that juice that is tomato juice and clam juice? Yuck. And actually what he had pitched was much worse. Because he had also inserted himself into the middle of the sketch, so he had basically pitched "Clamato: Now with a chocolate aftertaste!"

And when I attempted to point this out he accused me of both not "getting the joke" and not being fun. He literally said, "Can't we just have a good time?" In other words, once again, his white-man lens is the only lens. His definition of fun is the only way to have fun.

It is a classic move of this white guy.

Another time this white guy—a different white guy, but another white guy made from the same mold—was hired to run the show I was on. The show had been pitched without me to a network by a TV producer. That network suggested that the TV producer add me onto the show. The show was pitched to me, and I added my spin on it. It needed to be more inclusive in its scope.

Everyone agreed. At that point I was promised that it would be my show, in my voice, which was essential to me because I had gone fifteen rounds in my last project, and it had collapsed over fights about who was in charge. I wasn't going to do that again. I couldn't take it. My family couldn't take it. My health couldn't take it.

So the TV producer hires a showrunner. "Showrunner" is a made-up showbiz term that means exactly what it sounds like: the person in charge of running the show. In film that person is called the director, but in TV it is the showrunner. Showrunner is a very coveted title. Being a showrunner is the goal of all writers and lower-level producers. But the title has an inherent problem.

Showrunners always refer to the shows they are running as if they own them. They say "my show." It is inherently problematic when the show you are running has a star who has been told it is their show. The showrunner and the star either need to get on the same page really quick, or the showrunner better be fine with sublimating his ego. (I say "his ego" because nine times out of ten the showrunner is a "he," and also nine times out of ten, the showrunner is white.)

Now, this isn't a problem if you are Jerry Seinfeld and the showrunner is your old friend Larry David. You are on the same page because the show came out of a page you two wrote together. It is also not a problem if you are Conan O'Brien and your showrunner is Jeff Ross. Even though you two were initially thrown together, Jeff Ross understands his job is to support the vision of Conan, which is why his and Conan's working relationship has survived different shows, different networks, and the biggest backstab in the history of backstabs that didn't involve an actual stabbing. (Looking at you, Jay Leno!) Those two relationships are aspirational for me at this point. In my few years of working in TV, I have never had the time or good fortune to have those kinds of relationships. I have mostly dealt with the early-days-of-*Roseanne* version of showrunning. It was the showrunner on *Roseanne* who made the insane-sounding observation that Roseanne wasn't doing a good job of playing "Roseanne." It was my showrunner who told me that I needed to loosen up and have more fun . . . and let him hire some ladies to mud wrestle on the set of my progressive comedy show. And now, after that experience, I had a new showrunner in my life. I was determined to make this different, but that made only one of us. This new showrunner liked the old model: "I run the show; the talent shuts up and does as it is told."

Now, he couldn't say that outright. Instead, he took the tactic of saying yes to everything I asked and then just picking and choosing the things he liked, without checking in with me about what he was discarding. It is behavior like this that can lead a person to think that they are crazy. I had moments when I would think to myself, *I know I asked for this. I specifically remember him saying yes. And now here we are weeks later. We've already filmed the whole thing, but the thing I asked for didn't happen. Am I nuts?* When I would remind him of these things, he would inevitably say he had screwed up or forgotten—he was always "really sorry"—or that he had checked with the network and they hadn't allowed us to do the thing I asked. And this wasn't an occasional thing. This was an everyday, all-day-long thing. And it ultimately is about control and his need to control my body and mind. If you think I am making too big a deal about this, then you are most likely a cisgender, heterosexual white man.

He would control things as small as him not allowing me to wear a jacket on camera when I was cold, because he was worried how that would affect the edit. When I said I would happily wear the jacket the entire shoot if I put it on now, because I WAS COLD, he said the network didn't want me wearing jackets too much. This then caused me to go over in my mind how many times I had seen people on TV in similar shows wearing jackets. And in that one move, he had checkmated me. Because instead of him just handing me a jacket, he had instead created the circumstances through which he controlled my body—he was OK with me being cold, and he sent me down a nonsense path thinking about TV hosts and jackets instead of allowing me to focus on the work at hand: making the TV show that I wanted to make.

And he would control things as big as who was hired on the show. So even though I was promoting a brand based on diversity and inclusion, I was working on a show completely stocked with white people. And when I questioned this, I was told that because of where we were shooting, it made more sense for us to have an all-white crew. That made no sense to me because the place we were primarily shooting was a place called the United States of America. But basically the argument was made to me that structural racism was good for business. It is. It is good for America to continue to do its business the way America has always liked its business to be done . . . with little input from people of color, women, and people whose religion doesn't go down the heart of Jesus Street.

But also what having an all-white crew meant for me was that I had to make all the arguments for all people of color whenever a question came up during the shoot. It also meant that I was often on my phone during the shoot calling friends and searching Wikipedia pages to make sure we were producing the content I wanted, because nobody else was as invested in this being right as I was. The showrunner had the crew just invested in *content*. *Content* doesn't care about perspective. *Content* just wants to fill the allotted screen time. I knew that my stake in this was much bigger than just *content*. One of my bigger blowups concerned a segment where I was talking to the police. I actually said, "You don't understand. If I get this wrong, I can never leave my house again." I knew that as a Black man in America I couldn't come off like I was only concerned about content. Message was way more essential. I tried to explain this another way by saying, "Every decision that you make without me that I don't agree with is something I will be confronted with when the show airs." Nobody in the general public ever says, "That showrunner really screwed that show up." No, the fault and the failure always lands on the biggest star around.

And the shittiest thing about this is that I know that the showrunner knew this, but it didn't cause him to change his approach. In the middle of this project I knew that if this thing was to be a success and if we were to get an opportunity to make more content, then I would sooner walk away than go through this again. I had bet on myself way back when I left stand-up to work on my solo show, the main difference being that I was single and kidless back then. But one thing I had learned from watching my mom's journey through the years is that it doesn't matter how financially successful you are: if your job is making you crazy, then you will be a bad parent. I wasn't willing to accept that, no matter how much money it looked like it might cost me. Even with a wife and two kids, I was still willing to bet on myself, and bet against the tyranny of white men always being in charge of everything.

CHAPTER 7

My Awkwardly Awesome Parenting Skills

When I think about lessons I've learned about being a parent, of course I think about things my parents did that I loved, and I then try to replicate with my two daughters, Sami and Juno. One thing my mom did was always talk to me like I was a person. She never talked condescendingly to me because I was a kid. That meant that I always felt like my own person. It meant that when I was a kid I weirdly thought we were basically equals. As if we were roommates, but she was covering the rent and all the expenses. Don't get it twisted though. I had respect for her and I knew she was in charge. But I also knew she was my friend, that I could trust her in all situations, and that she always, always, *always* had my back. I'm modeling the same thing with my daughters. Sami, the oldest one, who is five, knows she can talk to me. She knows I will listen to her ideas. But she also knows I'm Dad. Actually, I'm Dada.

But most importantly to me, I know that me, Sami, and Juno (the two-year-old) are friends. We like hanging out. We like watching TV together. We like playing and reading books. That stuff may not sound like a big deal, but if you are parent, you know that it is not always that way with parents and kids. At the park, I always notice how parents and kids treat each other and interact, and sometimes the parent will look at me with that expression, "Don't you just hate your kid sometimes?" and I have to look back like, "Nope." I don't believe that *all* kids are jerks sometimes, I think *that* parent's kid just might be a jerk. If not, then, where else would adult jerks come from?

I also learned from my dad that men are only truly fathers when they work hard to provide a life for their families. When I was single, I turned down a lot of opportunities in comedy that just didn't feel right. I look back now and know that many of those times I was correct to turn those things down. But I also look back and know that some of those times what I was perceiving as things "not feeling right" was just my fear of the unknown. Now with two kids, while I still remain pickier than others may think I should be, I also regularly tell fear to go waste its time with someone who's not *more* afraid of their kids having to move in with their grandparents because Dad didn't want to do a college gig at Appalachian State in Boone, North Carolina. (I did the gig. It was lovely.) My dad also taught me that when your mom gets old, you take care of her. The one reason that I think my dad ultimately never commented on the closeness of my relationship with my mom was because he had the exact same close relationship with his mom. He would do anything for her. I think my dad quietly respected that I felt the same way about my mom, even though my mom clearly drove him crazy. She's good at that.

But I think one of the greatest lessons I've ever had in how to be a good dad was in the Martin Scorsese film *Casino*. *Casino* is my favorite Scorsese film of all time period. Not *Goodfellas*, not *Raging Bull*, not *Taxi Driver*, and definitely not *Wolf of Wall Street*.

It is *Casino*. I'm not saying it is the best. It's just my favorite. Something about it is a day-changer for me. On Kevin's and my Denzel podcast, we define "day-changers" as a movie that is on TV when you are about to leave the house, and when you notice it, you immediately know that you aren't going anywhere. Basically, the network TNT is the home of day-changing movies. *Shawshank Redemption, American Gangster, Ocean's Eleven* . . . if they come on I'm stopping . . . for at least a little while. With *American Gangster,* I know I'm not going anywhere . . . at least until a Russell Crowe scene comes on. I'm not anti-Russell though. If *Gladiator* comes on, I'm in *at least* until the scene where he screams the thing I've often wanted to scream onstage with a particularly bad audience: "ARE YOU NOT ENTERTAINED?!"

Casino is great for a lot of reasons. You get to see Robert DeNiro in a mob movie where he's not the heavy. You get to see Sharon Stone act her ass off. You get Scorsese's masterful use of music to tell a story. You get to see James Woods play a jerk so effectively that you actually start to wonder if he is even acting. (He's not. Go check out his Twitter.) And you get prime-era Joe Pesci. And it is the scene with Joe Pesci that caused me to file away a future parenting tip. It is during a classic Scorsese montage. The music, the film edits, the narration by DeNiro are all perfect. And toward the end of the scene—which is showing prime-era Pesci doing what prime-era Pesci does, murdering everybody in the general vicinity—the film shows how every morning after committing an evening's worth of felonies, he makes sure he's at home to make his son pancakes and send him to school. There was always something about that scene that I thought was extra sweet considering as a murderer he had every reason in the world to be a bad dad . . . and also every reason to sleep in.

Now, I'm not out in the middle of the night murdering people (I mean . . . I am killing people in the comedian way. I couldn't skip that joke. Sorry). But I do work late nights. I'm not always back at bedtime. And I travel way too much. But I always make sure that when I'm home I am *home*, as in present. And I also make pancakes. But I'm assuming mine are different from Pesci's character's pancakes. Mine are gluten-free, two-ingredient pancakes, made from two eggs and a banana. (Although I do recommend adding a little bit of vanilla, baking powder, salt, and cinnamon to bring up the flavor profile.)

And being a parent isn't all just making sure your kids have money to eat. Especially when you are raising kids of color. As much as Melissa was surprised by the woman who was upset by seeing us on our first date, she has gone all in on raising conscious kids of color. She pays attention to all the details from when her mom wanted to give Sami's first birthday party an animal theme and Melissa said to her mom, "Great! . . . No monkeys" (Her mom understood and said, "Got it!"), to how for the past two years, Melissa has taken Sami and Juno to a Martin Luther King Jr. teach-in in Oakland. That means for two years in a row Sami has made a Black Lives Matter protest sign, before she could even read it. My wife is not fucking around with our kids' survival.

But of course it hasn't always been that way for us. We weren't prepared for how #woke we needed to be when we first had Sami. But we learned very early on that the world outside of us had opinions about our family, and the world wanted in so it could give those opinions to us.

The story I'm about to tell happened more than four years ago. At that point, me and Melissa were new parents. New parents are like newborn calves trying to walk for the first time, except unlike newborn calves, you don't fully learn how to walk in one day. New parents learn how to "walk" every day. Everyday things that you did without thinking are suddenly brand-new.

Our first daughter, Sami, was born in 2011. Just a year later we would be getting ready to move to New York for *Totally Biased*. But that wasn't even a possibility at that point. The whole dad thing just completely blew my mind. The first time I changed a diaper became "OH MY GOD! THIS IS THE FIRST TIME I'M CHANGING MY DAUGHTER'S DIAPER!" And the second time I changed my daughter's diaper became "OH MY GOD! THIS IS THE *SECOND* TIME I'M CHANGING MY DAUGHTER'S DIAPER!" And the third time became "OH MY GOD! NOT ONLY IS THIS THE THIRD TIME I'M CHANGING MY DAUGHTER'S DIAPER, THIS IS THE *FIRST THIRD TIME I'M CHANGING MY DAUGHTER'S DIAPER!*"

Now, let me be clear, I had changed my share of diapers before . . . OK . . . maybe I hadn't changed *my share* of diapers, but I had changed *a share* of diapers. A decent share of diapers considering what I had been before marriage, so a single, childless, basically siblingless, not-an-uncle-or-even-a-play-uncle's share of diapers. Basically, I had changed like forty-seven diapers before my daughter was born. So it didn't make logical sense that it was such a big deal to me to be changing diapers, but it was. Because THIS time it was *my daughter's diapers.*

When you're a new parent, your brain is taking in so much information that it's overloaded, and when you walk through the world—especially with this new baby in tow—you are moving like the aforementioned newborn baby calf . . . a newborn baby calf that is learning how to walk while up to its ears in grape jelly. And also your five senses are on fire. Sights, sounds, smells . . . everything is bigger and brighter. It's like going from a thirteen-inch black-and-white TV to an IMAX movie theater. For the first few weeks, whenever me and my wife walked outside with Sami, we felt like Brooks, that old man from *The Shawshank Redemption* who gets paroled from prison after spending most of his life behind bars. He's completely overwhelmed by everything he sees and asks himself, "When did the world get itself in such a goddamn hurry?" The only difference between Brooks and Melissa and me was that Brooks had been behind bars for decades whereas me and Melissa had only been separated from society for the forty-eight hours it took for us to have that baby. But either way, the effect was the same.

All this is to say, the last thing we needed (or any new parents needed) at that point was to be interrupted by racism.

It was a classic new-parents situation. Me, Melissa, and baby Sami were leaving our apartment in San Francisco to drive down the highway to Melissa's parents' house in Monterey, California. Monterey is exactly like San Francisco minus the things that make San Francisco scary to people who live in places like small-town North Carolina or small-town Texas (or a small town an hour outside of San Francisco).

That basically means Monterey has temperate weather, delicious seafood, and not a lot of Black people. And unlike in San Francisco, Monterey's gay people aren't so GAAAAAAAAY that they've taken over a neighborhood. And instead of having a large proud Latino population in the Mission District neighborhood, Monterey keeps its Latinos next door in the city of Salinas. The Black people of Monterey County are kept in the city of Seaside, which I refer to whenever I'm with Melissa's family as "SEA-SIIIIIIDE!" (Pronounce it the way Snoop Dogg, Ice Cube, and many others said "WEST-SIIIIIIDE!" throughout the '90s. And if you don't know how that sounds, well then you need to make more Black friends . . . or cool white ones.) It always made Melissa and her siblings laugh when I did it this way. There was a sense of "How did you know that's how people say it down here? You're not even from here." I never responded with the truth: I've been Black all my life. I know Black things.

So the three of us are frantically trying to get out of the apartment . . . OK, well, actually only two of us are frantically trying to get out, me and Melissa. Sami is at that point a newborn. She's not frantically doing anything. Newborns are great. They don't do much. They are like footballs that eat, breathe, and poop. As new parents you can get seduced by how easy newborns are. You can take them anywhere: because they don't know how to move, you can just lock them into a stroller. They sleep most of the time. So even though you are exhausted from the lack of sleep (just because they sleep doesn't mean you do), you feel like, "Oh . . . I got this. This parenting thing ain't no big deal." Later, when they start moving and having opinions, you realize that *that* period of time is just evolution's way of giving you a moment to catch your breath before the perpetual onslaught of the next eighteen years truly begins. And don't get me wrong. When I say "perpetual onslaught," I mean it in a good way . . . mostly.

Making a kid is fun. Having a kid is fun (it *is* stressful). Seeing your kid grow up and take on the world can be fun (it *is* scary sometimes). Walking around the world with this new person who sees things differently than you and yet looks like you a little bit and is not afraid to call you out on your bullshit lack of knowledge is fun. ("Why can't we watch more TV? I mean, really, why?" "Because . . . Honestly I have no idea. That is just what parents are supposed to say.") And it's the calling-me-on-my-BS thing that leads to the thing I hate about having a kid: parenting. The ins and outs of raising a child (picking doctors, or picking a school, or coercing someone to eat something that they don't want to eat; explaining why we can't hang out with their "best friend" when you know that their "best friend," another kid the same age as your kid, IS A COMPLETE ASSHOLE!)—that stuff sucks. More on that later.

Back to this road trip.

So me and Melissa are trying to get out of the house so we can make the drive to Monterey. The goal was to surround this kid with grandparents so we can get some non–"What if something bad happens to my sleeping baby while I am asleep?" sleep. Or maybe we could just, you know, have some free time to do whatever we want. Revolutionary stuff when you are parent. But when you are a new parent, leaving the house is a process. Kind of like the process of getting out of your home when it's on fire. You grab everything you think you will need and want, get outside, and then look at each other like, "I FORGOT THE MOST IMPORTANT THING! I HAVE TO GO BACK IN!" Now, sometimes there is disagreement between the parties involved about how important that thing is, since you know that you want to get to the grandparents, and thus the sleep or free time, as quickly as possible.

"Do we really need her favorite blanket? Is it even *really* her favorite blanket? Does she even know it's a blanket . . . or that we put it on her all the time? Does it actually help her go to sleep in the car?"

"Do you *really* want to just leave it here and take the chance that it is the key element in her sleeping in the car?"

"Good point. *I'M GOING BACK IN!*"

The process of getting in the car . . . realizing that you forgot something . . . debating that thing's importance . . . and then going back inside to get it could go on forever, until one of you realizes that while time is indeed infinite, your time on this earth is NOT infinite, and eventually the grandparents will be asleep, *and then you won't be able to leave and your dreams of free time will evaporate in the wind like your dreams of seeing movies when they actually come out.*

So we finally get into the car and start to drive. We get about halfway down the block and Melissa turns to me and says . . .

"I didn't nurse Sami."

"Do you need to?"

"If we want her to sleep for the entire trip down, I do."

"*WHAT ARE YOU THINKING, LADY! NURSE THIS BABY!*"

At the time, we were living in a neighborhood called the Inner Sunset. The neighborhood is right above the historic Haight-Ashbury district, but mostly I knew it as a neighborhood where if you didn't already have a ride at the end of the night, then nobody who wasn't already headed that way was going to take you there. "You're going to the Sunset? . . . Nah, I want to be home in time for work tomorrow." It's not that it's that far from any other point in San Francisco—the city is only seven miles by seven miles, which means the borough of Brooklyn could eat it for breakfast and still be hungry well before lunch—but the perception was that it was waaaaaaaay on the other side of the city.

The Sunset is known for Chinese people, pockets of not-very-talkative Russian people, the famous San Francisco fog, and being the coldest place in the city—in a city already made fun of by Mark Twain for being too cold. This was all pretty ironic because it is also known as where the beach is. But the word "beach" in San Francisco means something very different from what it means in the rest of the world. In San Francisco, "beach" means a cold, bleak place to take a walk and wonder what went wrong in your life.

The Sunset is also right next to Golden Gate Park, which was important for our purposes. We had considered going back into the apartment to nurse Sami, but at that point that would have felt like straight-up admitting defeat. We knew that if we went back into the apartment, we would never, ever come out again. So we decided to head to the park a half block away, pull over on the side of the road in the park, and nurse Sami there, because since we have officially driven the car there, we are technically *on our way*!

So we did it. As Melissa finished up nursing Sami, she said, "We're low on gas. Let's drive around the corner to the gas station and then head out."

"OK." *Sounds good to me,* I thought. And then she dropped the bomb.

"Can you take Sami on a walk to the gas station so she can get some fresh air?"

File this under parent logic. She was talking about a thirty-second walk. I really didn't see how this walk was going to positively affect Sami's life in a profound way. But I had also learned that things like this were not battles worth picking. If Melissa thought this walk was important, then let's do it!

As I got to the gas station forty-two seconds later—apparently I was wrong about it being a thirty-second walk—I was carrying Sami, simply wrapped in her (maybe or maybe not) favorite blanket. I tried to figure out where to stand at the gas station so I could be out of the way of the constantly moving cars . . . *because I am a great dad*! I also kept my eyes out for Melissa and our car. Sami wasn't asleep yet, so she just quietly cooed on my shoulder.

A car pulled in—not our car. A white woman got out—not our white woman. She got out of her car, began to pump her gas. While she was pumping her gas, she looked around like everybody does when they are pumping their gas. That look of "What am I supposed to do with this free time that I didn't expect to come my way today?" In the midst of that process she looked over at me and Sami. The white woman's face turned all like, "Awwww, what a cute baby!" I smiled back full of pride as if to say, "Yup. I made this!" The white woman's face suddenly froze in a rictus. The kind of jolted expression that read like, "I shouldn't have smiled at that old lady, because she then fell on the icy sidewalk and rolled into traffic and was hit by a semi."

At that point—having seen white people freak out about things, only to later learn that not much was happening to be afraid of (for more information, see: white people's reaction to rap music in the early '80s)—I just moved out of her line of sight to a different section of the gas station, but before I could get too far, the white lady had a question for me, a question that I will never forget . . .

"Do you work here?"

What? And when I say "What?" I want to be clear. I didn't say "What?" out loud. Because this lady had stopped me (and Sami) in my tracks.

"Do you work here?"

I thought, *Is that what her problem is? She thinks I work here. And she thinks that a gas station is an inappropriate place for Take Your Daughter to Work Day? Well, fine, if that is her problem, then I can fix it easily and quickly by saying* . . .

"No."

I started to move, realizing I didn't want to continue the weird conversation with this lady. I was sure now that she knew that I *didn't* work here and that our conversation was done . . . but just like a late-night infomercial—"Wait! There's more!"— she wasn't done with me yet. She was twisting her mouth to say something else, but I could tell she was struggling with what that thing was.

"Well . . . I just don't think you should bring a baby to a gas station."

As soon as that sentence hit me, I froze like an overworked PC. And I don't mean I froze as in my steps froze. I mean my brain froze. Complete lockup. For a couple of reasons. First of all . . .

I had never heard that sentence before. It rolled over and over, back and forth in my mind. "I just don't think you should bring a baby to a gas station." Think about it. Most of the sentences people say to you in a day, you have either heard them before exactly . . . or you have heard some version of them before. "Did you go to the store?" vs. "Are you going to the store?" are basically remixes of the same idea: "Take your ass to the store, dammit!" (I don't know why I have created an abusive relation-ship in my example, but you get my point.)

Think. How often do you hear a sentence that you've never heard before? It's pretty rare. The Apple corporation is probably America's top creator of new sentences. Think about the first time you heard, "Have you seen the iPad?" Unless you worked for Apple—or are one of those freaks who doesn't work for Apple but keeps up with every little hint of a development—you were probably frozen for a second before you said, "What the hell are you talking about?" Apple has done that to us with iPads, iPods, Apple TV, and that U2 album that most people didn't want. "What do you mean it's already on my phone? I don't want it on my phone! WHAT DO YOU MEAN I CAN'T TAKE IT OFF???"

Those sentences were tricky the first time you heard them because they probably had words in them that you had never heard before. But this sentence didn't have unfamiliar words. It just had words I had never experienced in the same sentence. Check it . . .

"I just don't think you should bring a baby to a gas station."

It's like a Zen koan in that it poses the unanswerable ques-tion. But then it's MORE mischievous than a standard Zen koan because it doesn't actually even ask a question. And yet it is clearly a statement in search of a meaning.

"I just don't think you should bring a baby to a gas station."

On a good day . . . a day when I'm not a brand-new parent . . .

I could just walk away and ignore this. Again, I was living in San Francisco at the time. Ignoring people is part and parcel of living there, whether it's your neighborhood homeless guy who you just gave a dollar to yesterday and really don't have time to get back into that discussion about "What's reeeeeeeeeally happenin', though, maaaaaaan?!" or whether it is the millennial canvasser for Greenpeace, or Planned Parenthood, or one of the many people asking you to sign a petition for one of California's many inscrutable ballot initiatives.

"Would you like to sign a petition to get Proposition 37 on the ballot? It's a proposition to end all propositions on ballots."

But this wasn't a good day. This was a "new parent, everything is new" day. And one of the key elements about being a new parent is that you kind of feel like you may be doing everything wrong. So when this absolute stranger . . . this complete and utter nobody to me before this moment . . . this sack of DNA molecules . . . says . . .

"I just don't think you should bring a baby to a gas station."

I got scared.

I immediately thought to myself, *Oh shit. I have totally screwed up. I have brought my baby to a gas station. I didn't know that was a thing! I knew I should have read those stupid baby books that everybody gives you! Oh God! What have I done???*

Then my brain went further . . .

Well, what are you supposed to do when you take a baby to a gas station? What do people do? Is there a special place next to gas stations where you are supposed to drop off your baby? What's it called? How does it work? Is it like dry cleaning, where you drop off your baby and they give you a tag that you have to turn in when you come back to get your baby? Who runs these places? Are they licensed? Who gives out the licenses? Is it the same people who own the gas stations? I don't want Exxon or Shell in charge of who watches my baby! Have I really never seen a baby at a gas station?

Then, in one brief moment, my whole life began to flash before my eyes. Normally that happens when you're dealing with a life-and-death situation. But I was just dealing with an aggressive-white-lady situation. Instead of trying to remember all the good things about my life that I was going to miss or things I would regret, I was trying to remember every single time I had ever been to a gas station, then looking around in that memory to see if I recalled any babies at any gas stations. My first memory was when I was with my mom . . . at a gas station . . . I was a baby . . . *WAIT A SECOND!!!! I WAS A BABY AT A GAS STATION! THIS IS NOT A THING! YOU CAN TAKE A BABY TO A GAS STATION!*

Goddammit! I had let this random lady get into my head over her bullshit.

So then the question immediately becomes, what is this lady actually saying when she says, "I just don't think you should bring a baby to a gas station"? Now that we have determined that the sentence is meaningless, what is really going on? I'll tell you. (Thanks for asking.)

Racism.

This lady sees a Black man with a (white-looking) baby and her overseer detector went off. *Something is wrong here . . . But I don't quite know it yet . . . I'll have to investigate.*

But here's the thing . . . She didn't actually need to investigate. I'll admit that a man carrying a baby is not something you regularly see when you pull into a gas station, but again THIS IS

SAN FRANCISCO. San Francisco stakes its reputation on *stuff you don't see every day*. That should be the city's motto: "Come to San Francisco! And then go home with a story!" San Francisco is home of the Folsom Street Fair, a street fair that is pretty much just about naked people and BDSM gear. That's it! And again, *it's a street fair*. You could literally be walking down Ninth Street some Sunday in September, turn right at Folsom Street, and end up in the middle of a leather daddy sandwich, so a man and a baby at a gas station shouldn't even hit your radar . . . unless your radar is looking for Black people.

But fine. Let's say this lady was coming in from Marin County, which is over the Golden Gate Bridge. Marin is mostly known for being the place where the rich liberals and/or the rich showbiz people live. Liberals like Sean Penn, the late Robin Williams, members of Metallica, George Lucas, and even a young Tupac. A lot of those liberals moved there to get away from the weirdness of San Francisco—weirdness like Black men at gas stations with babies. So let's say she was coming in from Marin to go to the farmers' market to get her favorite dinosaur kale from her favorite organic farmer, and on the way back she stopped to get gas and saw me and Sami. Let's say that happened. And maybe she had just received an email forwarded from her aunt who lives back east in Toledo that warned of Black men who were showing up in gas stations with white babies and then were tossing the babies to people pumping their gas, and when the people caught the babies, the Black men would steal the people's bank information and social security numbers and sign them up on Fox News' email list!!! Let's say all that had happened. Now what?

You can be suspicious of something and mind your own damn business at the same time. I'll show you . . .

That's weird . . . Welp, nobody is breaking any laws. Nobody seems bothered by anything, nobody's asking for help, and it's got nothing to do with me, so I'll just keep it moving.

That's how you're supposed to act in that situation. That's how I was brought up to act. As Richard Pryor famously said, "Don't start none. Won't be none."

Well, white Americans regularly start "some," and then get surprised when there is "some"!

This lady had decided that she needed to insert herself in our lives. Had no real reason to . . . but then just kicked the door down anyway with the unneeded (but, yes . . . brand-new) sentence "I just don't think you should bring a baby to a gas station."

At that moment, Melissa pulled up in our car. I was at once relieved and frustrated that I was going to have to get in the car in a "mood" about some bullshit. Melissa got out of the car, began pumping gas, looked over at us, smiled, and said . . .

"Cute baby!"

Now this would not have been a big deal except for the fact that the lady—who still hadn't gotten any satisfaction from her baby–gas station salvo—was now going into full-on low-key panic mode. I could tell that she assumed from the way Melissa addressed me and Sami that we didn't all know each other. Because Melissa hadn't gotten out of the car and said, "Hello, my lawfully wedded husband and our biological baby!" this lady assumed that we didn't all know each other, which speaks to the invisible nature of mixed-race families. And this lady was also clearly afraid that Melissa was falling for the Black Man–White Baby Gas Station Scam. The look on this woman's face was, "Didn't this woman get the email I got? I really need to get her email address so I can put her on the Needlessly Worried White Person listserv."

I looked at Melissa and tried to communicate with her without talking. The message I was attempting to communicate was, "YOU NEED TO ACT LIKE YOU KNOW US! THIS WHITE LADY IS TRIPPING OVER HERE!"

These are the kinds of messages that Black people send to each other all the time. We don't have to talk. We don't even really have to know each other. It all goes back to the Middle Passage. Hundreds of West Africans below the deck of a slave ship were separated by language and culture (despite what Sarah Palin said about Africa being a country) and all united under one question. That question was simply, "WHAT THE FUCK IS GOING ON? How did this happen? Yes, Africans sometimes sell each other into slavery, but it's not like this! This is brutal! At least it can't get worse than this!"

And then they landed. And then it got worse.

So it was necessary from early on that Black people learn how to communicate without speaking directly to each other. And that's how you get the Underground Railroad, Negro spirituals, and Black people who don't know each other passing each other on the street and giving each other the nod of unity. For the first couple years that me and Melissa dated, when she noticed me nodding at Black dudes in public, she'd ask, "Do you know him?" "Nope." And then I'd smile broadly as if to say, "Ungawa! Black Power!" And then sometimes, I'd also think to myself, *Wait . . . Do I know him? . . . Wait. That was Philip from Penn.*

So needless to say, I had been trying to train Melissa how to read my "looks." It just felt like a necessary part of dating me. And a necessary part of my/our survival. Because sometimes there's not enough time to say, "We need to run right now! Don't ask why. We'll talk later." Sometimes there's barely time for a look that says, "Run!"

Obviously, teaching Melissa how to read my "looks" was an imperfect science. It took time. And at this point, even though we had been together for years, Melissa was at a Rosetta Stone Level 3 of Black Facial Expression Comprehension. Which meant sometimes I would look at her to say, "That cop is looking at me!" And she would say, "Do you need to go to the bathroom?"

Right now, at this gas station, we were having an "It looks like Kamau needs to go to the bathroom" moment as I was trying to communicate, "Look to your right. This woman is having an overseer moment. Make a tiny Underground Railroad so me and Sami can escape to freedom with you . . . or at the very least, we can escape to Monterey with you."

But Melissa just kept smiling with her "cute baby" look. And the woman to her right kept getting more visibly agitated. She kept looking back and forth from me and Sami to Melissa. So finally I said, baby still in hand, "This is my baby. That's my wife. We. Got. This."

What I really wanted to say was, "There's a white lady already in charge of this area." But I didn't have the guts that day. Also, honestly, I didn't want to risk escalating the situation. I just wanted to get in the car and go to my in-laws' house, and I knew that if we didn't hit the road soon that Sami wouldn't sleep. I didn't want any extra drama. I had plenty. I didn't want to be Black in that moment. I just wanted to be a dad.

It was the first time I ever felt like I had to defend my family's right to exist. It wouldn't be my last. It was the beginning of realizing I needed to become an activist, and not just in my work.

Awkward Thoughts
about 11/9

The night of the 2016 presidential election, there was an idea that most of the people that I know and follow on Twitter had. With all the many "last straws" that many of us assumed would break Donald Trump's gold-plated back, most of the people in my world just KNEW that it was time to finally prepare for the coronation of Hillary Clinton. Finally. Even people I knew on the left who didn't have much—or any—love for Hillary and/or especially Bill. (Bill had become like milk two weeks after the expiration date. "Wow! This used to be so good. What happened?") But around five o'clock on the West Coast on election night, sitting in my home with my wife, our kids, and a few other friends and their kids, we realized . . . Uh-oh. It started when we saw that tweet from Hillary Clinton's Twitter account. The tweet that was kind of like, "Hey, everybody! Thanks for coming to my party, but I'm going to head upstairs for a little bit and take a nap." The feeling in the room was so different than in 2008.

In 2008, the mood was so different. Again, I was at home. Some of the same friends were in my home as would be there four years later. Mike was there. And so were Jeremy and Kili. Mike is married with a daughter now. As are Jeremy and Kili. And I live in a different home. Instead of a house in Berkeley, it was a two-bedroom apartment in San Francisco. We were all just hanging out and having fun while the results rolled in. Don't get me wrong we were nervous. Even though all the polls said Barack was likely to win, we didn't trust them. (Back then I guess you *could* trust them.) My mom, who had voted early in Indiana, even came into town because she wanted to be with me when the final results came in. She wanted to be with me so we could celebrate Barack's victory together . . . or she wanted to be near me in case I decided we needed to hop in a car and head for the most convenient border (Canada would be closer, but Mexico is an easier drive) in case McCain won. McCain sounded like a dangerous choice to us back then. He seems so tame now. But if you think we were being hysterical about what that administration would have done, I have four words for you: Vice President Sarah Palin.

It is fascinating how different election night 2008 was from election night 2016. In 2016, it was like slow death waiting for the absolute final results to come in. But in 2008, when the polls closed in California, Barack Obama was immediately declared the winner. Everybody in my apartment actually missed the call, because everyone had thought the count was going to go late into the night. We didn't think there would be any rush to judgment. We figured the powers-that-be would not want to leave any vote uncounted, unscrutinized, or any chad undangled. But at like 8:02 p.m. PST, I looked at the TV and said, "Hey . . . Why is everybody cheering and celebrating? . . . Wait . . . What? He won already? Oh . . . Oops. And yay!"

But back to 2016. I assumed that once eight o'clock hit and the polls closed in California, something would happen. But nothing changed. Me and Melissa, Jeremy and Kili, and Mike were watching while our kids played. We didn't mean to have a 2008 reunion. It just turned out that way. And it felt right. These were friends who had seen the transition from a bunch of people who were just hustling to pay rent and pursue some dreams . . . maybe . . . to people who had careers and children. It was a great group of people to be with that night. But then it started slowly, joylessly changing. We had kids in the room who couldn't really put their fingers on what was happening, but they could tell things were getting tense and weird.

Suddenly we weren't laughing. Melissa was crying. Melissa, like many other women, had gone from Bernie supporter, to somewhat reluctant Hillary supporter, to full-on "I'M WITH HEEEEEEEEER!" Whereas I was more like, "Where I clearly see the differences between Trump and Clinton, I also know that due to the electoral college and its insistence on maintaining some slavery-era policies in modern-day America—combined with the fact that as a Californian I live in a reliably blue state, and combined with the fact that I believe the two-party system is far too simple a choice in a world this complicated," I was like, "What's up, Green Party?" Don't worry. Melissa hated hearing about that too. But to be sure, I was voting for the Green Party and not Jill Stein, the way many Democrats and Republicans in the 2016 election were voting for their party and not the person at the front of the ticket. Two of the most unpopular candidates in recent memory. At least not since World War II, when in Germany, Hitler ran against polio in a primary.

The next morning after Trump won, I flew to Santa Barbara, where I was performing *The W. Kamau Bell Curve*, the very same show that had turned my career around in the first place. Between breaks from doing *United Shades*, I was still performing at colleges all around the country. And I mean ALL AROUND the country. Places like Garden City, Kansas; Kutztown, Pennsylvania; Auburn, Alabama; Boone, North Carolina; Orange County, California; Kingsville,

Texas; Muncie, Indiana. These are not exactly home games. Sure, I also do liberal bastions like Stanford University and Vassar College. But I am out there in the field. So I was not surprised by the Trump victory at all. But that didn't mean it wasn't a bummer.

That day after the election I was like the walking dead. Me and Melissa hadn't slept much or well at all. I arrived at the school, and I needed Red Bull and coffee in rapid succession. I was also scrambling, because at its best, *Bell Curve* responds to the news. In large part, I couldn't do the same show that I'd done even *the week before*, even though I already had some Trump in it. For weeks, I'd been saying to the people who watched the show, "Hey, everybody! You gotta do something. Everybody's gotta do something. It's worse than we all think." But now everything was different. Even the calls I'd made the day before the election didn't make sense anymore. Instead of "Call me right away!" it was now, "Call me as soon as you are capable of focusing on regular life again, because you are of course currently contemplating the nature of existence right now. In other words . . . First, cope with the fact that Trump is president. Then, call me back."

For many people, especially my friends who lived in New York City, there was a strangely natural connection to 9/11. Obviously 9/11 is a tragedy that in America is singular in its devastation, but a few of the aftereffects were the same—like it felt really quiet outside that day, like it did the days after 9/11. Me and Hari had scheduled a recording of our podcast *Politically Re-Active* that evening of 11/9, and we opened like it was the day after 9/11, with quiet reflection instead of the normal jokey-bombastic opening that we usually did. It just felt more appropriate. Not because we are snowflakes who couldn't handle it. But because we are humans who experience a wide range of emotions. And we both knew that Trump's election made a lot of people feel like they needed to be prepared for an attack. Many Arabs and Muslims were right to be worried, as the postelection hate-crime stats prove. People knew their lives were (and are) at stake. That they could be killed or kicked out of the country and not allowed back in. Or just thrown in prison and not even be allowed to leave the country. That quiet was people realizing that it was all on us now. We have to put the pieces back together ourselves. We have to come together. Like we never have before. Whatever this thing is that is called "the left," it has to start putting its money where its tweets are. And those of us who are used to watching other people put their bodies on the line—see the 1960s Civil Rights movement and the disproportionate amount of Black people therein, and see the modern-era Black Lives Matter movement—have to put THEIR bodies on the line. They have to use their privilege as a shield.

But the afternoon of 11/9, I had a show at a college, which is always a little strange, to have a comedy show when the sun is still out, but often that's how colleges work, especially commuter schools, like the one I was at that day. More people are there during the day to go to a show, because at night they have jobs and families, and they don't live anywhere near campus. I was frantically screen-grabbing pictures from the Internet, updating references in the show that felt ancient even though they were only wrong by a few hours. I wanted to make sure the people who showed up *knew* that *I knew* what had happened. It was a lesson that Chris Rock taught me during *Totally Biased*. Always go new over old. If something happens that is more interesting or relevant than the thing that is in your act, then go with that new thing. Do your job and write a new joke. And now I was falling down a new shit hole!

One click quickly led to another. My head was swimming in the possibilities as it was also freaking out by how close it was getting to showtime.

I'm going to miss Michelle! I needed a picture of Michelle and Barack!

I also need one of Sasha and Malia!

But if I get that, then do I need a more recent picture of Sami and Juno?

I need a picture of that KKK newspaper that endorsed Trump.

Wait a second . . . That article was written by Thomas Robb? The same Thomas Robb who I "ate lunch with" on the first episode of United Shades of America? Oh God! Now I need a picture of him. That means I have to tell that story. WILL I EVER STOP TELLING THE STORY OF HOW I SAW A CROSS BURN????

I was scrambling, much like I had when Barack had won eight years ago, when I was doing *Bell Curve.* At this point I was onstage with my computer, using the school's Wi-Fi while the audience was outside waiting to come in. I couldn't stop. I yelled out in the darkness of the theater to whomever was in charge, "Just tell me when you absolutely have to let the people in, and I'll stop." And while I was doing this my Twitter was blowing up. Fifteen hundred students had left Berkeley High to protest the election. Berkeley High is so close to where I live that when they turn on the lights for the Friday-night football game, I can turn my light off to save money on electricity. So when their students walk out in protest (which happens somewhat regularly because the world sucks and we are Berkeley), my house can participate without leaving home. But this time I wasn't there. I wanted to be there, and I wanted to be there with Melissa and the girls. I wanted to follow the lead of those students the way that I had followed them the day I left home to run some errands but instead ended up in a Black Lives Matter rally that walked from Berkeley High through downtown Berkeley to the center of the University of California, Berkeley's campus.

But this day I was just in Santa Barbara, watching tweets go up, and pictures go up, showing me what was happening blocks from my home. So now, at the same time I was making the show, I was also sharing tweets about Berkeley High, trying to show solidarity. That felt as important (actually more important) than the show I was about to do in minutes.

Martha texted me to see how I was doing, and I told her that it felt like when I did the show after Obama's election in 2008, but upside down. I was feeling the same levels of franticness, the same levels of anticipation, and the same levels of my stomach being in knots. And I also remember being afraid in 2008 like I was in 2016, but in 2008 the fear was specifically centered on the show itself. Specifically, how was I going to be able to encapsulate everything that had happened in America around the election of Barack Obama, the first Black man to be the president of the United States of America? There was so much excitement and hope. Who was I to try to talk about it? I was afraid I would fail the audience. But in 2016, in Santa Barbara, I wasn't afraid of failing the audience. I wanted to do well, but I was way more worried about how America had just failed itself and it was clearly going to get worse. On some level, performing the day after the election felt like if that group of musicians on the *Titanic* had said as the boat went under, "Naaah, let's keep playing. It'll be fine."

It was a full audience at Santa Barbara. And that's not always true at college shows. College shows pay a lot more than shows in clubs or regular theaters, but in return you have no idea how the show will go down. I've done shows for handfuls of people where I made thousands of dollars. And when they booked the show at Santa Barbara, they weren't imagining these circumstances. The bookers knew it was going to be the day after the election. But back then, they, like most of America (based on the popular vote) thought it was going to be Hillary. I could feel the energy was tweaked from everyone I dealt with at the school. I knew I'd be stumbling through the show, but because of everyone's energy I knew it would be OK. Everybody was stumbling around me. When the show began I told the audience that this wasn't the show I normally do. That I just wanted to talk. They were totally with it.

The show was about 65 percent or 70 percent what I normally do, but even those parts felt different. It all felt hyper-real. Stuff that normally gets laughs didn't, and not because it was bombing. It was because the audience was listening more intently than they normally do. Also it was because I was saying things more intensely than I normally do. I'd been talking about this all for months, but it meant more today. And I knew it would mean even more tomorrow.

I could see in the audience the thing that usually happens in my show was happening but to the extreme. The people in the audience were having different experiences while they were all watching the same show. Many of the white audience members had a sort of Droopy dog expression of "I'm sorry" but also "What am I supposed to do? I'm just a simple white person who was born with a silver set of privileges in my mouth." And mixed among them were the people of color who spent major chunks of the show cheering and clapping. And I don't think it was because I was great. They were using this experience as a reckoning, as a cleansing, as a catharsis. There were shouts throughout the show from the POCs. *"Yes, you tell them! TELL! THEM!"* At the end of the show the audience stood and applauded, but I knew they weren't applauding me. They were applauding to energize themselves to go do the work. The work that those of us who have higher hopes and expectations for this country than this country has of us know what we have to do . . . and quickly . . . and fervently. There was a reception right after the show. I talked to the students and faculty for about an hour. All the conversations were deep dives in short periods of time. In like thirty seconds a person would tell me their greatest fears for the future, their most petty angers about the present, and their hopelessness that felt eternal. And each white person asked some form of the question white people asked, "What do we do next?" I don't know. Go talk to your white people who voted for Trump. "But I don't know any white people who voted for Trump." Yes, you do. Because all white people are *your white people*. Just like Ben Carson is my people, even though I don't know him, have never met him, and every night I go to bed and pray to Black Jesus that I never do.

It wasn't the most fun show I ever did. I had certainly not "killed," as comics say. But I didn't feel ashamed because it wasn't as funny as it usually is. It had a lot of laughs, and it ended funny. Although the ending was much harder for me to get through than it usually is. No matter what changes I make in the show it always ends with me talking about Sami and Juno. (Well, at least it has ended that way since there have been a Sami and Juno.) The show has always ended on my personal life. *Bell Curve* has evolved from being about "my white girlfriend" to "my white wife" to "my pregnant white wife" to "my white wife and my Black and mixed-race daughter" to now "my white wife and my two Black and mixed-race daughters." Near the end of the show I put up a picture of Sami and Juno. And one this day, the day after the election, the picture, which I normally look at with a father's pride, nearly broke me onstage. I had to force back tears to get through it. I'm not afraid to cry onstage, but I could feel that this was going to be one of those big ugly, snot-nosed cries—like the kind Black people have when they watch the film *The Color Purple* and Celie and Nettie start slapping hands with each other and singing, "You and me will never part . . ." I knew it was going to be sloppy like that—not a dignified Denzel Washington–*Glory* tear situation—so I held myself back, but it was close. That show was the beginning of a two-week trip of college gigs and filming for *United Shades*. And if there was ever a time that I didn't want to be away from home, it was then. I wanted to be with my family. I wanted to be around those two awesome little future ladies. I wanted to help Sami understand. She knew that we didn't like Donald Trump. And she said she didn't either. If you ask her why, she says, "I don't like his rules." To me that's as salient a point as most of the talking heads on cable news have made. My daughters were both born during the Obama presidency, but they're going to grow up during the Trump presidency. Most likely they'll have way more Trump memories than Obama ones. That's awful. Kind of like I have way more Reagan memories than Carter memories. But Trump makes Reagan look like Martin Luther Gandhi Winfrey Jr.

One of the conversations I had after the show in Santa Barbara was a long one with a white student. He was probably around nineteen. He said, "You said that good white people need to have white pride . . . but what does that mean? What do we do?" I told him that he had to figure that out himself. He had to put himself out there and try new things. He wanted more. He wanted marching orders. I gave him a name of some organizations. I told him about SURJ, Showing Up for Racial Justice, an organization for white people, run by white people, about . . . white people. SURJ was trying to be all the conversations people should have been having: about America's history of racism, about the toxic nature of white privilege, about the need to use your white privilege effectively for racial justice, and much more. At least that's what I think is going on. I've never been to a meeting. White folks need to be able to have these awkward conversations on their own. In the same way that my mom wasn't inviting white people into her living room when she and her friends were railing against "crackers." I told this young white man that he needed to start calling the worst elements of his people out on the carpet, the way Black people have always called out our Hall of Shame. I pointed out a Black man standing nearby and said, "If I had said something up there on that stage today that was crazy, that Black man—even though he doesn't know me—would have pulled me aside and asked me what the fuck I was talking about. I told him that white people need to do the same thing. He wasn't buying it. He said he was, but like a shopper who realizes his eyes are bigger than his wallet, I think he left his shopping cart at the register and ran out the door.

Every person of color knows what to do now that Trump is president. Because we grew up in this life. People who are full-time activists and organizers are saying, "I just need to do more activism and organizing. I need to get up earlier, and I'll just have to go to bed later . . . And I'll skip going out for lunch. I'll just eat at my desk." Those people know that they just need to do more of what they were already doing.

But those of us who know that the Trump thing hit us out of nowhere need to finally do something real. And once you do something real, every now and then you have to check yourself to make sure you are really doing something. It's like going to the gym—you need to keep setting new goals as the current work gets easier and easier. And don't just be satisfied with what you're already doing. If you're thinking, "I put a filter on Facebook that takes the words 'Donald Trump' out of my Facebook feed, and I deleted my friend from high school who I don't want to talk to anymore," that's not doing something. That didn't help. Everyone needs to be honest with themselves, figure out what they're doing, and figure out how to do more.

The biggest thing that white people can do is really get comfortable having conversations about race and racism in this country. And the way you get comfortable is that first you get awkward by putting yourself in the middle of it. Read books—actually read Ta-Nehisi Coates's *Between the World and Me* instead of just putting it on your shelf. Read Michelle Alexander's *The New Jim Crow*. Go to websites like *The Root*, *Colorlines*, *Very Smart Brothas*, *Blavity*, and also *The Establishment* and *Indian Country Today*, and read Lindy West, wherever she's writing at currently. And support the artists, TV shows, and films that support the America that most Americans want. Don't take any of these choices for granted.

And finally, white people reading this book right now (and the people of color who believe in them and want to help them), you need to confront the white people in your life who you think don't exist but actually do exist. I talk to liberal white people who say, "I don't know anybody who voted for Trump!" But of course you do. We all know that guy at work who we don't want to talk to.

Everybody has that uncle at Thanksgiving who they don't want to talk to. Even I realize I have to start having these conversations with my wife's cousins. I know I have to put myself on the line in ways that I didn't before.

People of color are used to putting ourselves on the line like that, because we put ourselves on the line every time we walk out of the house. White people have to get used to putting themselves on the line in uncomfortable situations. Some of that is joining organizations, but some of that is actually having real conversations with other white people in their lives about what America actually is and what most of the country knows it should and could be.

Every parent reading this right now knows that at your kids' school they are surrounded by people who are different from you. There's no way you're not surrounded by voters of all different stripes, even some people who voted the same way you did but for different reasons. And at some point, bring up gun control or underfunded public schools or parents being ripped form their kids over nonsensical immigration laws. People say you should avoid talking about politics, but I say lean into it: the full Sheryl Sandberg. Lives are at stake.

When people say you can't change people's minds, they're usually just talking about one conversation that didn't go well. Well, change doesn't happen all at once. It's often glacial. We like to think that people change like Edward Norton's neo-Nazi character in the movie *American History X*. Edward Norton goes to prison and after a few sessions of doing laundry with a Black guy, Norton's character does a complete 180 on race relations. Like, "Well, if that Black guy can fold T-shirts, then the entire Black race can't be that bad!" It's a perfectly fine movie, but it's never gonna go down like that in real life. People get caught up in one bad conversation on Facebook, and then they never try again. Do you think the Civil Rights movement would have worked if they gave in that quickly? If they thought after one conversation, "Well, THAT didn't go well? I guess we should just get used to not voting and never being able to live up to our dreams." Fuck that! They said, "Bus boycott, sit-ins, civil disobedience, arrest us all, get strength from the Black church, join the Nation of Islam, march on Washington, and do this by all means necessary!"

And I know people can change. When I met Melissa's grandfather, I could tell I was not exactly what he expected from his granddaughter's future husband. It was just a feeling. A very strong feeling. A very strong feeling that lasted years. It made sense, even if you just looked at a picture of the two of us together (not that those exist). At best we looked like an unlikely buddy cop comedy from the early '80s. *"This summer . . . Jimmy Walker and George Burns in . . . Who's Idea Was This?"* Melissa's grandfather was a septuagenarian, Sicilian-American, Fox News addict. And I was . . . me. The only overlap we had was the Food Network. And that was not enough to build a relationship on.

For years we were like two people who worked in the same office building but on separate floors. But over the course of years, I kept showing up. And we kept being around each other. I didn't confront him or push him, I was just there. And he saw me and his granddaughter building a life together. And he saw this completely unsuccessful stand-up comedian get one TV show, and then another TV show. And at the same time he saw one adorable great-granddaughter show up and then another one. And he saw how hard I worked to provide for my family, which I can only assume reminded him of himself. And then one day out of nowhere he was asking me about my travels and he offhandedly said, "I keep telling my friends that I can't keep up with my grandson. He's all over the place . . . In New York every other week it seems." It took me a minute to realize that the grandson he was referring to was me. For a kid who grew up without any grandfathers (my mom's dad died when I was a baby, and my dad's father died before I was born), it was a big deal. I held some tears back that day too. Change is possible. It is not always loud and fast, but it can happen. And one small change doesn't always mean everything changes. Because after much consternation, "my grandfather" voted for Trump. But it's fine. Pops lives in California. Neither of our votes really counted anyway.

CHAPTER 8

My Awkward Failure as
a Late-Night Talk Show Host

B y 2010, I was doing my solo show, *The W. Kamau Bell Curve,* pretty regularly at small black-box theaters around the country and I was occasionally getting some local college gigs. It was one of my main sources of income and it was changing (or giving me) my reputation. I wasn't in the clubs as much as I had been, and some comics had fun with the fact that I had gone the one-man-show direction (the theory being that when comics aren't successful, they just talk slower onstage and do it in theaters). But I knew that I wasn't doing that. I was using all my chops as a comic and adding new ones. I knew I had gotten way funnier in the process and the material was way more interesting. One night, one of my comedy heroes, Marc Maron, was in the Bay Area and came to see the show. By this point it was really doing well. It had become a well-oiled machine, but was still organic and had a feeling of *who knows what happens next* that is a main ingredient of Bay Area art.

La Peña in Berkeley was packed with about two hundred

people. I had a good show that night. And afterward from the stage I gave Marc a shout-out. Marc was experiencing his own new level of success through his runaway-train hit podcast *WTF*, so a lot of people in the audience knew who he was. It felt like his presence was knighting me as someone who was relevant.

After the show, we talked briefly and he said he had enjoyed it. Marc was not known for giving the love, so I took it as a high compliment. I had been a fan of Marc's since the early days of Comedy Central, when he hosted *Short Attention Span Theater*. And by moving to San Francisco, I had become a part of a scene that he had a lot of love for, and where he had spent significant time. He just seems, now and then, to have a base level of respect for comics from San Francisco. It's like he knows we're all a part of a secret society. I had a bunch of friends on the SF scene who were good friends of Marc's. And as they all slowly made the move to LA or NYC for (hopefully) fame and/or fortune, I kind of got grandfathered into being friendly with Marc. He'd occasionally pitch me jokes in the greenroom before he went on—the highest honor a bigger comic can bestow on a younger comic. He let me be on his podcast, and he put me in a couple of pilots he was working on. I was never sure why. I just assumed it was because he considered me to be in his circle.

A couple of years later, when I was trying to figure out what to do at a key moment in my career, I decided to call Marc, which I wasn't really sure I should do, because we weren't really friends like that, but he had given me his number. He was happy to talk to me, which meant a lot at the time because I didn't know what I was going to do, and I needed help making one of my first real showbiz decisions. He boiled it down to one sentence: "Show business isn't your parents." He meant that all of us comedians needed to stop seeking validation from these execs, producers, managers, and agents who at the end of the day are only thinking about us if we could make them more money at the start of the next day. I have thought about that advice ever since.

Marc's advice led me to sign up with my manager, Keri. Keri was running a small boutique management company. I had a chance (at least I was being led to believe I had a chance) to sign with a bigger management company. But I just trusted Keri. It also helped that she managed Kevin Avery as well. And Keri basically hand-delivered me to William Morris Endeavor, WME. When WME had a meeting with me saying that they wanted to sign me, I didn't really believe it. William Morris was so associated with Hollywood that even people who knew nothing about showbiz had heard of them. They were the most mainstream of the mainstream. And I was a thirty-seven-year-old late-blooming stand-up comic. At one point I got so suspicious during the meeting that I said, "I want you to sell me . . . to me. Tell me why you think I should be here." This wasn't what I suspected they usually heard from unsigned talent in these meetings. But they took the bait, and one of the agents even mentioned Bill Hicks by way of comparison. Bill Hicks was a deep-cut stand-up comedy reference. Bill had been a '90s-era Lenny Bruce before Bill died of cancer. I knew I wasn't as good as him, but I did enjoy the smoke up my ass. After the meeting, me and Keri walked to the car and talked about whether or not I should sign with them. I had no other choices and they had been great. We called them from the parking lot and signed right away!

I was still doing the *Bell Curve* regularly, and by 2010 I had replaced Martha as director with Paul Stein, who I had met at the Comedy Central Stage in Los Angeles. Paul was in charge of the theater that Comedy Central used to produce cheap pilots and to scout new talent. *Tosh.0* and *Mind of Mencia* had come out of that theater. Paul was a more technical director than Martha. He understood lighting and theatrical pacing better than either me or Martha did. At the time, we both relied on our good instincts (now Martha has caught up in that regard), but Paul had actual theatrical training and experience. I thought he would be a good addition to the show. I also let Paul know that Martha would still be developing the material with me. Martha—like Jason and Melissa—is my person, to put it in *Grey's Anatomy* terms. It was bigger than the show. Paul said he understood. He helped get the show into theater festivals and submitted it to writing programs, and he let me do the show in LA at the Comedy Central Stage three times—two more times than most people get—in front of talent managers, execs, other comics, writers, producers, and fans. Each time I thought it was going to be my BIG BREAK! It never was, but all the shows were good, and I was getting more confident that there was a place for me in showbiz.

At the first show down there, I met . . . Let's just refer to him as Runner. He was a white comedy writer and producer. Runner called me the next day to tell me that one day I would have a TV show. OK, whatever, TV guy. Me and Runner had met over the phone about a year before, when he tried to hire me and Kevin Avery for another project, which fell apart. So I knew he did know things, but I was determined not to have smoke up my ass this time. But I have to give him credit; he was right.

In October 2010, I was doing the *Bell Curve* at a one-off show at the Upright Citizens Brigade Theatre in New York City. UCB had become the new epicenter of all that was cool in comedy at that point. And when I say "all that was cool," I mean "cool" as defined by recent liberal arts school graduates who also happen to be white and usually also liberal, although sometimes that liberalism feels like it is in name only. Many of them were the kind of white liberals who say things like, "I can say 'nigger' because I know that it's wrong to say 'nigger.' I'm not saying 'nigger' the way a real, like, Republican racist from the South would say 'nigger.' I'm saying 'nigger' like Lenny Bruce said it. The way Louis C.K. says it . . . I'm saying 'nigger' ironically . . . NIGGER! . . . Why are you getting so mad? If you don't get the joke that's *your* problem." UCB, in the twenty-first century, was occupying the same hip space that Second City had taken up in Chicago in the '60s. A similar space to the Improv in New York City in the '70s. The way that the Groundlings and UnCabaret had been cool in LA in the '90s at the same time Luna Lounge was cool in New York City.

And UCB had done one very important thing. They had torn down the "wall" between improv comedy and stand-up comedy, which was as cold as a cold war could be, even though many people spent time on both sides of the wall. Before UCB, when improv performers talked about stand-up comedians, it was the same way BMW drivers talk about Toyota Camrys. Well, UCB had enough of that nonsense. UCB integrated stand-up and sketch the way the Civil Rights movement had done with the lunch counters at Woolworth's. Although the lunch counters at Woolworth's had way more Black people.

The irony that I was doing the *Bell Curve,* a show where I promised to "End Racism in About an Hour," at one of the whitest places in Manhattan was not lost on me. Once again, I was a Black without borders. Me and Keri had worked hard to make sure that the audience that night was not mostly white. UCB wouldn't let us do the "bring a friend of a different race" ticket offer that I had used since the beginning of the show's existence, which was usually my way to guarantee a mixed audience. Instead, me and Keri just had to hit up organizations and friends to get the correct people in there. But it worked. UCB felt like my crowd that night. I had a great show. And like most comedians, I can hate on my performance even if others think it was good. But this one felt good.

Afterward, I was backstage, standing around, feeling pumped and proud—I still haven't found a productive way to use that energy. (It's the kind of energy reserve that leads comedians to drugs and drinking problems . . . or even to too-many-desserts problems . . . and worse.) Then suddenly as I was standing there, talking to one of my new agents from WME, Keri walked backstage looking like she had just seen a ghost. And just as I took in the look on her face, I saw the person floating behind her. It *was* a ghost: the ghost of my comedy future, Chris Rock.

I would later come to understand that look on Keri's face as the way many people react to Chris's presence, especially the first time they are around him. When people weren't expecting to see him and he suddenly apparated, like out of thin air, they would often look dumbstruck, like all the adults in those Christmas movies where they find out that Santa Claus is real. Kind of like, "Oh shit. I thought you were pretend. This is so exciting!!!"

Chris walked up to me and at first made small talk. "My name's Chris . . . Nice to meet you . . . Runner told me about you . . . blah, blah, blah." As if to say, "Let's try not to act like I'm one of the biggest comedy stars of all time." And then he got down to it . . . sort of . . .

Chris: "Yeah . . . you were funny . . . Take it for what it means. I think like eight guys are funny and you're one of them."

Lemme be clear here: the whole thing had a "but whatevs" quality to it. Like he was aware of his power to blow people's minds and he didn't want to just give it away. I respected that. But of course I would have preferred, "I HAVE FINALLY MET THE ONE! THE ONE TO TAKE THE SWORD OF COMEDY FROM ME AND CONTINUE TO SPREAD THE WORD!" He didn't say that. And he wouldn't have said that. Chris still very much carries and wants to keep that sword. He works harder on his act, even when he's not on tour or about to go on tour, than most comedians who need to be funny, or risk not putting food on the table. (Like me for instance.)

Then he asked a couple of questions.

Chris: "Where do you live?"
Me: "San Francisco."
Chris: "Move. There's nothing there. You have to move where the action is. I was just talking to Seinfeld and . . ."

I would come to learn from Chris that by "nothing" he meant, "There's no showbiz there." And he really didn't think you could be a real comedian and not be where the real showbiz was—i.e., New York City or LA. I knew I wasn't moving anytime soon. We had fairly recently found out that Melissa was pregnant with Sami, and we weren't about to have that baby in a new city where we couldn't lean on/exploit our friends and family for help.

And then he asked the question that still haunts me.

Chris: "How old are you?"
Me: "Thirty-seven."
Chris: "Don't tell anybody that!"
Me: . . .

Outside I think I laughed, as people are wont to do around Chris. One, because he is very funny, even in casual conversation, and two, who doesn't want to say that they shared a laugh with Chris Rock? But inwardly I was thinking, *Oh shit. Am I really too old? Am I really too old to be funny? What the hell am I supposed to do about that?*

All my life I had felt like the youngest. I was the youngest on both sides of my family by a mile. That feeling was mostly gone by age thirty-seven, but I still thought I had a little of it. It was gone in one moment, because here was Santa Claus in real life saying it was so.

Chris talked with me for a few minutes. Coulda been two minutes. Coulda been twenty minutes. Coulda been a year. I don't really remember. One thing I would later discover is that Chris-time does not hold to our simple human understanding of time. He is like a wizard. He can change the air around him. I would soon come to learn how powerful his magic is and how much he could change the air around me.

A couple months later I got a call from an unlisted number on my phone. Unlisted numbers on my phone were one of two things: my dad or a bill collector. Either way, it was going to be a long phone call with a bunch of questions about money and why I didn't have more of it. Not to say my dad wasn't supportive of my career, but he had sacrificed all artistic ambition to provide for his family. I knew he'd been a professional photographer, and my mom swears he wrote poetry during their courtship. But now he was a businessman. And he had money. He liked this much better. And he saw a lot of himself in me: I was a struggling artistic type who would soon learn the value of the dollar. Sometimes I felt like he was just waiting for that "money gene" to kick in. It still hasn't really. And sometimes I wish it would too.

But this phone call was not from him or from a bill collector.

I answered the phone with a tentative "Hello." And the voice came back, "This is Chris Rock."

I immediately responded the way you should if you want this big career moment to be a good story later. I replied, "No, it's not."

Yes, I really said that. My first phone call with Chris and I basically called him a liar. Not totally my fault, though. Runner had indeed told me that he thought Chris was going to call me. (Me and Runner had stayed in touch.) And I was so blown away by the possibility that I had told my wife and a few friends, including my friend Jeremy. And if I had one friend who was going to fuck with me over this, it was going to be him. Not fuck with me in an asshole way, but more fuck with me in a "Don't get too big for your britches!" way. It says a lot about my expectations for mainstream success at that point, that even when I knew from a good source that Chris was going to call me, I still assumed that I was being screwed with.

But I wasn't being screwed with. It was Chris Rock. In my defense, it wasn't the *Chris Rock voice*. He wasn't doing it that day. It wasn't the voice of the guy who panther-walks the stage and performs jokes like rap songs, with hooks and choruses. This voice wasn't dropping truth bombs with screamed punch lines. This voice was the voice of a dad with two kids who was taking a moment from the Bulls' playoff game to reach out to me with an idea. But at first he had to let me know that it was really him.

> Chris: "Don't be the guy who doesn't believe it's me when I call him and then one day I'll be sitting on Leno talking about how I tried to help this guy out and . . ."

He was turning up now. He was segueing into character. Now he was beginning to sound like "CHRIIIIIIIIIIIIIIIS ROOOOOOOOOOOOOOCK!"

I jumped up from where I was sitting. And where I was sitting was in the office building of Pandora in Oakland. Pandora had decided to get into putting stand-up comedy on their platform, and they had recruited a few Bay Area comedians to help refine the process. All the comedians were young and fairly new to comedy, except for one: me. I had swallowed hard and decided to apply for the job. Melissa was due to give birth to Sami in a few months, and I got that kind of money-grubbing greed that only comes from being a new parent. This wasn't the kind of empire-building greed that my dad had, but it was close enough for him. He was happy I had a regular job.

I jumped up in the middle of the office. It was the end of the day, so only a few people were still around. One of them, Dave

Thomason, was one of the young comedians. Dave is a tall, good-looking, hilarious white guy. I liked him from the start. And I especially liked him because, despite all of his wins, he didn't take advantage of it in his act. He had what I refer to as the classic "goofy white guy" act. That's not a slam at all. It just describes a genre of comedy that is best seen through the act of the stand-up legend Brian Regan.

I walked over to Dave and mouthed the craziest sentence I had ever mouthed in my life: "It's . . . Chris . . . Rock." Now, I didn't need to tell him who was on the phone. Maybe I was humblebragging, or maybe I just wanted a witness in case the world came to an end during the middle of our phone call. But either way, I immediately ran into one of the conference rooms and closed the door.

After the small talk about the Bulls' playoff chances was out of the way, Chris uttered the phrase I would never forget (and, strangely enough, occasionally come to regret):

"I want to do a show with you."

Before I had a chance to even begin to say yes—or, even more important, before I had a chance to ask what "do a show" meant—Chris was off to the races.

> Chris: "Un-famous Black guys never get TV shows. Un-famous white guys get TV shows all the time."

And although I knew that wasn't strictly true (anybody remember Chris Spencer's brief tenure hosting the late-night talk show *Vibe*?), I knew that the overwhelming numbers were in favor of what Chris was saying: Conan O'Brien, James Corden (un-famous in the United States at least), Zach Galifianakis, Tom Green . . .

Chris: "You're gonna need help. But maybe you don't want my help. Maybe you already have somebody helping you. Maybe you're like, 'Fuck this guy . . .'"

I wasn't like, "Fuck this guy." Although one day in the not-too-distant future I would certainly have days when I might have wanted to say that. And I'm sure he had days when he at least thought, "What the fuck is wrong with this guy?" But today I was in my head going, STOP TALKING SO I CAN SAY YES!

He eventually did take a breath. I said, "Yes, I want your help." And then, a couple weeks later, I flew to New York City to meet with him at his offices with Runner. Runner was a part of the mix because he had "discovered me," according to Chris, and because they were boys, according to me. Runner had also worked on a bunch of Chris's projects. It seemed fine to me at the time, but there were also signs of things I needed to watch out for. Like it immediately struck me that both me AND Runner were starstruck by Chris. It made sense for me to be starstruck. I had just met the dude. But I didn't understand why Runner was so taken aback by Chris. Runner had worked for Chris on and off going back more than ten years at that point. Why the hell was he nervous and fumbling his words like I was? And what was that going to mean if this show actually happened?

Months later. We have the show. After too many bad titles to remember, one day me, Chris, and Runner got on the phone and came up with *Totally Biased*. It is weekly on FX and doing fine. Not great, but OK-ish. Luckily we were getting cover from our getting too much criticism from all the criticism Russell Brand was getting. He also had a weekly talk show on FX, and because he was famous, he was getting waaaaay more attention than I was. And his show was quickly proving to be a beautiful mess. Russell is an extremely talented comedian and actor, but he clearly was bristling against the confines of what was done in a late-night talk show. (I could already relate.) But instead of doing what I was doing, which was basically keeping my head down and hoping I could figure it out from the inside, Russell was wielding his great big comedy phallus to blow up the show's format and redo it seemingly every few shows. First it was a twenty-two-minute monologue. Then it was a more traditional talk show with a guest but squeezed into twenty-two minutes. Then it was an hour-long talk show that was live. If Russell's show was going down, it wasn't going down without a fight. I admired that.

Totally Biased wasn't that dramatic on camera. Once we found a format, we basically stuck with it: topical monologue, field piece or correspondent piece, and finally a guest. Occasionally there would be a small piece of comedy to close out the show. I hated that. There was never enough time to do anything interesting in that time, and we inevitably just threw to a wacky video, the kind I never watched when I was left to my own devices. But overall, the feedback I was getting was that it was working . . . ish.

Chris had basically hand-sold the pilot to FX. HBO didn't want it. Chris was their guy but not on this. At that point HBO was good with Bill Maher being their political comedian of choice. This was years before John Oliver came along and said, "Are you sure that's enough?" So Chris just had lunch with the president of FX, the televisionary John Landgraf. And John agreed to do the show. No pilot. No "Let's make another pilot and see!" No "Let me meet Kamau first." None of the usual (and reasonable) things people do before a big deal like this. John went with his gut . . . and of course he also went with Chris's gut. If Chris was my foul-mouthed Yoda, John was like my Southern Californian version of Obi-Wan Kenobi. John is one of the coolest people I've ever met at that level of showbiz. And, John, I'm sorry I didn't do better with the show.

The pilot that Chris showed John that sold the show was funded by Chris. Runner ran the show on the pilot, hiring everybody and leading the creative direction. That second part was the main problem. I was already having to talk Runner into my ideas instead of him just helping me execute them. He had his own ideas about how he wanted the show to be, which was of course necessary, but I was getting the feeling that he was just paying lip service to my ideas. And I usually gave into his because, one, I wanted to get along with everybody. My fatal flaw, I would come to discover. And two, he was the TV guy. Maybe he knew something I didn't. He often did, but not always. Not even close.

Plus, once the show was up and running, I had noticed another issue with his leadership style. Runner would often say he hated meetings. He would rather things just sort of happen. I also think he hated any kind of checks and balances, because without oversight he could hide out better. And nobody would notice that he wasn't doing much. He had never run a show before, but that didn't stop him from acting like a chief. He could be abrasive and generally had what I would refer to as an old-school *Mad Men*–era management style. This filtered into his comedy pitches and writing. I grew exhausted from telling him that I didn't want to say the word "bitch" in a joke. He thought I was being politically correct. I thought I was trying to not be an asshole. That's not all we disagreed on.

I will say that *Totally Biased* was incredibly hard, and there were days when my soul felt like it was being sucked out. I felt like the show was a meat grinder. It was my job to put meat (comedy) into the grinder, but if there was no meat that day, then I just had to put *myself* in the grinder. It was making me crazy. I'd come home not wanting to talk to Melissa about my day, and not wanting to play with Sami. I was just done. Sucked out of emotion. Those challenges almost led me to abandon my family because I felt I had to pick one over the other. (And maybe I did have to pick. I think I picked my family.) And as much as the quality of work that came out of *Totally Biased* varied wildly, especially once we went daily, I know that the best work that came out of *Totally Biased* will forever be some of the best work of my career. The first show, possibly, had the best work I personally did on the show.

Our show was scheduled to premiere on August 9, 2012. On August 5, a white supremacist army veteran killed six people and wounded four others at a Sikh temple in Oak Creek, Wisconsin. He then killed himself. As tragic as it was, I knew we needed to figure out a way to talk about it on our show. I just wished our show had maybe more than zero episodes into our run at the time. People always ask me, "How do you make jokes out of such tragic events?" The key is two things. One, you don't make fun *of them*. You make fun *out of them*. I'm not going to mock a victim, obviously. But if I can find an angle that feels like it reveals something . . . or even poses a question, then that's what I will do. And what helps you do that is the second thing: Figure out how you feel about it. What makes you angry about it? What makes you confused about it? What is ridiculous about it that nobody else is pointing out? I heard Jerry Seinfeld once say that if you are angry about something, then there's a joke in there somewhere. We could talk about it on the show. We just needed an angle.

We were all sitting around the table in the writers' room, trying to figure out how to crack this. There was talk of just skipping the story altogether, but to me that felt dishonest, especially on the very first episode. I knew we needed to stake our claim. I knew I needed to show that we were not a regular late-night comedy show.

But how? We were sitting around the table, the writers, at the edges were some producers, Runner, and me. Also, Vernon Reid, my hero and the guitar player from Living Colour, was there. I'd been a huge fan of the band since Rob played them for me in high school. And when I first got on Twitter, I had noticed that he was on there, too. And he was super interactive with fans. I took a chance and invited him to a show when I was performing in New York City. Surprisingly, he came to the show. Afterward, we talked and weirdly became friends. Eventually we started a podcast together, *The Field Negro Guide to Arts and Culture*. Technically, we are just between episodes right now, even though it has been years since we've regularly posted them. Vernon has become more than a hero. He is mentor, a friend, an older brother, a guide, and an example of a Black man living his Blackness his own way and thriving (two Grammys and dozens of other accolades). But on *Totally Biased*, I brought him in to do what he was known for, write and play music. He wrote the theme song. I still can't believe that happened. And that day, he was just hanging out and he ended up pitching ideas into the mix, too.

What came out of that room was that we noticed that multiple respected people in the media and government (including presidential candidate Mitt Romney) had confused Sikhs, the people who were killed at the temple, with sheikhs, an honorific title for Muslim men. It basically came down to many non–Muslim Americans thinking that anybody who looked Middle-Eastern-ish and who also wore anything on their head—anything that wasn't a baseball cap or a cowboy hat—had to be a Moos-lim. Many Sikhs wore turbans. Some Muslim men wear turbans. Also Sikh—when pronounced the way most of us Americans do—sounds like "seek." In fact it is pronounced more like "sick." We ignorant Americans also pronounce "sheikh" like "sheek" when in actuality it is pronounced more like "shake." While we were talking about the story we kept tripping over "Sikh" (like "seek") and "sheikh" (like "sheek").

At some point, somebody said that maybe that's all we can do. Maybe we can just get people to know the difference between the two. The idea clicked instantly. It was nearly perfect. It was topical to the story, but we weren't going to have to spend time going through the tragic details in ways that would make it too hard to tell jokes. And we were writing something that we legitimately thought would help the situation. And as a (tepid) Christian, I would be demonstrating intersectionality in the first episode. And that's how "Sikhs vs. Sheikhs" was born. The day of the taping I knew that if this hit, we would then really be establishing ourselves. After a few warm-up jokes, the segment started out solemnly enough, but quickly I pulled up a huge grid on my giant screen. And I went through the different people in order to separate them into categories.

Picture of a man in a turban—"This is a Sikh."

Picture of a Muslim man in a ghutrah, the traditional headress of Saudi men—"This is a sheikh."

Pointing back and forth—"Sikh . . . Sheikh . . . Sheikh . . . Sikh."

Picture of a Muslim man with his head uncovered—"This is a Muslim . . . A Muslim can be a sheikh . . . but not a sikh."

At this point, people in the audience were laughing and clapping along in the sort of collective agreement that says, "Thank you for saying something!" But now we really needed to turn up the juice and make it funny. "This is Shaq. Shaq is a Muslim but not a sheikh or a Sikh." "This is Nile Rodgers. He is from the band Chic!" "This is Mark Zuckerberg. He's a geek!" "This is Shaq drinking a shake." "This is Shake Shack [picture of the restaurant]. This is a Sith [picture of Darth Maul from *Star Wars: Episode I—The Phantom Menace*]." It devolved into silliness. And the audience loved it! And at the end, it took one more turn . . .

"And the one thing that all these people have in common is that none of them should be shot."

We went to commercial at that point. Looking back, I realize I should have said, "None of them should be shot . . . Except for Darth Maul." Just to sell the fact that we were a comedy show first. But that's the big thing with late-night TV, you only get one chance with jokes. As a stand-up comedian you can constantly tweak and rewrite. In late-night you better get it right the first time. Because you will hear about it the next day if you don't.

I don't miss it. The pressures were so hard for me to deal

with, and sometimes I felt like I was crumbling from the inside out. And the guy I was supposed to turn to for support, Runner, was not there for me, mentally, spiritually . . . and sometimes physically he wasn't in the building.

Much of the best work on the show actually came from the other writers who were comics. Aparna Nancherla, Janine Brito, Hari Kondabolu, Guy Branum, Eliza Skinner, Kevin Kataoka, my old friend and mentor Dwayne Kennedy, and others would perform pieces on the show that they had pitched. It gave the show a band-of-misfits look and attitude that I liked. Women and men of different ages and different races, and, most interestingly, different types of comedy. Best of all, it gave me a break from being on-screen. And it introduced new voices to America— well, at least to the small sliver of America who was watching. It was clear to the audience my best work wasn't in the studio. My best work was out in the world.

The pieces that were the most successful were my man-on-the-street segments. Whenever I got to go out in the field, I could do and say whatever I wanted. It was freeing. I often wished that I was allowed to *only* do man-on-the-street pieces. Me and the Universe didn't realize at the time that a producer named Jimmy Fox would soon be conspiring to make that happen.

I didn't even want to do the MOS pieces when the show started. I hated those when I saw them on TV. It usually featured a smug person with a microphone making fun of a person who just happened to be foolish enough to interrupt their day to talk to a stranger. I didn't want any part of that. But Chris insisted. "You have to get out there and mix it up and meet the people." He was right again.

The first segment we did was on the NYC stop-and-frisk policy.

I was super nervous. The policy was on everybody's mind in NYC. Stats had come out that showed that cops were overwhelmingly stopping and frisking Black and Brown people. And the stats also showed that overwhelmingly these people weren't guilty of anything . . . other than being Black or Brown. I had no idea how I was going to make that funny. Runner had the writers pitch a bunch of extra gags and props that we could use to bump up the humor (a fake cop, a break-dancer).

But at the end of the day, the best part was just my conversation with the people. They told their stories. I listened. And we would share the kind of gallows humor that oppressed people have learned to use to get through the day. It was that simple. That piece, another one called "Who Would You Gay-Marry if You Had to Gay-Marry Someone?" and one called "Do You Have Anything to Say to a White Guy?"—where a new writer, Ethan Berlin, came out on the street with me so people of color could tell a white guy (Ethan) anything they wanted. It was so funny—again, some of the best work that I had ever done.

When the show was weekly, we would usually work twelve-hour days, or more, from Monday through Thursday. Thursday was the taping day, and then on Friday there would be a little bit of breathing room. It was a much slower day. People would spend time basking in the glow of the previous night's show. And big groups would go out for long lunches. I enjoyed the break in the schedule too, even if I wasn't always able to go out on those long lunches. As the host AND an executive producer, I always had stuff to do. Friday was the day to catch up on the stuff I hadn't gotten to all week. It should've been the same for Runner, but it usually wasn't.

In my opinion, Runner liked the camaraderie of comedy writing as much if not more than the comedy writing itself. He liked the hanging out and the inside jokes. It was very much a men's club in his office. And if any woman dared speak up or cut her eyes as if to say, "Seriously?" he would then put the blame on her. "Come on. We're just having a good time." In my opinion, it's behavior like that that keeps some women from wanting to stay in those rooms once they deal with all the sexist shit that it takes to get in there in the first place.

As the show continued, it proved to be like a major league baseball player who hits home runs but bats .225. It was clear that the show had potential, but the problem was raising its batting average. One Friday in the middle of this, I was in my office, physically and emotionally exhausted. We had just barely gotten the show on the air the night before by the skin of our . . . the skin of MY teeth. The feeling in the air was that "Friday feeling." The big question of the day? Was the big lunch going to be at that fried-chicken place or Red Lobster? The big question was not: What the fuck are we going to do with Mike Tyson? And for my money that was the ONLY question worth asking.

We had a shoot in a hotel room with the extremely controversial former undisputed heavyweight champion of the world, Mike Tyson. Why did we have a shoot with him? Well, because one of the people at FX knew Mike and had excitedly let me know weeks before that Mike had agreed to do something for *Totally Biased*. Yay?

Now, look: When I was young, I was a huge fan of boxing champ Mike Tyson. And through living during the time of his rape conviction, I had come to understand something very important when you are a man: no matter what time someone shows up at your doorstep, that person hasn't agreed to have sex until they have verbally agreed to sex. More than once . . . Throughout the experience. But after Mike served his time in prison, I had sympathy for his struggle to figure out what was next for him. I knew he was far from a perfect story of prison rehabilitation, but I also knew that he wasn't the ignorant buffoon that people (including comedians who often employed him to this effect in their projects) made him out to be. But one thing I didn't know was what the fuck to do with him on *Totally Biased*. I was trying to establish us as a hyper-relevant and extremely left-leaning comedy show. I was trying to, as the *San Francisco Chronicle* put it, "Make *The Daily Show* seem like something your dad watches." It wasn't easy with Runner walking around like HE was the dad that the *Chronicle* was talking about.

I didn't know what to do with Mike Tyson. So I did what I had been told to do: I turned to the writers. So I (well, me and Runner) asked the writers to pitch ideas for the Tyson shoot, which was only a few hours away. There wasn't a ton of time, obviously, so they only had like an hour to get something together. Now, if we had any type of real organization, we would've had these ideas done already, earlier in the week, but we didn't. Thanks to Runner's laissez-faire management style, every piece of comedy on the show was an all-hands-on-deck situation. There wasn't much breaking people into teams. It felt like everybody was trying to do everything. Which tends to make it always feel like the boat is sinking.

After the writers wrote for an hour, they turned in their pitches. And then most of them went off to the long Friday lunch.

I sat in my office with Kevin and we went through the packets. I quickly realized that there was not much there. Good ideas, sure, but many of them required props that we either weren't going to be able to find in an hour OR, more importantly, those props would lead to the kind of comedy that I didn't like but that Runner enjoyed. I still don't envy the writers' difficult position. They were serving two masters for most of the show. And by the time I "fixed" that, it was way too late.

The reason why it was only me and Kevin in my office was that Runner was out to lunch too. Again, he loved a good hang. And that was certainly going to be more fun than figuring this piece out. I was at this point beginning to panic. I was about to meet with one of the most famous knockout artists of all time, a man who had a more violent past outside the ring than in it, and I was taking up his time for what looked like nothing. Fuck. Me.

An hour or so later, Runner moseyed on back from lunch with the writers. The only reason he came back when he did was that it was time to go to the shoot. I let him know that we had nothing, and I wasn't happy. Then Runner got to do what he loved to do: ride to the rescue like the cavalry. Again, when everything is chaos, the person who screams, "EVERYBODY JUST CALM DOWN!" can look like the voice of reason, when in reality they are just slowing things down even more.

I grabbed Dwayne and told him to come with us. Dwayne had known Chris Rock since way before Chris was "CHRIIIIIIIIS ROOOOOOOOCK!" Chris would often say that Dwayne was funnier than him . . . back in the day.

Dwayne made things funnier just by being around and talking. Kevin was coming too. The four of us—me, Runner, Dwayne, and Kevin—hopped on a subway, and I stood about five feet from them as they scrambled to come up with something. When we got to the hotel room where we were shooting, the camera crew was all set up, waiting for us to tell them what we wanted. We still didn't know. I was in full-on quiet panic mode. The guy from FX who had set this up to help this little show he believed in was there too. I made small talk with him while I tried not to jump out the window (something I would increasingly spend time doing).

Eventually the four of us squeezed into the bathroom and started to come up with some loose ideas . . . Too late. Mike had arrived. When I walked out of the bathroom and up to Mike, I was being trailed by Runner, Kevin, and Dwayne. Mike looked like he was afraid of what he had gotten himself into.

The VP of FX introduced me to Mike. I remember noticing how huge Mike's head is. And I couldn't help but get the feeling that maybe he was keeping it together the same way that Mark Ruffalo as Bruce Banner, aka the Hulk, does in *The Avengers*. When Captain America wonders how Banner stops from being angry and turning into the Hulk, Banner responds, "That's my secret, Captain: I'm always angry." Mike seemed at peace on the surface, but I imagined currents roiling underneath. So the last thing I wanted to say was, "Hello, Mr. Tyson! We have brought you here today to completely waste your time!"

Runner shoved some hastily scribbled and mostly illegible note cards in my hand. I sat down on the couch that me and Mike were to share. I shoved the note cards under my butt, knowing that even if they contained the greatest idea in the history of comedy, it was too late now, and I just decided to talk to

Mike. It was over an hour long. It was winding and weirdly seemed like therapy for him and a fishing expedition for me. But it was a good conversation. He is an interesting dude.

I'd like to tell you that our conversation turned into the viral hit of 2012, but you know it didn't. And the fact that that Mike Tyson clip was never put online, even though it is one of our few comedy segments featuring an actual celebrity, should tell you how much I liked the end product. Don't get me wrong. Mike was great and patient and funny and thoughtful. But *Totally Biased* was a mess. And it was revealing itself to be messier and messier. That day, I left the shoot completely broken. This show was clearly never going to be MY show under the current conditions. Something snapped in me. I was done trusting Runner, but that didn't mean I didn't still regularly acquiesce to what he wanted. You know the expression: "Any port in a stumbling late-night talk show."

Things never got better with me and Runner. In fact, they only got worse. But despite all that, we got through the next thirteen episodes, and things developed a little bit of a structure and schedule—much of that due to Kevin, who was hired as the head writer. And then I was invited to a swanky dinner with Chris; Obi-Wan himself, John Landgraf; and one of his vice presidents. They lavished praise on the show, which was strange and didn't happen often. And then John Landgraf made an offer I couldn't refuse but definitely should have . . . or at least I should've thought more about. And to be clear, it wasn't really an offer, or even a question. By the end of that meeting, I had been informed that *Totally Biased* was going daily beginning the next September. It was moving to a new network, FXX. And I was going to be the face of that network. None of that stuff was on my bucket list, even though it sounded like stuff I was supposed to want . . . except for the FXX part. Everyone on *Totally Biased*, including Chris, was suspicious of this "new network."

After a not-really-too-restful summer break, we were back and we were gearing up to go daily. FX had sent out several of their executives to guide the launch. I was doing press for it every morning. Chris was around a lot more to help and also to "help." "Help" consisted of lots of good, legitimate advice but also taking us all out to lunch when we were already behind, because there was no schedule in place that was being followed. Runner should have handled it, but he often threw up his hands like, *What do you want me to do?* Umm. Your job.

But the day had come when we were doing the premiere of the daily show, and everything was even more chaotic than usual. This was not a good sign for us for going on four days a week. Anticipating that, I had flexed some muscles and gotten Martha hired as . . . Well, I didn't give a shit what her title was. She was the floor producer, but really she was just there to get my back at all times and also to help talk me off the ledge . . . soon to be an everyday thing. Usually it happened right after lunch . . . the lunch I was too nervous to eat.

But the cake was pretty much baked at that point. I, Sisyphus, pushing the TV boulder uphill every day. My body was breaking down on me. I had had cataracts surgery a couple years before. (Yup. Cataracts at thirty!) I had a plastic lens in my right eye. Well, the lens had begun to slip and I was basically blind in that eye, making reading the teleprompter, something I was never good at, even harder. My right eye was not great at its best. It was lazy and wander-y, probably from too many years of sitting up against the TV screen when I was a kid. Also I was losing friends on the show, and no one was having any fun at all. One day Hari came into my office. It felt like he had been "elected" by the writers to confront me about being a bad boss. Me and Hari had been super close before the show, but I was losing him too. I knew he was right, but I didn't know how to change things. I was in deep survival mode. I broke down in front of him and Martha. *"I just want to go home. I just want to go home."* Even at my lowest point it wasn't lost on me that I was basically quoting Daniel-san from *The Karate Kid*, a movie I had always related to but felt damn near prescient now: a dude moves to a new town full of optimism but can't stop the daily butt-kickings he is getting. And as much as I have serious enmity toward Runner, I know it is ultimately my fault. If I had been better at my job, onscreen and off-screen, then the show would have been better. But I also knew that I needed someone in Runner's role who had my back. I'd read both of TV critic Bill Carter's books on NBC late-night talk show wars. In one he described the relationship that Conan O'Brien had with his showrunner, Jeff Ross. It was described that when Conan left the room, everyone knew that Jeff spoke for Conan. Whatever Jeff said was straight from Conan's mouth or might as well be. I didn't have that with Runner. In fact, I had it on good authority that sometimes when I left the room Runner would say things like, "I don't know what his problem is."

So two months later, the show was canceled. Obi-Wan John got me and Chris on the phone and politely and regretfully broke the news. The weird thing for me was that even though we were canceled, we still had to do our last two shows of the week. I had mixed feelings. But none of them involved wishing it would continue. What very few people knew was that I had actually called my lawyer a couple days before to see if I could get out of my contract. I didn't have Dave Chappelle's money or contacts, but I was seriously thinking about getting away to my own personal South Africa.

And at the last taping, when we had gotten the very last line that I needed to say, and Arthur, the Zen-like stage manager, signaled that we were actually done, the audience clapped. The applause had the sense that the audience knew it was really over-over. Many of the people in the audience seemed truly moved. We had built a loyal following in just about a year. I respected and appreciated that. But I was burned out. The writers turned and looked at each other. Maybe there was hugging. Maybe there was smiling. I don't know. My gaze was narrowing. The one thing I do remember is Dwayne Kennedy getting teary, which I had never seen in the nearly twenty years we had known each other.

And as a Sikh man wandered the stage dressed like Captain America not knowing what to do (I had decided to cut his on-stage bit at the last minute due to me not wanting to actually try to be funny anymore), I beelined off the stage to the elevator. It was basically a straight shot of about twenty-five feet. Martha looked at me as if to say, "Do you want me to come with you?" And I looked back at her as if to say, "FUCK YES!" And we rode that elevator down to the ground floor. I don't remember exactly what was said, but when I think about it, the words that come to mind are . . .

OHTHANKYOUGOD!   OHTHANKYOUGOD!
OHTHANKYOUGOD!   OHTHANKYOUGOD!
OHTHANKYOUGOD!   OHTHANKYOUGOD!
OHTHANKYOUGOD!   OHTHANKYOUGOD!
OHTHANKYOUGOD!   OHTHANKYOUGOD!
OHTHANKYOUGOD!   OHTHANKYOUGOD!
OHTHANKYOUGOD!   OHTHANKYOUGOD!
OHTHANKYOUGOD!   OHTHANKYOUGOD!
OHTHANKYOUGOD!   OHTHANKYOUGOD!
OHTHANKYOUGOD!   OHTHANKYOUGOD!
OHTHANKYOUGOD!   OHTHANKYOUGOD!
OHTHANKYOUGOD!   OHTHANKYOUGOD!
OHTHANKYOUGOD!   OHTHANKYOUGOD!
OHTHANKYOUGOD!   OHTHANKYOUGOD!

When we got down to the ground floor and walked outside, the security guards were there for me like they always were. (Usually a few of them would've been on the elevator with me, but I think I left far quicker than anyone would've predicted, even highly trained security guards.

Those dudes (and that one lady) who ran the security were all really cool. And I was going to miss them. Because even though they were paid to get my back, they made me feel like they actually really wanted to get my back. Maybe that was part of their training. But whatever, I appreciated it. I let them know I didn't need to be walked to a car or escorted anywhere. They responded, "Are you sure?" as they always did. I said, "Yeah."

And me and Martha just started walking. Walking and talking. It was absolutely the happiest I had been in months. Ten or so blocks later, I said I was going to get in a cab and head home. Martha asked me if I wanted her to come. I said, "No, I will be fine." She said, "Are you sure?" And I said, "Yeah. YEAH. I'm great." Me and Melissa had worked through our shit to the extent that I had moved back home with her and Sami. So I was truly going home.

The next day, when I asked Martha about the wrap party and she told me some of the details—people asking about me, people feeling all the feelings, people making out with people in surprising combinations—I immediately knew that not going to that party was the first good decision I had made in my newly unemployed life. I felt like I had a clean slate. And let me be absolutely clear . . . Chris Rock and *Totally Biased* completely changed my life for the better. It raised my profile in the business. It led to every opportunity that I have now. And my mom got to hear Henry Louis Gates Jr. say her name on TV when I interviewed him on the show. (He had one of her books.) And my dad, who was living in New York City at the time, got to walk around like he was the president of showbiz every time he came to the set. He got to hang out with Chris Rock and explain super-nerdy insurance regulations with him. My dad will forever be proud of me because of that show. It changed our relationship too. The only problem I had post-*Totally Biased* was how was an unemployed guy going to pay for an apartment in New York City that cost seven thousand dollars a month? It was a serious problem.

Awkward Thoughts about the Democratic Party

The Saturday night after 9/11, I went to see Lewis Black at Cobb's Comedy Club. He was flying in from New York—despite everything that was going on, he still wanted to fly to San Francisco and do the gig. Unfortunately, I was late. I got there in time to see the doors open as he got a standing ovation and came out of the room. You could see that he had done a great job. He had done everything people wanted him to do and captured everyone's emotions. I also remember walking through the neighborhood of North Beach to get to the club that night. North Beach is the San Francisco version of the neighborhood where I sold condoms in Chicago. It is the nightclub spot for people who don't live in San Francisco, and I remember it feeling like New Year's Eve, with people laughing and having a good time, and they were extra loud and extra boisterous like people are on New Year's Eve. They were determined to get back to "normal" after all the country had been through that week. And I was surprised—I certainly wasn't ready to do that yet. I remember thinking, *We're all pretending that we're going to be OK.*

In late 2016, I found myself watching a lot of CNN. And on TV, I saw people saying, "Well, you know that Trump said all of those horrible racist, Islamophobic, xenophobic things, but he IS our president-elect now, and we do need to give him a chance." We're pretending these things didn't happen in the effort to become a country. We want things to make sense. But it's a luxury if you can do that. If you're a Muslim immigrant and you don't have your green card yet but you're working on it, or if you're a refugee, you don't really have time to think, *Oh, let's just give it time and things will go back to normal.*

Trump directly targeted groups of oppressed people during his campaign. And since he's the president, that doesn't mean that those people no longer feel targeted just because he told his supporters to "Stop it" on *60 Minutes.* I'm a six-foot-four African-American male who already felt targeted during the Obama administration—not by Obama, but I didn't feel like Obama had my back all the time. I always felt like at any moment I could turn my back and get killed by a police officer and my family would have to sort through the details.

For many people, things are instantly worse now that Trump is president! Right after President Trump's victory, we filmed an episode of *United Shades* in Dearborn, Michigan, where there's a sizable Muslim population. While we were there, there were stories about Muslim women getting their hijabs ripped off nearby at the University of Michigan campus. Just by virtue of Trump's victory, people felt like they could say the things and do the things that they've always wanted to say and do but didn't feel like they were allowed to say and do. So even if Trump never says those things again, he's given license to the people who are saying them now.

So things are instantly worse for so many people already, and they also don't know how bad it's going to get. You can't tell anyone who's Muslim, "Oh, they would never do a Muslim registry." You can't convince them of that. There's no way to talk them out of that, to say that would never happen. We're already through the "that would never happen" part of world history entitled "President Trump."

I think everybody who's anti-Trump has to make a commitment to themselves and to their communities to do more and get less. Less sleep. Less caught up on their favorite shows. Less satisfaction from fighting with Internet trolls. I think that if you're an activist and an organizer, you're already out there in the streets. It just means you've got to get up earlier and stay up later; you're already doing the work. But if you're a Democratic suburban white mom who changed her Facebook avatar to "I'm with Her," and that's all you did . . . then you need to do more. And those women's marches all over the country were great. My wife went to one. When's the next one? You cannot expect to combat this through Facebook avatars or through a single event. Martin Luther King Jr. and his cohort were already planning the next march while they were at the March on Washington. For many people, this was a wake-up call. But most people I know were already awake. So I feel that the people who normally do nothing have to start doing something.

Democrats offering to work with Trump on things like infrastructure are normalizing him. If you're looking for common ground with the man, then you're meeting him on his territory. My least favorite thing in politics is the Al Smith dinner, which happens right before the election. It is one night during every presidential election when the campaigns stop working for our votes, and they put on tuxedos and treat the elite (and us at home) to an evening of stand-up-comedian-style roast jokes. I hated it when Obama did it with McCain. I hated it when Obama did it with Romney. And I hated it when Trump and Hillary did it. Because it gives the impression that this whole thing is a game. If you take this so lightly that you can go into a room, put on your finest finery, and lob friendly jokes at each other, and you have the audacity to broadcast that on television, what you're saying is, "I don't respect the work that needs to be done. I don't respect that people are suffering." And I think it's absolutely disgusting. It's left over from a time when that dinner happened in a room with closed doors, when the servants were afraid to talk about it because they'd get fired. But now we broadcast it on TV. I don't even like the White House Correspondents' dinner. Those things are for the people in the room, but when you start broadcasting them on TV, you're mocking the people who never have the ability to be heard by the people in that room.

So when the last Al Smith dinner happened and Trump actually talked real shit about Hillary, I thought, good for him. He doesn't ac-tually respect you, and he doesn't want you to win, and he doesn't have that much good feeling toward you, so why should he pretend like he does. He was like, "I'm not telling jokes." He was the white, rich, Republican version of Bernie Mac's "I ain't scared of you mother-fuckers." These things create the impression that this is not as serious as life and death, and it makes me crazy. When Democrats say they're going to ignore Trump's white supremacy, xenophobia, Islamophobia, ableism, and racism because they're going to find common ground, they're letting him dictate what the ground is.

I feel the same way about the Democratic Party now that I felt about the Republican Party in 2012: It's time for a reboot. Some people are saying, "Oprah should run!" I don't actually know if I want Oprah to be the president. I like Oprah, but why should we just look for the most charismatic billionaire who's politically active to be the president? So I think the Democratic Party should do what the Re-publican Party should have done (and they still should have done this, because even they don't really want Trump. They've just sold themselves out for him): look to groom younger leadership.

Awkward Thoughts about the Democratic Party

One of the big problems with Hillary is that whatever people think about her, she became an obstacle to new blood. The conventional wisdom was that 2016 was her turn, especially after Barack Obama had taken her turn before. Someone who actually thought they might make a good president wouldn't even entertain running, like Cory Booker or Elizabeth Warren. And I love Bernie, but nobody was more surprised at his success than he was. He started as a protest candidate and almost had a shot at winning the damn thing. Democrats need people with audacity. Barack Obama in 2008 had the audacity to go after the presidency, even when it didn't make any sense.

In the future they have to encourage new leadership and groom people, and give the party over to a new generation. The whole situation with Debbie Wasserman Schultz? It was like the party was the *Titanic* running into an iceberg. They didn't even try to steer clear of it! They just thought, *We can take that iceberg down.* People are talking about Keith Ellison, and I think, sure, we should give a Black Muslim a shot. And Elizabeth Warren is great, but what about Kamala Harris? What about people who are under the age of fifty? Julian Castro? What about under forty? I'm not mad at older people, but still. Barack Obama came from *seemingly out of nowhere*, and other people can come from *seemingly out of nowhere too.*

I think the Democratic Party needs to embrace their progressive base the way that Trump embraced the white supremacy base of his party. And Democrats get uncomfortable with progressivism; they think it's the crazy uncle wing of the party. I'm here to say that yup, it is. But we're crazy enough to be in the streets for what we believe, even when TV cameras aren't there. We're crazy enough to do online campaigns when the very idea of #BlackLivesMatter scares some of the same people who claim they are on our side.

We're crazy enough to show up. Embrace us, Democrats. And if you don't? Well prepare for *2016: The Sequel* in 2020.

I've had several arguments with my dad about this: I don't think anyone's smart enough to explain to me why the electoral college makes sense. If the Democratic Party supports the electoral college going forward, then they clearly misunderstood the problem. If they try to run Tim Kaine for president, then they really misunderstood the problem. I've seen some Tim Kaine 2020 murmurs, and I think those people also really didn't understand what happened.

Everything the establishment does to control the vote serves to disenfranchise Black people and communities of color. The Democrats have to get really wonky and nerdy and embrace the nerds, the political wonks, and the freaks out in the streets doing the heavy lifting, and fight about gerrymandering—real nerd shit. Because when Democrats run away from these fights, Trump is what we get. Hillary won by more than two million votes and yet that was a loss? When politics is treated like a game, then this country elects a game-show host. All the talk about the elites and the ruling class, and all the people who hate the elites voted for Trump. He's like the king of the elites! He's a billionaire (maybe . . . we still need those tax returns) who inherited money from a millionaire! How is he not an elite? I'm just aware that the next four to eight years are going to be about pushing even harder than we've ever pushed before. And that's good in some sense, because we needed to push anyway. If Hillary had been president, maybe people would have backed off, but I'm inspired by the people from Black Lives Matter. Black Lives Matter didn't endorse anybody because they are aware of the fact that none of these people actually have our best interests at heart.

Awkward Thoughts about the Democratic Party

When I think about my utopian future, these two parties are gone. Why are we acting like these two parties are enough? Like there are only two different versions of humanity. My goal is to spend the next four years focusing on people and causes and forgetting parties. I stopped wanting to go to parties when I was never invited to them in high school. We have to stop letting Democrats and Republicans lead us into believing that it is their way or no way. I feel like right now we are in the era of "No way!," which means we need to find a new way. People feeling like they had to pick a box— or worse, feeling like they couldn't pick a box because of the choices—got us where we are: the eve of dystopia. The day before *Mad Max* begins.

Chapter 9

My Awkward Joking Around with the KKK

No comedian grows up saying, "One day I hope to get a show on CNN!" But by this point in my career I had learned, for better or worse, that I just didn't do things the way most people did them.

The day after the last episode of *Totally Biased* aired in November 2013, I found out that the head of MSNBC was interested in meeting with me. Rachel Maddow, who I consider my Patronus, had set it up. I was still stunned by everything that had happened in the last few days. I was only twenty-four hours removed from having the show, but I wanted to go to the meeting. I felt like I was being recruited, like a draft pick.

Shortly after that, me, Melissa, and Sami went on vacation, or at least we tried to. I was still in shock about the last year or so and I had no idea what to do next. College dropout, stand-up dropout, late-night TV dropout. I was depressed again. Sami was about two and a half years old. My agent said, "MSNBC is great, but let's take some meetings." Jeff Zucker from CNN wanted to meet with me, and I was like, *Huh . . .*

The only thing I knew about Jeff Zucker is that I'd read he'd screwed Conan O'Brien out of *The Tonight Show*. I had heard this during my effort to become a better talk show host during *Totally Biased* when I had read Bill Carter's book *The War for Late Night*. In the book, Jeff was painted as the enemy and Conan was the hero. I was honestly reluctant to meet with him. The comedy world had been knee-deep in the Jay Leno/Conan O'Brien thing. But I got over my reluctance pretty quickly because Jeff was in the middle of transforming CNN from a straight news network into a news and relevant-programming network. And they employed some people whose work I loved. Anthony Bourdain, Morgan Spurlock, Mike Rowe, and Lisa Ling had recently gotten shows at CNN, and Jeff was clearly letting them continue to do the good work they were already doing. And ultimately, the meanest thing Jeff has ever done to me was to have my show follow Bourdain's show. It was a lot of pressure. But I also knew it showed how much he believed in the show.

Jeff was behind his desk with about eight thousand TVs on and his computer up. He was clearly short on time. There was a lot going on in the news that day. (Remember when there wasn't a lot going on in the news?) I didn't blame him. He got right to it—"So, your show got canceled. Congratulations. It was good. So, do you pay attention to the news?"

"Yeah, I sure do."

"So you know what's going on? Here's a quiz . . ."

And he gave me a news quiz. I was like, OK . . . I had been waking up to the news alerts on my phone, watching the news shows at night, and listening to NPR since the early days of the *Bell Curve,* so I shouldn't have been worried, but I was. How deep would this quiz go? Would he ask, "How do we solve the problems between Israel and Palestine?" "Give me a cost benefit analysis of the Keystone Pipeline!" But it was more like a game show about the news. "Do you know about Bridgegate?" It was 2014 by then, and I was still living in New York City. I don't know how anybody wouldn't know about Bridgegate. Basically, if you watched CNN for ten minutes, you'd know all the answers. Luckily, nobody expects comedians to be that smart.

I was aware I wasn't just one of many comedians that CNN was meeting with that day. Which is what my career has always been like—I end up places other people aren't even trying to go to. I'm not really competing against anyone; I'm just trying to do what I do and make it better. Which is good for me—there are so many comedians who think they're competing with Kevin Hart; some are, but most aren't. I know I'm not competing with Kevin Hart. I think it's weird that I can even claim that I have the same job: comedian.

After I passed the quiz, Jeff left and brought a couple of his vice presidents in. I was happy to see that they weren't all dudes. It was two women, Nancy Duffy and Amy Entelis. It became very clear that they didn't want a late-night talk show. That wasn't what they brought me in for. They told me that a production company had pitched them an idea called "Black Man, White America," where a Black man would travel across America and visit all white places. And I thought, *That idea seems horrible,* although I liked the idea of a travel show. I'd written up a pitch for a show called *Don't Go There,* so I pitched them my version. I told them I wanted to go to more than just white places, because I was from the Bay Area, and I wanted to see all kinds of cultures I don't know about, not just white places. I joked, "I already have white in-laws." They liked my twist on the idea.

I went to other meetings at other networks, but CNN called me back and told me they took my idea back to the production company that had pitched it, and the production company liked it even better. They set up a phone call with Jimmy Fox, the head of the production company. Jimmy told me they'd changed the name to *United Shades of America*, a WAY better title, and a way better feeling for a show like this. He wanted to hire an executive producer named . . . Let's call him Showy. Showy had a long résumé and had run another show that I liked a lot. That show was funny but more important, it was smart. It was a natural fit.

We talked about the first idea for the show. I was the one who said, "The Klan." I had been thinking about the Ku Klux Klan all my life. You can't learn about the history of America without reading about the KKK, America's own terrorist group. My mother is from Indiana, which was a big Klan stronghold. I had heard about a Klan museum in South Carolina. I would regularly go on the Klan website—I mean, not every day, but I'd always kept my eye on them, to read the rhetoric and work on the Klan jokes in my act. It was something I had always been interested in, and if we were going to do it, I wanted to go all out. Jimmy had originally thought of the show as a broad comedy show, but I saw it more like Anthony Bourdain's show—a serious take on something from someone with a big personality. I'm a big personality, and I'm funny, but I wasn't doing this in a funny way. Some of the ideas were like, "Kamau could go to an Indian wedding!" and I just thought, *What does that even mean?* They're Indian. If they get married, I'll go to their wedding. I give Jimmy lots of credit though. Every time I pushed back on something, he would listen. He allowed me to explain what I, a Black man who wanted a show based on inclusiveness, needed from the show. Jimmy was a white guy and a TV executive who had produced many, many shows. He had lots of reasons *not* to listen to me. But more often than not, he did.

So I kept saying, "What about the Klan?" and one guy actually said at one point, "Is it too on the nose?"—a classic showbiz thing! People are so inside their rabbit hole they don't see the outside perspective. Do you see a lot of shows about *Black* people visiting the Klan? *You know that* Chappelle's Show *sketch wasn't real, right?*

We settled on it, and the production team started looking for Klan members we could talk to. But the bigger conversation among the team ended up being about representation. Because I sat down with Jimmy Fox and later the whole the production team, and I realized that they were all white people. And mostly dudes. I was already feeling, OK, I'm not going to be able to rely and lean on these people in the way I was expecting. They aren't going to get it on the same level as people of color. The difference between two people talking about cancer. If only one person has cancer, then the person with cancer has to spend time explaining cancer to the other. If they *both* have cancer, then they can get past the explanation and directly to the conversation about *having cancer.*

We got to Kentucky. Ethan Berlin, from *Totally Biased,* was there. Ethan was the "white guy" from the *Totally Biased* field piece, "Do You Have Anything to Say to a White Guy?" He found out from the YouTube comments that many white guys feel like his Jewish-ness outweighs his whiteness. I love Ethan. He matches an extremely dark sense of humor with a sensitive soul. He gets me. But with most of the crew, I just felt like they were a TV production crew. I didn't get the feeling I was with people who had any interest in, or empathy for, the subject. I really felt alone and isolated.

Part of that may have been that the first day of work was also the day we shot with the KKK. The night before we shot was the first time I had met most of the crew. It felt weird to do something so vulnerable with a bunch of strangers. The guy in charge of security was a FORMER LA POLICE OFFICER! I thought, *Greeeeeeeat . . . Now who's in charge of protecting me from him? In case he has an LA riots flashback while we are shooting?* It was just another example of how whoever was in charge was *not thinking* about how these decisions would affect me . . . or worse . . . Maybe they didn't care. The ex-cop ended up being a good guy. We had some really interesting drives, which will force communication to happen. Not that I'm suggesting every Black person be forced to take an eight-hour car ride with a cop.

But this was a classic example of the problem of the lack of representation in show business. No one was thinking, *Oh, Kamau should probably be surrounded by people who understand what he's trying to do here.* I was having to translate my ideas to this white crew, hoping they could understand them so they could then translate them to the screen. And it's awful. I couldn't just make a good show; I also had to manage my relationship with the crew. And hold a diversity training seminar that no one had signed up for.

The ex-cop was Mexican-American, so he understood where I was coming from, but he was WAY more ex-cop than current

Mexican-American. We ended up laughing a lot more than I expected. But he got it way more than anyone else there, although during the shoot he had to pretend to be white. The Klan said they wanted no other people of color there. The producer said that the reason there were no other people of color in the crew was because the Klan didn't want that. And I thought, *Why do they get to pick?* Why are we putting them in the position of power? Also, that didn't explain why there weren't POCs in the remaining seven episodes either. Let me be clear: Occasionally there were POCs on the crew as production assistants or editors on the show, but there were none in positions of authority. None existed in the positions that mattered.

Early on the first day of shooting, we walked around town and did some man-on-the-street stuff. I thought, *Oh, I'm talking to people, being funny, this is OK. I know how to do this.* And while we're filming, some white guy recognized me and said, "Hey, *Totally Biased*!" which was great, because the crew weren't necessarily fans of *Totally Biased*. To them, I was just this guy who was the star of the show. I understood. They had all worked on hundreds of productions. This was just another day at work. So when people recognized me, I'd think: See? Hey, guys, I'm actually *already in showbiz.*

At the end of the first day, we went to a clearing in some trees off a dirt road. We pulled up, and there was a long wait getting the KKK ready while I sat in the car with Patrick, the director of photography who I would eventually come to love like a brother, the sound guy, and the ex-cop. There was a long wait—maybe five minutes, maybe an hour. It didn't make it into the show, but I was singing Tom Petty: "The waiting is the hardest part . . ."

We finally pulled into the clearing where they were going to burn the cross, and there was a guy with some sort of rifle. They had told me no one would have a gun, but the LAPD guy tried to reassure me by telling me that the guy with the rifle clearly didn't know how to use it. And I thought: That actually makes me MORE worried. *He might* accidentally shoot me. The ex-cop told me that no matter what happened, he had my back and he would do whatever it took to get me out of there if the shit hit the fan. "Better to be judged by twelve than carried by six" was his mantra. Only time I would hear a cop say that and feel good about it.

They finally waved the car in. I got out and walked toward the group. When you watch it on TV you can hear me say, "I've had some bad ideas . . ." I wasn't acting. I immediately felt like this was a dumb idea.

There was a phalanx of Klan members in front of me in full regalia, ironically dressed in all the colors of the rainbow. There were several in white robes but also one in blue, who I took to calling Klanny Smurf (in my mind) and a young blond woman who looked like an eighteen-year-old Britney Spears, who looked like she wanted to kill me the entire time we were there. Klanny Smurf got all up in my face talking about Ferguson and policing in America, about how Black people can't be policed. Showy stepped in to calm him down, because that wasn't going to work for the show. We needed conversation, not a '90s-era Jerry Springer show. I had been worried that some of the KKK members who were on the periphery would really not be OK that I was there. I was worried that someone was going to run up and attack me. But when someone did run up, he handed me a bag of Skittles and iced tea, which is what Trayvon Martin had bought before he was killed. He handed it to me, clearly trying to insult me, and I laughed it off and said, "Oh you got jokes?" I thought: Why didn't you do that on camera? We should have got that on film!

I was trying to pay attention to everything, looking all around me. Things began to settle down, and I started to feel comfortable enough to be funny. At some point the crew stopped filming because they had everything we needed in one conversation. I pulled Showy aside and I told him, "You need to tell me when you stop filming, because I don't actually enjoy talking to these guys." I realized, again, that they just thought they were making a TV show. They didn't realize I was a Black guy TALKING TO THE KU KLUX KLAN. I was paying an emotional toll for being here. He just said, "Oh, I'm sorry." But it was a big indicator of how our relationship would not work out over time. He was always just making a TV show. He never realized that in all the shows we made I was paying a human cost.

We filmed the cross burning. It was incredible. It was surreal. It was sad. I couldn't help but think about all the Black people who had been in positions like me with the Klan, but were *not* there to make TV shows. The burning cross was probably the last thing they saw before they were murdered. Showy came up with the idea that we should end the episode with the image of the cross. He was right. It was dramatic that way.

By the end of the shoot, it was weird. We had been there for serval hours, and several of the Klan guys were laughing with me, except for Klanny Spears. I found out that she was fourth-generation Klan. I felt bad for her. She was classically Hollywood-looking. She looked like if she could sing she'd be on *American*

Idol. I wanted to tell her: You're filled with so much anger and enmity, and it's just because you're in this town *and you are disappointed in your circumstances.* And you think it's my fault. You think that Black people are the problem. *Come to Hollywood! I'll make you a star!*

I think a lot of the people there were like that. They lived in a town with no industry and not a lot of jobs and not a lot of future. They weren't educated well, and they just blamed it on Black people. I had empathy for them. I laughed with them, but mostly because I wanted to get out of there.

Later during the shoot, me and the crew were in Harrison, Arkansas. I was standing in front of a barbershop with a huge Confederate flag. We were told it was owned by a man who was part of the Klan. It was nighttime, and I couldn't tell if anyone was inside the barbershop. I had a walkie-talkie in my back pocket, and I could hear Showy saying, "Get closer to it! Get closer to it!" And I thought: Dude, there's a guy in there who might be with the Klan. Do you understand? This is real. I'm REALLY walking toward a place where a guy who might be in the Klan could shoot and kill me.

I just stopped and started crying. And instead of asking me if I was OK, the crew sort of backed off. I realized I had to pull it together, because nobody really knew how to handle it . . . or worse, they didn't give a shit. Ethan was there. And he came to me. Showy told him to get out of the way.

I don't hate Showy. We had different working styles. He's a talented, funny dude. He was a big part of why the first season went so well. But I was spending too much time arguing for things to be more inclusive, or less stereotypical. Smarter. And I had no one else on the crew who I could turn to and say, "You tell him." Again, lack of representation is the problem. It was crazy. My show about inclusion had a problem with inclusion. The show wasn't creating an environment where the person of color—who was the star and an executive producer—felt like he could be successful. But that's showbiz, and that's America. People think that representation doesn't matter, but it does. It makes a difference. The problem is that sometimes people of color in show business—and this is true of women too—think that they just have to eat it. They don't want to hurt anybody's feelings or be an asshole or be looked at as overly sensitive. I was certainly that way during *Totally Biased*. But now I think, *Fuck that*. Why am I not naming names? Why am I protecting white men's feelings? They weren't protecting my feelings. *I don't have to be in this business if it doesn't work for my family or my soul. There's always work at Starbucks.*

Later, we started editing the show, and a lot of the funny moments were edited out. Showy had said, "When you start making jokes with the Klan, it makes it seem like they're in on the joke, and we want them to appear scary." And I thought, *White man, the Klan is ALWAYS scary*. If I make them laugh, I have power. If I make the Klan laugh, then they're submitting to me. Then I'm winning. If you take out the laughter, then I just look like a Black guy who showed up and got *lectured* by the Klan.

We went back and forth, and I had to argue to get things in that were funny. But I'm glad I did. I got some of it in. And those things ended up being talked-about moments in the show. (There was a riff about how Klanny Smurf didn't believe in gay marriage because of the Bible, but he did believe in eating at Red Lobster even though the Bible was clearly against eating crustaceans. Holy cognitive dissonance, Batman!) And in season two, we have replaced a lot of people. (Showy is gone. He's found other work, because—again—he's good at what he does.) But there are still moments when there are ghosts in the machine. If I learned anything from dropping out of Penn, it's that I'm always ready to leave. Being able to say no is the most power you can ever have. It is either a luxury when you can afford to leave, or it is necessary for survival when the cost to stay is waaaaay too high.

Awkward Thoughts about Missing President Obama

Now I realize I'm going to miss Barack Obama. There are things he's done that I've liked, and things that I haven't liked. But there's also the simple fact that he's Black. I know it's a symbol, but it's a pretty big symbol. I had two kids born in the era of the Black president. They see a Black family in the White House and think that's what it is. And that's a big deal. I'm going to talk as a Black person for a second—it's just been nice to have a Black president in the White House because sometimes he talks directly to Black people in a way that white people have gotten from every other president. And sometimes it's directly, like with the My Brother's Keeper initiative, but sometimes he's subtler, so only the Black people and the cool white people know what's going on. The people of color and the Black people are like, "We know," but it goes right past some white people. Like the time he said, "Sometimes you've got to brush the dirt off your shoulders," and we all said, "HE'S QUOTING JAY Z! Mama, get in here! The president is quoting Jay Z!" Meanwhile, Tea Party white people are thinking, *That's another reason I don't like him! He's got dirty shoulders! I don't understand why he's got dirty shoulders!*

It's also fun to have him right now because he's starting to be clearly just done. He's had enough. He's got that Danny Glover look in his eye, like, "I'm getting too old for this shit." Or like, "Soon y'all are going to have to deal with this yourselves, because I'm gonna be in Dubai, writing poetry and growing out my Afro. Writing my memoir: *I Can't Believe Nobody Shot Me Either.* I'm getting out of here, so you guys are gonna have to figure this stuff out." He's like a senior who's got all the credits he needs to graduate, so now he's just hanging out with his feet up, just doing what he wants to do.

And now I think he's talking about race stuff more, being more direct. A big moment when I realized I was going to miss him was when he gave a eulogy for his friend Clementa Pinckney in South Carolina. He was giving that eulogy, and he was *so Black* that day. He was doing that thing where it's clear he's been practicing his Martin Luther King Jr. impression. He was dropping his *g*'s at the end of verbs. He was using words that only Black people and white Southerners know: "We're fixin' to get out of here—" *Fixin'*? He's up there being so Black, and I think, *Oh God, I'm going to miss this so much.* And then he got to the end of the speech and said, "Clementa Pinckney had grace. Amazing grace." And then he took a pause like, *Am I about to sing?* And he did. And I thought, *Oh my God, this is SO BLACK.* Bernie Sanders ain't singing! He'd be like, "Amazing . . . Oh, you know the words! Aaaaargh, capitalism! Big banks!" Hillary Clinton ain't singing! She'd call Bill up there. But Barack started singing, going into the next verse, and all of a sudden there's a gospel choir that appeared out of nowhere, and a Black guy playing the organ just fell out of the sky. *Oh my God, this is SO BLACK.* He's, like, hitting my Black G-spot. I'm gonna miss you, Obama.

CHAPTER 10

My Most Awkward Birthday Ever

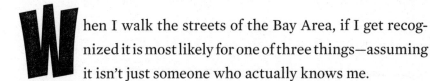hen I walk the streets of the Bay Area, if I get recognized it is most likely for one of three things—assuming it isn't just someone who actually knows me.

1. "KAMAU! I LOVED *TOTALLY BIASED*."
2. "KAMAU, I LOVE *UNITED SHADES OF AMERICA!*"
3. "Kamau! I still can't believe what happened in that coffee shop."

The first two things that people recognize me for are always said with pride, like they are a member of my family. It's one of the reasons I knew that I needed to move back to the Bay Area after *Totally Biased* was canceled. I knew I needed some of that. I needed some of that old-school *Cheers*-style "Where everybody knows your name" love.

But the third thing is not said with pride. It is said with a headshake, back and forth. It is said in hushed tones, like they don't want to embarrass me. But then depending on their race, there are other things added that let me know where they in particular are coming from. People of color usually add a resigned sigh that says, "The more things change, the more things . . ." But white people always seem like they are talking about someone who died, even though I'm standing right in front of them. Although I'm pretty sure the person they are mourning is the person who *they themselves used to be* before my story proved to them that racism is alive and well in the liberal outpost of Berkeley, California.

"The coffee shop thing" happened all because I wanted to do Melissa a favor on my birthday. Melissa comes from a birthday family. They do birthday weeks. When I was a kid, I loved big birthday celebrations. But as I got older, I started to really crave low-key birthdays. Being a comedian, especially once you start to see some success, you end up feeling like it's your birthday a lot. People are constantly clapping and cheering for you when you just step onstage. And the more famous you are the more those cheers and applause get louder and mean more. I started to realize I was expecting cheers and applause when I went home. It was truly fucking me up. It really came to a head during *Totally Biased* at the time when me and Melissa lived apart for a couple weeks. I promised myself that I wouldn't get caught up in that nonsense anymore. A low-key birthday was a way to zig when everybody else was zagging. I even turned off my birthday on Facebook, the ultimate "love me" day on social media, so I wouldn't have to deal with all the "love" from "friends." But as the Yiddish saying goes, "Man plans and God laughs . . . and institutionalized racism ruins your birthday." At least, I *think* that's the expression.

And so it was my birthday, January 26, 2015, and it was super low-key, just like I wanted it to be. But Melissa wanted to take me, and then-thirteen-week-old baby Juno out for a birthday breakfast after we all dropped Sami at school. I had been on the road doing college gigs and this was my first Monday back in a bit. Melissa picked the Elmwood Café, a beautiful all-day brunch spot that she LOVED. When we moved to New York City for *Totally Biased,* just two years before, it had been Ozzie's, an old-school soda fountain. Melissa had loved it then, too. But gentrification had turned it from Ozzie's into a high-end brunch spot. And even though Melissa is as troubled by gentrification as I am, she is also a sucker for runny eggs, scones, and lemon curd. I blame *Downton Abbey.*

So we had breakfast there. Well, me and Melissa had breakfast while Juno mostly slept. Breakfast was fine other than the hair I found in my food. We told a member of the staff. They apologized and brought me new food. I never freak out when stuff like that happens. I always figure it could happen to anybody. And after all the retail I've worked, I'm not trying to make anybody's day harder unless I have no choice.

After breakfast, I went down the street to Espresso Roma, a low-key coffee shop, unlike Elmwood, where I could work on my MacBook Air. Melissa and Juno went to their mom's group, a bunch of women who had been in a class together when they were pregnant and were now having look-at-this-cute-baby-I-made reunions . . . and also probably having adult conversations. A couple hours later, Melissa ended up back at the Elmwood Café for lunch with a few of these moms and their babies. I was happy she would get to hang there twice in one day. I was happy that the

Elmwood made her happy. This was the kind of easygoing, Bay Area day that you don't get often enough in New York City. It was one of the reasons we moved back. We were now living our dream.

When I was done working, I walked back down College Avenue to rejoin her and meet her new friends. I was just carrying my laptop with no bag because I knew I wouldn't be out for long. On my way back I stopped at an independent bookstore, Mrs. Dalloway's, right next to the Elmwood. There was a new children's book in the window display, and I knew I had to have it. I knew *my family* had to have it. It was called *The Case for Loving*. It was about the Lovings, the Virginia couple who went to the Supreme Court in 1968 and successfully argued for the striking down of laws that banned interracial marriage in seventeen states. Without this couple, maybe me and Melissa wouldn't have gotten married. And maybe there'd be no Sami and Juno. And I would definitely be a sadder person if I didn't have the family I have now. After I bought the book, I was filled with pride and joy and also feeling like I had just *dad'ed my ass off* by buying that book. I knew I was a surefire first ballot Dad Hall of Famer. And then everything went pear-shaped . . .

1. After I bought the book and decided not to get a bag for the book, I walked next door to the Elmwood Café.
2. I saw Melissa and her new friends all happily chatting and holding their babies while sitting at an outside table. It struck me how well my wife fit in with these new friends.
3. I walked over to them. Melissa introduced me to them.
4. One of them asked about the book I was holding.

5. I showed her the book.

6. Seconds later there was a loud series of knocks on the window of the Elmwood Café. They were coming from the inside of the restaurant.

7. I looked up and saw one of the Elmwood Café employees staring daggers at me.

8. The employee then jerked her head to her left aggressively, and I saw her mouth something to the effect of . . . "SCRAM!" (OK. Maybe it wasn't exactly, "SCRAM!" Maybe it was, "GIT!" Or maybe it was, "GO!" Whatever it was, it was certainly directed at me. And it was certainly telling me to make myself scarce. And it was also the kind of direction you should only give to a dog . . . a dog that you, yourself, own. A dog that you own and . . . that you hate. Or maybe you would yell that at a dog you don't own, but a dog that you are afraid is going to attack a group of moms and their babies.)

I was stunned. Caught totally flat-footed. Melissa saw the look on my face. Later she told me that what I heard was, in fact, the second round of knocks on the window. Melissa apparently thought it was a person who recognized me from my work and was just overly excited to see me. But when she saw the hurt expression on my face, she knew it wasn't a fan. It was racism . . . on her husband's birthday . . . and at her favorite coffee shop. Damn.

I quickly told Melissa, "A woman inside just told me to get out of here." Telling Melissa also meant that I had to awkwardly tell these new women, who I had met like a minute before, what had just happened. I didn't want to tell them. I was trying to make a good impression. But now that this had happened, I didn't give a shit about my impression. I wanted to run away. I was actually strangely embarrassed, as if I had done something wrong.

In my life's work, I have learned of the many ways that oppression works from the inside. I felt numb, like I was going to pass out. And then a different employee—at the time I thought it was the same one, but later I learned more than one person in that coffee shop wanted me gone—walked out of the café to once again deliver the "Get out of here!" message. I guess since I was still standing there, the café figured I hadn't heard it the first time. But then the employee hesitated and looked around. And I guess she realized that no one at the table was bothered by my presence. We were in fact only bothered by *her* presence. We were bothered by the fact that we were currently standing in Berkeley, California, a city so allegedly liberal that even the most progressive-y progressives make fun of it, and yet thanks to institutionalized racism being alive and well and embedded into the fabric and the buildings of America, Berkeley is where I, as a Black man, was being told to "GIT!" like it was 1963 in Selma, Alabama, and I was crashing a meeting of the New Moms of the Confederacy. In that moment, the employee delivered the line that has become an instant classic in our family:

"Oh, we thought you were selling something."

We thought you were selling something???

What the hell was that supposed to mean? "We thought you were selling something." So you thought you'd tell me to "GIT!" . . . for selling something. You didn't think to first WALK OUTSIDE TO FIND OUT EXACTLY WHAT WAS GOING ON? And is "selling something" enough for you to bark at me through a plate-glass window? And is the equivalent of "Oops!" enough to get you off the hook? The answer to the last two questions is "No."

At this point Melissa couldn't take it anymore.

Melissa: "He is my husband."

Elmwood employee: "I'm sorry."

Me: "This is my wife. That is my daughter. I just ate here earlier today."

Elmwood employee, not even looking at me: "I'm sorry."

Me: "I bet you are."

And then I said to whoever was listening, "Well, I'm going to take a walk and think about racism." Yup. I actually said that. I'm not sure why. I just wanted it to be known that that was exactly what I was going to do . . . on my birthday.

But Melissa wasn't having any of that; she quickly gathered herself and Juno and caught up with me. And we headed to the car. But just as we were about to get in Melissa said, "I can't. I have to say something." She approached the employee as the employee was about to go back inside the Elmwood. Melissa explained in the kind of calm yet stern and emotionless tone that I had come to understand meant that she was *really, really pissed*. She told the employee that although we had eaten at the Elmwood twice that day, and even though she loved the Elmwood Café, that we would not be back after the racism that we had just experienced.

That's when the Elmwood employee reached into her well of white privilege and told Melissa, "I don't think it was a race thing." That was hilarious to me, considering that the only Black people in this whole story were me and Juno. And Juno hadn't bothered to weigh in, so that made me the only person in the story qualified to make those kinds of judgment calls.

Because in actuality, a Black man being told to leave a restaurant because the restaurant believes that his very presence constitutes harassment of four white women and their kids, even though there is literally NO EVIDENCE TO SUPPORT THAT, is textbook racism. It is so old-school that it has a wing in the racism museum, right between the sit-ins at lunch counters and a Southern redneck telling a Black man on a business trip, "You ain't from around here, are ya, boy?"

My wife told the employee in no uncertain terms that we absolutely knew it was a "race thing." Melissa looked the employee right in the eyes and said, "We live with this shit every day." I heard about this exchange after it happened, when we were headed home. Because while Melissa was talking to the Elmwood employee, I was cooing at Juno in the car for two reasons. One, I loved my daughter's fat cheeks, big hazel eyes, and baby breath. And two, I knew if I stood over my wife with my six-foot-four, 250-pound frame, that it could very easily be spun that I was standing over this employee—this innocent-looking, tiny white woman—and maybe it would be spun that I was trying to intimidate her, *or even worse*, that I was getting aggressive. I didn't want to end up a hashtag if I could help it. (I probably can't.) I live with this shit every day.

And look, I understand that on College Avenue in "Berserkley," the Elmwood gets some characters coming through their establishment that they might not want to serve. And it is their right to refuse service. For example, when we had breakfast that morning, there was a white guy with dreadlocks sitting directly across from the doorway. He was spare-change-ing everyone who went into and out of the Elmwood. And I could understand if a business thought he was bothering people. And I would understand if that business had asked him to leave. But he was there the entire time we had breakfast, at least an hour, and I didn't see anyone tell him to "SCRAM!" But when I stood amicably talking to my wife for a few minutes, it was a different story. I think me and that white guy were both even wearing hoodies, so it can't be how I was dressed. Plus, mine was a super-cool-expensive Oaklandish, one that Oaklandish had given to me because I rep the Bay hard. I guess in his hoodie he had a more Mark Zuckerberg–type of feel than I had.

And then me and Melissa went home with our mixed-race baby, my MacBook Air (that I certainly wasn't selling), and our new book about an interracial couple whose love was so strong that it changed the world. And me and Melissa cried. It just sucked. We had gone through it the past couple of years in a good way mostly. But the move home was us betting on our family and our community and hoping that I could figure out showbiz from the hinterlands of Northern California. But we couldn't just leave everything with the Elmwood the way it was. My parents raised me better than that. I immediately realized that if this had happened to me, then it was happening to other people. And those people likely didn't have the way to get the message out that I had. And Melissa is Catholic, and she's one of those Jesuit-social-justice Catholics. We were a united front. I had Melissa take pictures of me wearing the same clothes I was wearing at the Elmwood while holding the book on the Lovings. I posted it to the Elmwood's Facebook page. I suggested that they Google me since they clearly didn't know who I was. I didn't blame them for not knowing me. But I did hope that maybe someone from there would look me up and discover how ridiculous that whole situation was. And how so mishandled it had been from start to finish. I was really hoping that they would reach out to me. But nope. They didn't.

A couple days later, me and Melissa were still raw from the experience, so we cowrote a blog post about it for my website. We went back and forth on it. She would take my computer and rewrite things to clear up my arguments. She was an academic for real. I would complain that I needed to keep in jokes that she thought were extraneous. She would prove to be right. We were doing what we do best. We were deep in the fight together, turning it into art. Once we were done, my finger huddled over the touchpad. I knew once I sent it I was going to be in the middle of something. I could feel it. But I had no idea how big it would be. I turned to Melissa. "You ready?" She responded confidently, "Yup." Send.

I uploaded it to my website. And then I also shared it to Facebook and Twitter. It was a really long blog post. I didn't want to confuse people—or take the chance that people could think I was manipulating the story—by shorting details. I knew it would take a bit for even my most ardent and excitable fans to get through it. And then it started happening. People began responding. At first it was overwhelmingly supportive. And then (of course) some of it turned all *"How do you know it was racism?"* Because as a Black person who has lived all his life in America, I have a PhD in racism.

But then it kept getting bigger. People from all over the country flooded the Elmwood Café's Yelp! page with negative reviews. I didn't support doing that . . . but it was hilarious. The first good laugh me and Melissa had allowed ourselves in a few days. Then local newspapers began hitting me up for a comment on Twitter. By that night it was the local story du jour. Perfect for a slow news day. "Black comedian who jokes about racism claims he was kicked out of a restaurant because of . . . and get this . . . racism! Well, the jokes write themselves!" I got to hear my name, "Kamau," pronounced multiple ways within one news story. The anchor would do it one way and the reporter would put their own unique spin on it.

At some point that first day, the owner of the café reached out to me through my manager, Keri. Keri said he was frantic and wanted to do anything to resolve the issue. He said his café believed in social justice, and that it supported good causes. I had seen that on the website. He was a white male liberal and he wanted credit for all his good deeds despite what had happened. But racism is like eating food. Just because you had a kale smoothie on Monday, it doesn't mean that it's OK to eat three dozen chicken wings on Tuesday. At first I didn't want to talk to him. My picture had been on his Facebook page for two days, and I hadn't heard from them. This could have been resolved quietly and quickly. But nothing then. But now—of course—that the media was all up his ass he wanted a solution. It was a microcosm of how Black South Africans defeated apartheid. Get the world's attention, and wait for previously unreasonable people to suddenly become very reasonable. I kind of wanted him to stew in his juices.

But me and Melissa knew that wouldn't accomplish anything. We finally talked to him later that day. He was full of sorrowful apologies and promises of a new day. He talked of firing the employees involved, even though me and Melissa said we didn't want that. We both knew that firing a couple employees like *they were the problem* was bullshit. I don't for a second believe that these two people showed up to work that day and decided on their own to kick out a Black guy. (Kind of exactly how it works with police and the police department.) The employees were obviously just carrying out an either spoken or unspoken policy of who belonged in the restaurant and who didn't. I was in the "didn't" category.

We told the owner that all we wanted was a meeting with him to discuss why the whole thing had happened. We wanted to have a public conversation with members of the community there so that they could voice their opinions. We wanted this to be something we could build from. The owner suggested that we could do it at his café. He would even close early for it! He clearly had no idea who we were and how we do things. I wanted something bigger. Much bigger.

A month and a half later me and Melissa, the owner, a panel of activists and academics, a moderator, an ACLU lawyer, and the most #woke high school senior in the history of all time period, Khadijah Means, were sitting on a stage in a gymnasium at Willard Middle School in Berkeley. There were a few hundred people there. It was packed. People were turned away at the door, including friends of ours. There were multiple local news crews outside. It was impressive that this had all happened because of our little incident, but the number of people of all races who showed up also was indicative of the fact that our family was not the only one that had experienced that kind of racism in the so-called liberal Bay Area. It was beautiful in its full-throated response. It was also weird to be at the center of it.

Everyone on the panel did their thing, but Khadijah was the clear star. Once she had been invited, I realized that she was the Berkeley High student who had led a Black Lives Matter march that I stumbled into one day right outside my house. That night I learned the terms "microaggression" and "implicit bias." Both are fancy ways for describing racism that isn't necessarily fatal. Racism that often doesn't physically injure you. Racism that is hard to prove. Racism that makes our so-called white friends ask, "How do you know it was racism? . . . I mean that sucks, but how can you be sure?" This is the kind of racism that drives you crazy. Death by a thousand racist cuts.

The owner of the Elmwood Café clearly loved these terms. I think he loved them because it meant people said the word "racism" less. It meant he had to feel less guilty. At one point in the middle of the meeting, the owner was using "microaggression" and "implicit bias" in order to turn the problem from *his problem* into a problem "that we all have." This was in *no way* his job to do that. His job was to say, "I fucked up" and ask, "What can I do to help?" His job was to listen. Not the strength of many white men. Or even many men, for that matter.

Melissa couldn't take it anymore. At one point she asked— although really it was a rhetorical question, always the academic—"Can we stop saying 'microaggression'? Can we just call it what it is: racism?" This caused many in the audience to applaud and cheer and yell things like, "TELL IT!" Many Black women in the audience nodded along in approval. Me and Melissa had come a long way since the burrito incident. We were family.

Whereas the owner of the Elmwood continued to deflect. He continued to "mansplain" and "whitesplain." At one point he even recommended a book that he thought the audience should read . . . like we weren't in Berkeley . . . a college town . . . in a room filled with academics and activists. Like this book he was recommending wasn't—I'm sure—unfinished on his nightstand. He was doing everything I had learned not to do, as a cisgender, tall man. Everything that Melissa, Martha, my mom, and many other women had worked hard to teach me. The owner didn't know the value of shutting the fuck up.

He also pitched a plan to the crowd. He said he was working on an initiative to create a list of best practices for businesses regarding implicit bias. He said this had never been done before. Many people in the crowd vocally disagreed with him. He said he wanted to be the leader of this. He actually said that WE, me and him, would be the leaders in this. This was news to me. He had been to my house and told Melissa and me about this, but I had no idea we were doing it together. Melissa also noticed that he only mentioned me and him when he talked to us in our house and when he talked about what had happened. He left Melissa out, even though the incident happened to her too. It happened to us with other people during this time. There's a wrongheaded idea that racism only affects people of color. Sure, it primarily and initially affects us, but it spreads easily into affecting the quality of life of whoever is nearby, especially if that person is the partner of a person of color.

The owner went on. He said he wanted to change his business, then the ones in that neighborhood, then all of Berkeley, and then . . . I don't know . . . maybe the whole universe? As much as it had come out in a ham-fisted manner, I wanted to believe in him. I knew that people who believe in freedom needed people who *don't get it* to get involved, no matter how much ham-juice they get on everything.

The night ended. People felt like something had happened, although nobody quite knew what exactly. I knew that we probably needed to have meetings like this once a month. And remember, this was in 2015, way before people were interested in regular meetings, unlike now. Now we need—and many are having—those meetings daily.

Parts of the meeting and the story ended up on the radio show and podcast *This American Life*. I had been pitching them ideas, and when the Elmwood thing happened it seemed appropriate. Especially since it happened on my birthday. "Happy birthday! Here's some racism for your act! You needed new racism, right? Hope it fits! One size fits y'all!" The *TAL* story ended with me talking about my need to talk about racism to my kids.

Before the Elmwood, me and Melissa had both put our toes— or at least our older daughter Sami's toe—in the race pool. But we had not put even the slightest hint of a Sami toe into the *racism* pool. Yes, those are separate pools. The race pool is filled with positive stories of Black achievement, African-American role models, books and TV shows featuring diverse characters. Our race pool even has Kwanzaa.

But Sami's racism pool was completely drained with a lock on the gate, and we ran past it every day on the way to the race pool. And every day that went by, I felt guilty. The racism pool is treacherous. It's not fun to swim in. And if you aren't careful, you drown in the sorrow of the Black experience in America. The incident at Elmwood really kick-started Melissa and me to talk to our daughters not just about race—*"Flojo was the fastest woman at the Olympics!"*—but also about racism—*"Harriet Tubman knew those white devil slave owners weren't shit, so one night she escaped to freedom. And then she came back repeatedly and got more of our people free."* Or something like that. So I guess I owe the owner a debt of gratitude for that. The smallest debt possible. Like "the alt-right's budget for reparations" small.

But it has become clear to me that the owner of the Elmwood Café is not interested in hopping into the racism pool. It's been more than two years since I was ordered to leave the sidewalk outside the restaurant. And he stopped returning my emails over a year ago. Or maybe for some reason he never got my last email. Maybe it didn't go through. Anything is possible, right? You know what? I'm going to email him now, just to make sure. As far as I can tell the only thing the Elmwood has done differently is that they now have one of those "Everyone is welcome here!" signs that started popping up during the election after Trump and the alt-right began to really double-down on demonizing Muslims, immigrants, and refugees. It features an illustration of a woman wearing a hijab. Every time I pass the Elmwood I think to myself, "Everyone is welcome . . . Everyone but me." One day I'm getting a selfie with that sign. It would make me laugh.

In my life if there is one thing I've learned, it is that laughter can be healing in hard-to-resolve or figure-out situations. And if there is another thing I've learned in my life, it's that if liberal white people have the chance to disappear back into their liberal bubbles, out of the fray and back into the comfortable embrace of white privilege, they will do it most of the time. And that is how we got President Donald J. Trump. Since most white liberals felt like he wasn't their specific problem, they let him *Trump* all over everything in his path. And now he is the entire world's problem. When you are Black . . . or any person of color . . . or openly gay . . . or disabled, you are supposed to handle everyone in the world who is like you when they screw up. Every trans person on planet Earth had to have a Caitlyn Jenner conversation, even though many trans people had never had a "Bruce Jenner" conversation in their lives.

And the owner of the Elmwood may be content to disappear into his familiar life and not confront these awkward but important issues that affect him whether he knows it or not. But I see other white people now doing more, doing better. There's an organization called Showing Up for Racial Justice (SURJ) that is a white privilege organization founded by white people specifically for white people to talk about racial justice without the pressure of *doing it right* that happens when people of color are in the room. White people reading this, if you don't know about SURJ, then stop reading this right now and Google your local chapter. And if there isn't one near you, then you do what people of color always have to do: START ONE YOURSELF! Up! Up! You whitey race! You can accomplish what you will! (Sorry, Marcus Garvey.)

Because despite everything that happened at the Elmwood, I do believe in people's ability to learn new things, in a business's abilities to conduct better practices, and in a country's ability to rebound from a loss and confront evil. It's a key component to my intersectional progressivism. But that doesn't mean you get to have my family's patronage as you go about your learning curve, or my family's respect simply because you are the president. And you *definitely* don't deserve my silence. Nobody is just going to scram because you said so. Because as much as it is easier to let it go, if I did that, I wouldn't be fulfilling my duties as a member of the advisory board of Race Forward, a racial justice organization, and I certainly wouldn't be living up to my responsibilities as the ACLU's Racial Justice Ambassador. And I'd definitely be neglecting my role as the son of Walter Alfred Bell and Janet Cheatham Bell, and the husband of Melissa Hudson Bell, and, most importantly, as the father of Sami and Juno Bell, the two greatest kids of all time period. Yup, thankfully I have a little bit of a platform to try to prevent this from happening to anyone else. Wanna climb up here on the platform with me, everybody?

Epilogue

'm in Puerto Rico. No, I haven't relocated here because Trump is president. That would be stupid since Puerto Rico is a part of America, something I don't think most Americans realize. We are doing a Puerto Rico episode on the second season of *United Shades of America*. We wrapped the second season yesterday, so now I'm with my family. I brought them out here to be with me because it felt stupid to be so far from home in such a beautiful place by myself. Also it makes me feel more like a person to have them here and less like a TV person. We haven't edited this season yet, but things are smoother. We hired a new executive producer. I told Jimmy Fox, the white producer who came up with the initial idea for *United Shades*, that I needed more diversity on the staff, and he got it. The new executive producer is named Donny Jackson, a name only slightly less Black than Barack Obama. He's an experienced Black television producer who gets the show. That doesn't mean that we always agree. It just means that when we have discussions, we know we are coming from similar places. Last season I was the only person of color on the field production team, and now there are six, including me. Six people of color out of fifteen isn't exactly the

Wu-Tang Clan, but it is a much healthier and more creative environment for me than ever before in my TV experience.

Me, Donny, comedian Ron G, and a producer named Christine often ride together in an SUV, and we talk about *The Shade Room*, the Black tax, Kevin Garnett's enthusiasm, and other Black things. We laugh about Shirley Caesar's viral Thanksgiving hit. We laugh about it over and over again. Because even though we each have separate Black experiences, we all have that one in common in some way. We call the rental SUV the Black Van even when it's not Black. We also talk about other non-Black-specific issues, like bathrooms in North Carolina, the ridiculous nature of border walls, and how we are all strongly #NoDAPL. We don't always agree. But we do always laugh. And we always have each other's backs. And it is glorious. We even talk Trump. And after I interviewed an alt-right white supremacist for *United Shades*, the Black Van became a safe space for all of us to vent. Again, we all had each other's backs. And nobody had to ask. It was like we just got to be people without interpreting our experience for others. We got to be ourselves. It's nice. I look forward to more of that, whether other people want me and my people (of all races, sexes, genders, immigration statuses, religions, political persuasions, humanities) to be ourselves or not. We can't be stopped, because I have two little girls/future world-beaters depending on it. If this book was the end of the movie *The Matrix*, I would fly away at this point, but it's not so I'll just say, "See you soon."

ACKNOWLEDGMENTS

I never knew how many people it took to make a book. If you like this book, these people get the credit; if you don't like it, the blame rests with me.

Thanks to my literary agent, Anthony "The Velvet Hammer" Mattero and the Foundry.

Thanks everyone at Dutton, led by my editor, Jill "The Hammer Hammer" Schwartzman. Thanks to everyone there who worked hard on this book: LeeAnn Pemberton, Amanda Walker, Liza Cassity, and Elina Vaysbeyn.

Thanks to WME, especially Stacy Mark and Ben Simone. Thanks to KALW, Earwolf, First Look Media, and Seamus Kirst. Thanks to Jeff Zucker, Amy Entelis, and CNN. Thanks to Jimmy Fox, Objective, and Main Event. Thanks to Tara Kole and Gang, Tyre, Ramer & Brown. Thanks to Keri Smith, who believed in me and knew this was all going to happen. Thanks to Sean Lawton and Keppler Speakers.

Thanks to my *Totally Biased* family.

Thanks to the San Francisco Bay Area comedy scene, specifically Nato Green, Robin Williams (RIP), Margaret Cho, Greg Proops, Dan St. Paul, Robert Hawkins, Laura House, and Will Durst for teaching me what it means to be an SF Bay comic. Thanks to the Punch Line and Tom Sawyer and Cobb's Comedy Club.

Acknowledgments

Thanks to Kevin Avery, Bruce Pachtman, Molly Schminke, Jeremy Townsend, Hari Kondabolu, Dwayne Kennedy, and Chris Rock for being so important to who I am and how I got here.

To my family: Mom, Dad, Melissa, Jason, Martha, Sami, and Juno. Thank you all for being patient with me.

ABOUT THE AUTHOR

W. Kamau Bell is a sociopolitical comedian who is the host of the hit Emmy Award–nominated CNN docuseries *United Shades of America*. Before *United Shades*, Kamau was best known for his critically acclaimed, but criminally short-lived, FX comedy series *Totally Biased with W. Kamau Bell*. The series was nominated for both an NAACP award and a GLAAD award. Kamau is also the host of *Kamau Right Now!*, a public radio talk show that airs on NPR radio station KALW in San Francisco, and a cohost of the podcasts *Politically Re-Active* and the memorably named *Denzel Washington Is the Greatest Actor of All Time Period*.

Before pursuing a career in stand-up comedy, Kamau lived with his mom all over the country. He was born in Palo Alto, California, then moved to Indianapolis, Indiana, then Boston, Massachusetts, then Chicago, Illinois, with several extended visits to his dad's house in Mobile, Alabama, mixed in for good measure. Today he lives in Berkeley, California, with his wife and family.